Painting on Glass

ALSO BY JESSICA AUERBACH: *Winter Wife*

JESSICA AUERBACH

Painting on Glass

A NOVEL

W · W · NORTON & COMPANY

NEW YORK · LONDON

First Edition

The text of this book is composed in Avanta, with display type set in Garamond Oldstyle. Composition and manufacturing by the Haddon Craftsmen Inc. Book design by Marjorie J. Flock.

Library of Congress Cataloging–in–Publication Data

Auerbach, Jessica.
Painting on glass / Jessica Auerbach.
   p.   cm.
   I. Title
PS3551.U384L4   1988
813'.54—dc19   87–18750

ISBN 0-393-02545-4

W. W. Norton & Company, Inc., 500 Fifth Avenue, New York, N. Y. 10110
W. W. Norton & Company Ltd., 37 Great Russell Street, London WC1B 3NU

1 2 3 4 5 6 7 8 9 0

For Josh

❖ ❖ ❖

I WISH TO THANK the National Endowment for the Arts for the generous grant which supported the writing of this novel.

Thanks also to Claire and Baxter Garcia for sharing their memories and insights about expatriation.

There are Six Essentials in Painting. The first is called spirit; *the* second, rhythm; *the third,* thought; *the fourth,* scenery; *the fifth, the* brush; *and the last is the* ink.

—CHINGHAO
fl.925, "Notes on Brushwork," from *The Spirit of the Brush*

It takes two to speak the truth—one to speak, and another to listen.

—H. D. THOREAU

Painting
on Glass

CHAPTER ONE

RACHEL WAITED two weeks to get his first letter. Had he been there, next to her, she would have strangled him for keeping her waiting so long. She'd have punched a fist against his chest and told him he was a real idiot.

But he wasn't there. He was on some island near Toronto, though in what body of water she'd no idea. She'd have to look at a map. Definitely in another country, though, and not coming back real soon. Not coming back at all.

"Why an island, Jake? Why not downtown Toronto? An island puts you farther away. Now I need to take both boat and plane to reach you out there where you float. Write soon, tell me as fast as you can, how often do the boats go out there?"

"On a really crystal clear day," he wrote back, "I can see New York State, flattened and dark, way out across the other side of Lake Ontario, and for an exile, Rach, that's a whole lot better than no view at all. There's a beach, of sorts. Not exactly the highly touted white sands of the Caribbean, but it's all right. The boat crosses from Toronto on the hour in summer, a couple of times a day in winter. My cottage is nearly dead center on the island, about three short blocks from the ferry slip. I could meet you at the dock, whenever you say.

"It's quiet as hell out here. No cars are allowed. People have wagons to bring their belongings from the mainland. They pile them up with groceries or firewood and pull them onto the ferry. I found a wooden wagon with built-up sides under my front steps when I moved in. This is definitely not like the real world. That's why I like it. There's a sense of sanctuary.

"Come summer of course, I'm sure the place will smell like popcorn and be noisy and trashy, but I don't care. Maybe it'll make me think I'm on vacation. A brief stopover between part A and B of life. That'll help to keep me from defining my exile too well."

And then another hiatus without letters, though she churned them out to him, daily. She imagined him sitting on the floor of a shack with a blanket thrown around his shoulders for warmth. No electricity. Sitting in a corner in the dark.

He sent a picture postcard of Ward's Island. "News from the Islands," he'd scrawled on back as though he were in the Bahamas. The photograph showed a stark little place with rows of tiny cottages. Not hovels, though. Genuine summer houses. "My new home," it said at the bottom.

Next he sent a ferry schedule. No letter. She couldn't believe it. No letter? She turned the envelope inside out. She thought maybe a note had gotten stuck inside somehow.

She gave him hell. "If you don't tell me more, you're doomed, Jacob. You're there and I'm here and a ferry schedule is very much beside the point. What the hell is happening in your life? Did you get Landed Immigrant Status? Can you get a job? Have you gotten one?

"Do you need money?" she wrote to him. "Write to me, damn it."

And then another long white envelope was visible behind the glass door of her post office box. She bent down low and peeked through before she even dared turn the combination lock so as to avoid disappointment, and she saw, yes, it was his handwriting, that oversized R of Rachel serving as testimony that Jake was the sender.

"Sorry," his letter began. "There's been so little time. I've been trying to set this place up so it feels like home (or somebody's home that I'm visiting, at any rate) and looking for work, which is the world's greatest bitch here, believe me. Rachel, I want to talk to you, not write letters, I want to hear your voice. I've thought of calling, but I haven't because I think it'll just set me back. There are moments when I maintain sanity only through tremendous effort of will. I don't have a phone and won't for a while because I have no money for luxuries."

She saw, as she read her own letters, that they bordered on vulgarity with their passages of phoney cheer. She wanted to write: it'll get better, you'll see. It'll be over soon. What is it, she wondered, you're supposed to do for the You Can't Go Home Again Blues?

"Tell me about the border crossing," she wrote, her hand forming the letters clearly to make sure there was no ambiguity as to what information she sought. "Tell me details so I know what you went through. So I feel it with you, Jake." Then she fought with her need to tell him how she missed him, how she had so much to say that needed answers now, not next week after her letter travelled across two countries and his travelled back again. And below her name she wrote, "I miss you something awful, Jake." And immediately thought to toss the paper out—why tell him he's missed here when there's nothing to be done about it? But they had this agreement: no ripping up letters. No rewriting. First thoughts. True thoughts. So she sent it.

After Jake left, Rachel started training to be a Resistance counselor. She read through all the printed materials and attended the first training session. But that was all she could take. She went back to stuffing envelopes and running the ditto machine.

If there had been real guidelines, good solid correct answers you could give to people, it would have been one thing. But there never were. You were supposed to emphasize in the counselling sessions that there were only options, not solutions. Depending on who you were, there were some options that were slightly better than others. Depending on this, depending on that.

So, supposing you got as far as deciding to emigrate. You still had a million other choices to cope with. Where to cross, for instance. Everybody said go through at Quebec even if you were headed for Toronto. It was the long way round, no arguing that, but at Windsor, the major Ontario entry point, the word coming back from American exiles was harassment. There were some people who believed that unless you went all the way to the west, the odds of getting in were only just even. Jake had opted for Quebec. "Just go clean shaven," one of the counselors had advised, "and you'll slip right in, sweet as can be."

"Tell them," Jake wrote, the voice of experience now; the draft-evading border-crosser, "that even in Quebec it's rough going. They should be telling people this," he advised. The letter was so long, the envelope bulged with the delicious promise of much, much news. He'd had to use scotch tape to keep the flap closed over the thick contents. Rachel savored his words, rationing them out to herself in small segments; a page to be read after class, another after dinner, and the last of his yellow legal sheets to be saved till she had gotten into bed. Here finally were the details; the coffee shops he'd stopped in, the motel that smelled of fish, and the quality of light when he stopped briefly along the Maine coast. But mostly, how he had made that transition from here to there. "I hadn't expected a long line—that's why I'd come so late at night in the first place. I thought, hell, everybody and their mother is trying to beat it out tonight. I went nuts sitting in that car. Sometimes I turned the motor off, sometimes I just let it idle and played the radio. I was getting French-speaking stations by then. I thought, maybe there's some special bounty being offered tonight, with prizes given to the border cop who tosses the most Americans back over the fence. Or maybe the final quota had been reached and I'd get to the booth and the officer would announce, "Sorry, sold out," and slide a glass window across the space between us. Then the damn Chevy started stalling out and I began having visions of being towed all the way back to Boston and starting all over again, as in, 'Go back three spaces, miss a turn, take your induction physical over again.' People were coming over to offer the usual advice about flooded motors, though nobody was suggesting what I knew as truth, that the car was desperate to stay on American soil. But I finally got it going and rode it coughing and bucking all the way to the booth. I held that damn wheel so tight, that car wouldn't have dared to stall again. Then, of course, I didn't just get waved on like the cars before me, but got told to go into an office for more questioning. I'd expected that because I was asking for immigrant status, but I got a new wave of panic (and crippling nausea, I might add) when he told me to park the car. I felt really weird going down that corridor: my legs were stiff and longer than I'd remembered them being. I was tripping all over myself.

"This next part was like a real interview. I got asked all the stuff we'd anticipated: how much college did I have, did I know French, did I have relatives, friends, in Canada, the whole bit. We predicted that all pretty accurately. He put numbers in little boxes every time I answered. He kept sliding the paper left and right while he asked me questions, and I couldn't take my eyes off it, as though I was sitting across from a neurologist instead of an immigration officer.

"I made a real ass of myself trying to explain about how I had no proof of acceptance at the College of Art, saying no, I hadn't actually applied yet, in fact, in truth, actually, come to think of it. He started rolling a pen between his palms. I sat there listening to the pen click across his wedding band, and I thought, Hey, this is as far as I'm going to get. And I felt relieved. OK, so they're going to throw me back, I said to myself, and I started sweating, but I felt good, like something'd come clear finally, so I sat back and said, 'It was a sudden decision to emigrate,' because I figured I had nothing to lose anymore being reasonably honest. He started writing again, and I watched him move the pen up and down the columns of numbers and he wrote some stuff and passed it across the desk and I signed. He took me over to another desk and I traded the form for another one and the guy behind this desk started dealing out papers to me. I wanted to say, Crazy Eights or pinochle? But he was reading what I'm sure were rules and regulations, but I can't for the life of me remember any of it, because I kept expecting to hear the phrase Draft Status—the air was hot with the promise of those words—but nope, he didn't say a word about armed service or war or draft or evasion. Then he shook my hand and that was it.

"When I got back in the car, I went through all the papers and pulled out the ID card that said Landed Immigrant Status. It had my name, spelled all right and proper, written out on it. I put it into my wallet on top of my driver's license, so it showed out through the plastic window. Then I took all the cards that were in my wallet—social security, Boston Public Library, Boston Food Coop, and draft registration and put them on the dashboard. First wastebasket I come to, I thought, in they go. I could feel my speeded-up heartbeat pumping away, not just in my chest, but in my gut, and my neck, and my ears, so hard it hurt.

"And I started driving. Rachel, it was endless. It's just a big black open road going on forever. Here was where the first fantasy got blown sky high: I thought I'd see the sights, take in the terrain and start to understand my new country. The only thing the lights of my car illuminated was black macadam. To the left and right were cavernous vistas. And when the sun came up, I was too crazy, too strung-out tired to notice. I started thinking the stuff around me was moving on continuous conveyor belts, and I was standing still. A mere illusion of moving through space. I thought I'd never get there. I hit the brake a lot, thinking maybe I should pull over because I must have gotten on the wrong road. I'd lost all sense of how far I was supposed to be travelling—after all you can bridge the distance with an outstretched hand across a map. And then I got this idea, and it seemed real, and frightening, that the highway had been tampered with, cut off from its regular path and sent veering off somewhere else. I was on my way to the top of the continent, and I was going to drop off into the frigid northern waters. I must have been exhausted, though I didn't register what I felt as fatigue. It was more like being really high, with the requisite paranoia thrown in for color. When I got hungry, I really started to freak because there were no places to stop. No roadside Ho Jos with blueberry toastercakes and orange juice for breakfast. Nothing was familiar. Then I let my eyes close for a second or two, and had to start slapping myself to keep awake. I was convinced that if I stopped I'd be ambushed by highwaymen or shot by snipers or mauled by rabid bears. Those images kept me awake for a while and I started talking aloud to myself, too. 'Real freedom, huh?' I started to shout, and I could feel the noise of my words reverberate in my head. Why'd I do this if I'm not safe here? I kept thinking. What was that border for if it didn't grant me peace? Then I saw the cards, the library card and all on the dash, and I grabbed them and put them back in my pocket. A little while after that I pulled off to the side and slept for a couple of hours. If I hadn't stopped then, I'm sure I would have totalled myself out in another five minutes.

"When I finally got to the city, everything was gray and overcast. I could see the lake as I drove through, and it was as vast-seeming as an ocean; so much larger than maps made it out. I almost cracked up the car trying to see where the other side began, where what I'd left, somewhere, back there, had now slipped off to.

"I stayed the first few nights at an Amex house. They got me connected with my little island rental. Eventually I'll try to move to the Annex where most of the other American exiles live. (Notice the difference in language between the two countries? Back home I was a draft evader and a member of the Resistance. Here, I'm an American Exile and a member of Amex.) I've got a temporary job, out beyond the city, being a janitor. Eventually, I'll get something more real. I think eventually I'll get something in a gallery. Eventually. I keep using that word, don't I?

"And I didn't write all this before because I kept waiting for it to be Eventually already. I thought if I waited, I'd be able to write: 'I'm home at last, Rachel. All is well.' Maybe tomorrow. I know the worst of it's behind me, and that I'm safe, but the sense of being the stranger in a strange land persists. I'm still waiting for something. And I'm bothered by something about Amex: It's not Canadian. Nor is it American. Amex and I are the new hybrids born of these times."

She wrote as often as she could. When she had no news, she detailed political events, writing of every move Lyndon Johnson made, every word he uttered. He wrote back, "There are newspapers here, you know." His criticism stung, and her foolishness seemed too obvious. So she wrote of the weather changes, football games, or her reading assignments. Anything, so long as he'd have to respond, react, and write. When he grew angry or impatient with her, she was not wholly displeased. That meant he'd taken off listing his own ills for a time.

This moodiness was not new. Even when they were kids, she'd always been the one to shake him of his despair. She could handle this. "Hey," she wrote, "what are friends for?" when he said he couldn't bear to write such depressing drivel to her, and that he was going to start editing himself. "No," she wrote back. "Tell me everything. This is between friends. Very old friends. We agreed: I send the Letters from Home, you send the News from Another World."

She imagined each piece of correspondence he sent having to travel backwards down that same long long route he'd taken between Toronto and Quebec, the letters piling up on top of one another in the Blackpool border crossing office. Dead-ended. But the letters did arrive. Sailing through space in some inexplicable way like radio waves, oblivious to all barriers. She kept her letters coming, kept them aimed at him, like tiny arrows directed toward the emotional center of his brain. "You'll be all right. And the war only gets worse, Jake. There are no other options now. This is the solution."

His letters began to fall into a pattern. One page long. Beginning in calm, cool reporting. My Life as an American in Canada. The political mood of the city. The newest Amex meeting. An analysis of his reasons for emigration versus someone else's. Then three quarters of the way down the page, he'd let loose the pain: "I took down the mirror," he once wrote in the loopy letters that marked his transition to truth. "I wake up mornings and feel so different from who I once was. Am I changing? I thought the glass might show I'd faded, so I'd rather not look. I've let my beard grow again—so if I were to run into someone from home, I'd be recognized. Anyway, there's no longer a mirror here, so I can't shave. If you come to visit, will you know me? Damn, how I long for the freedom I've surrendered, along with my right to bear arms for my country, of being able to visit you."

She told him the island seemed, after all, to be a good place for him. He had written of the political struggle of the islanders to be declared legal owners of their homes. The government claimed the land and had for generations been trying to raze the homes and turn it into park land instead. It was an intense issue; all islanders were committed to the fight, and every islander would be personally affected by its outcome. Jake envied them that, he said. He had wandered so far away from what he had been fighting for, he had trouble remembering the arguments for his side. The islanders don't forget for a moment, he said.

Here, Rachel believed, was a community that would take him in and make him part of itself. She wrote that island rights sounded like a good issue in which he could get involved. "Do you feel connected to this cause?"

His answer disappointed: "This is a very small community, Rach. I can walk up and down every street of it in under half an hour. I board the boat each morning with all the other commuters and we stand together, leaning against the railing. There are few enough of us that the launch can be very small. Too small for such luxuries as benches, or a cabin for protection from the elements, so the weather dominates conversation.

"No one's exactly rushed me socially, either. There are the vague, polite gestures: 'You ought to come by sometime.' 'Yes,' I answer, 'when things quiet down.' They don't ask what things, so I figure, the invitations are empty. And there are things that need to quiet down, though I don't even know what they are, myself.

"As a renter, I'm an outsider even to the outsiders here. My roots simply don't reach down deep enough for me to be embraced within their cause. Physically we ride out the storm together, on an island that is nowhere at all, part of no nation; a shifting sandbar ready to wash back into Lake Ontario. We are all homeless here, though I can make no claim even to the squatters' rights they hold. Once more, I live my life by sidling along the edges of the illicit."

And what was politics, anyway, he asked her? A way of making our own motives acceptable? He wrote that at the last Amex meeting someone had brought American beer ("not really as good as Canadian beer, if you're honest") and they'd gotten into drunken truth tellings. "There's a lot of bad guilt here. It doesn't matter how thoroughly you believe that the U.S. is acting criminally in Southeast Asia, there are times when you have to see what you've done as skin-saving. In daylight, without the beer, we think of ourselves as committed political creatures. But it wears thin for me. A rally at which I don't know the patriotic songs that the Canadians have been singing since the cradle, makes me feel all the more the outsider and intruder. I keep going to Amex meetings, though, because I want to hear those Boston and Brooklyn accents. They're sweet, sweet music to an expatriate. Also, no one there ever asks questions like, 'If Canada goes to war, will you run away then, too?' That seems the first thing Canadians want to know of us. How can anyone answer such questions? Every war, every cause is different, I usually say. Every case must be examined for its own merit. But people who ask such questions don't want such answers, believe me, Rach."

When she got nowhere with politics, she wrote about art: "What are you painting?" She didn't say, are you painting? She knew the answer to that would be negative. "Go find a supplier and get yourself some canvas," she instructed.

He bought canvas, but despaired: "You cannot imagine the

feeling of failure. The quiet. The expanse of time and space that is all around me."

"What size is this canvas?" she wrote back. When he sent the dimensions in the next letter, she wrote, "Go out and get smaller canvases. Take a small piece of your head and put it down. Think small. Start somewhere. Start, Jacob."

A week later he wrote, "I haven't touched the canvas yet, but I did a tiny water color, about the size to fit in an old pocket watch. It's of you, Rachel, with your light-colored curls. In fact, it's mostly curls. You haven't cut it, nor let it grow, have you? I don't think I've got your eyes quite right. The blue seems too soft, but I'm not sure. Anyway, it's a start. You were right about that. I have an idea now for an acrylic series involving the cottage."

The paintings of his house began to come through the mail. "So you'll know where I am," he wrote. "I dream of pulling the ugly plastic from the windows when spring comes. If I paint it red this spring (the real house, not the canvas replica, you understand), do you think it will seem less run down?"

She was relieved to see he'd begun to ask questions that went beyond the narrow definition of himself. The paintings that he sent arrived one after the other, identical in their brown paper wrapping and string, and with her name scrawled in two-inch-high letters. They came at intervals of about a week. And they were wonderful, dark, eerie things that drew you into them, despite the scary mood. She wanted to linger, to move in along the roofline toward the next cottage, to stare into those shapes that might be rocks, might be animals, and to know more.

"I have the houses (your house, your paintings) up in my room," she wrote to him. "The shadows are black and unremitting. No Haystack Series sweetness for my Jake. What you say about shadow (in the paintings) is what we really do feel about shadow, that it is invasive, insidious. Cold, certainly. We feel the presence of shadow as a malevolence (am I getting too extreme?), though it has no substance. You have palpable, tangible shadows. Correlatives of our fears. I think you're brilliant. All we need do is convince the rest of the world.

"Is it really like that, is your house so towered over by trees? I assume it isn't simply metaphorical because the trees appear unchanged in size in every painting. Is this part of what makes the paintings so compelling, that the mind knows that this island, this summer community built on sand couldn't support such trees, yet they seem so right, so indigenous? Anyway, paint more."

These canvases were small. When she was alone, she'd sometimes prop one in her lap and study it. She imagined the house passing through the seasons, the plastic down, the coat of paint already applied. Flowers, perhaps large declarative sunflowers. "What you need is a garden," she wrote back. "I think I'd be good at gardens. I told you that you should have let me come." She sent along a seed packet. Nasturtiums. She dashed off a sketch of his house surrounded by flowers. She took a set of colored pencils from her drawer and gave the house its red face-lift, made the flowers all colors of the rainbow. He sent a wildly exuberant and corny thank you note about her bringing color into his life without his having planted a single seed. "Your drawing shows there's hope of better times. And you've convinced me: get up here and plant me a garden. I'm glad you like the paintings. I'll send you every one."

"No," she said. "I love them, but you need to get yourself some kind of backlog for a portfolio and so you can make slides, and take them around to galleries. So you can get serious."

And to amuse him, she wrote: "Have just gotten a letter from my father saying he is glad I didn't rush off, 'nipping at Jacob's heels.' I laughed till I cried. Would that I could only have the chance to bite at those voluptuous heels of yours, my dear."

"The Parents must have their fantasies," he wrote back. "But then, we have led them on and teased them so shamefully."

Every step he took beyond the sand of his island, she applauded. He wrote about a wonderful exhibit of Fauve paintings ("Please Jake, no green faces just now," she'd written back), and then a great deli with New York–style water bagels. There was almost always something about his art now in his letters. And then there was a casual mention of "a woman I have met," taking him to a bizarre hole in the wall shop that sold, among other exotics, gargoyles.

"Why are you so deliberately cryptic?" Rachel demanded. "I'm interested in what kind of gargoyles (old? new? media?), but I'm a damned sight more interested in who this companion, this 'woman I have met,' is, dear Jake. So let me in already on this. Tell me, are you at least (since, alas, dear Parents, Jake and I aren't) lovers? I love you madly, Rake."

She laughed at herself as she reread the letter to see that she'd signed her childhood nickname, the one The Parents had given her, so as to make her a more neatly matched set with Jake. She thought to reshape the letters of her signature to her real name, but hesitated. He'd enjoy such silliness. And it was clear, he still needed all the cheering he could get.

CHAPTER TWO

D AMN, she missed him. She missed the life they'd led, hanging out together with his friends. The friends, too, had disappeared, some of them graduated and gone off every which way even before he had, scattered to the winds. Sometimes one of them would call her, long distance, though she knew it was mostly to get news about Jake or to talk about the war resisters, but always to tell her about the complicated patterns they were each weaving for themselves, without her and Jake.

Her girlfriends had taken her plight very seriously, too seriously, she felt, and set up a stream of dates with guys from the Coast Guard Academy. These were not just any old dates, they told her, but guys who liked classical music, who did a little dope now and then (off base only, of course), and who were very, very good looking. ("Imagine this, Jake," she wrote, "guys with their hair cut so short it's practically invisible being described as sexy.") Her friends wasted their time, though. To Rachel the dates seemed a string of look-alike, sound-alike, reactionary, overly cautious people. She mumbled apologies to Jake and swore off the military. "Don't be such an extremist," one friend, engaged to a Coastie, lectured her. "The Coast Guard is not the military."

They told her she would dry up and die emotionally if she didn't start dating again. They threatened ("We'll tell the shrink you're suicidal"), coaxed, and begged. To shut them up, she followed her roommate Jennifer to Yale one weekend for a blind date. "A really relaxed guy," Jennifer told her. ("Translate relaxed, here, Jake, to heavy drinker.") Rachel's date passed out and she took the midnight bus back to school, leaving him unconscious on the floor of his fraternity house. ("I leave out the grotesque details in the interest of good taste.") Jennifer was terribly apologetic, begged to be given one more chance to fix her up with a left-wing type she'd met, and Rachel went along with it. She liked David, but he turned out to be a homosexual who wanted a photograph of Rachel standing next to him to send to his mother so she'd get off his back. Rachel had obliged. So she told her friends, Hey, don't worry about me, I'll just wait. And they said, wait for what? and she said she didn't know.

Then she went back to Yale on her own. She left on an early Saturday bus and spent the morning studying in Sterling Library. Around noon, she walked over to Davenport, Jake's old dining hall. She hung out for a time in the public rooms, looking at the ancient photographs of crew teams which hung over the piano, reading the notices in the corridors just beyond the dining room, and watching for a familiar face as Yalies filed into lunch in conversational packets of twos and threes. When a guy with a Resistance button over his pocket came in who looked vaguely familiar (though she admitted to herself that he probably only looked familiar because he had the same color hair as Jake did), she joined the lunch line behind him. She tapped him gently on the shoulder and asked, "Can I buy myself lunch here?"

"I'll buy you lunch," he said. That was how she met Ben.

It turned out that Ben remembered Jake. They hadn't been friends, but he had known him by sight he said, and knew he had been thinking about resisting. He said she looked familiar, too. That he might have seen her there with Jake sometime.

He asked questions about where Jake was living. "I'm thinking about Canada, too," he told her.

After lunch Ben invited her back to his room. It was a great room. His mattress was on the floor, with just a big fluffy dark green quilt thrown over it—very European looking. And he had stuff all over the walls—newspaper articles about Staughton Lynd going to Hanoi and a poster (the same poster Jake had had in his room in Boston) saying, "Do you remember Norman Morrison?" And then a picture of Morrison (was it him? Did anyone take a picture of him as he burned in front of McNamara's office window?) and a picture of a Buddhist Monk setting himself on fire. At the bottom of the poster were the words, "Protest. End the War." Ben had scrawled across one wall with pencil, "Johnson: pull out like your father should have done."

He told her he liked the way she dressed. He said he really liked boots on a girl. And hers were fabulous boots, really good soft leather. Were they handmade? No, she said, but they were British, which she supposed was almost as good. He needed new ones, he said and he showed her how the sole was nearly worn through on the left foot, but he said he liked them most when they were that far gone. They got real soft then. Like they were part of you, almost. He put on a Stones album.

The water pipe was in the closet, the plastic bag of grass under the mattress. He scraped away all the old ashes from the pipe and picked through the grass, pulling out the larger pieces and flicking them to the floor. "You get such junk these days," he explained to her. "I like it powdery fine, so it fills you like a gentle dust. You'll see," he told her, "how much easier it is on your throat when it's small this way."

When they were high (though not very high—he wanted to show her what he called a fine high, where you held back and smoked less than you thought you needed—and definitely not stoned), he lifted her long necklace and moved his hand from one purple bead to the next as though he were counting them. His fingers grazed lightly across her chest, but didn't pause. She held her breath, waiting for those fingers to move closer, for his arms to pull her toward him. "They're glazed pottery," she said, her words hard and short-syllabled for lack of full breaths. He touched her hair. "You look a little crazy with this huge head of curls all gone wild," he said to her.

"I am crazy," she said, and wondered if that might frighten him away, now that he was near enough so that if she bent her head just slightly, she could rest it against his, so she added, "just a little crazy. Only the tiniest bit."

"Our hair's the same color," Ben said, and he caught a strand of his hair on his fingers and one of hers, and tried to weave them up together. She kissed him. "We'll go slow," he said, putting a hand on her cheek, barely returning her kiss, and she felt exposed as an aggressor, and longed to retrieve the kiss and move backward in time. "Jake's hair was this color, too," she told him, grabbing for another subject, working at shifting Ben's attention away from her transgression.

"Was?" he asked, and he laughed a very silly-sounding grass-high laugh. "This friend of yours isn't dead, is he?"

"No," she said, and put a finger across his mouth to shush him, "don't say dead, it'll make me cry." He kissed her gently, a welcome kiss after he had so recently chased her away.

"Are you waiting for Jake?" he asked her and she laughed at his anachronistic phrasing.

"Saving myself, you mean?" He nodded. "No."

He kissed her again and said, "Save yourself for me, then," and he sat back and with one hand began to undo the buttons of his workshirt.

"Hey, what happened to that whole idea of going slow?" she asked him.

"We are going to go slowly. We're not jumping into this, and we're not even going to think of making love yet. All I want you to do is wear my shirt, not yours. No nakedness. But wear my shirt, then later, when I wear it, I can feel you against me without even touching you."

Her breath was uneven, tossed around by the way he managed to turn things upside down and make clothes more sexual than nakedness. She watched him take off his shirt and she reached out to touch his bare chest just where the blond hairs curled every which way around his nipples, but he held her hands away. "Not yet," he said. He kissed the fabric of his shirt, just about where her breasts would brush against it when she put it on. He turned his back, waiting while she removed her shirt and replaced it with his. When he faced her once more, his fingers moved smoothly down the shirt's center, engaging buttons in button holes and then his hand glided across the surface of the fabric, touching, though barely touching, her breasts through the chambray. He brought his mouth to the fabric over her nipple. "We take it very slow," he reiterated as he lifted his head.

When it came time for her to give him back his shirt, he watched her change, but stood at a distance and didn't reach out, even then, to touch her bare skin. "Stay for dinner," he whispered to her. Could he possibly believe she could leave? She needed to know what would come next, when, and for how long. Still later, he asked her to spend the night, though she'd had no plans to board a bus and depart. She was saving herself for him now.

They stayed awake through much of the night, touching and holding at precisely the pace that Ben allowed them. Till finally, in the darkest part of the night, Ben asked permission to consummate their relationship, which she granted. "Next time we do it," she said to him, "what will we call it?" for she had nearly swooned at his use of the word consummate, and its quality of the devout. "Each time," he explained, "will be a consummation, for each act will be entirely new." On Sunday, he walked her to the bus station and she went back to school.

How she wished Jake were there to meet Ben! It would be nearly impossible to explain each to the other. She would write to him, though, and try to capture something of it; try to explain how Ben was unlike anybody she'd ever dated before. No one else had taken so much time, so much—pleasure— that's what it was, with sex before. And it wasn't just sex he approached that way, it was everything—smoking, eating, walking, breathing. With Ben you didn't have to be up all the time, you could get into the thing you were doing, even if it were just sitting silently in a room together.

She thought of the first sentence of her letter before she even left Ben's side: "I've got a new life now," she'd begin, explaining that this was not one of her "brief but torrid affairs," as Jake had labelled all her past relationships. But his letter, the one that was waiting for her on her return to Connecticut College, was filled with self-pity. There was some conflict about whether he wanted to invite this new woman—Elizabeth—to his house.

"I don't want to say to anyone, come back to my place, because I don't want to lend stability to this existence. I drift, hoping, I think, that this sandbar will one night cast off and float to the southern shore and I'll step off and be home. Man, have I got the Blues."

"Invite her, damn it," Rachel wrote back. "Subject closed. And then invite the whole damn Amex crowd over. Maybe their combined weight will cause the island to break away from its moorings. It's worth a try, isn't it?" She mentioned she'd met Ben, but gave no details. Those could wait till he pulled out of this latest slump.

Rachel telephoned her mother to tell her she wanted to stay in New Haven for the summer. "To go to summer school, Rachel?" her mother asked. "I thought you said Yale didn't have a summer school. What is it exactly you do want to do in New Haven, Rachel?" Rachel's only real plans were to double up with Ben wherever his bed was, but there wasn't any way she could tell her mother that.

"I want to get a job and make some money for next semester."

"You have a job, Rachel. Daddy has it all set for you to be his receptionist for the summer."

"I've done that already for three summers, Mother. It's time for something new. Working for my father is too protected. Too unreal. I need genuine work experience."

"You can try the department stores. They always want girls for the summer for their College Boards. They'd give their eye teeth for someone from Connecticut College for Women, I'll bet."

"I can do that in New Haven. There's a Macy's there," she said.

"Don't be foolish, Rachel," Alice said and slipped into a description of the floodlights Ed had just finished mounting over the patio.

In other conversations, Alice said to her daughter, "Rachel, it isn't right, an unmarried girl away from home." Such words made Rachel feel the heat of her mother's kitchen, the summer dampness of red and white checked cotton dishcloths and the interminable advice ("Remember, Rachel, if you use silver, it doesn't tarnish"). She remembered days and nights of other summers with her mother following behind, arranging luncheons with her friends ("Mother, you go out with Mrs. Ewing and Mrs. Moss. I'm fine by myself") and her mother's voice, routinely as clockwork, asking, "Happy?" Soon, perhaps in just a few days, her mother would begin calling her about details of the annual welcome-home party the two sets of parents would have planned for her and Jake—but not Jake this year, just her—details of renting the tent, of the menu, and the guest list. Alice would be picking out three dresses for Rachel, bringing them home, laying them out on Rachel's bed so they'd be the first thing she'd see when she went upstairs to her room: summer dresses in pale pastel shades. ("Pink brings out the natural color of your complexion. Blue makes your eyes sparkle.") This year there'd be nowhere to run. "Jake, is that you?" she heard herself shout, somewhere in the future, in the dark, out onto the pond. And to Alice she said, "Mother, this isn't pre-World War II America, anymore, you know."

It had always been easier not to tell her parents about her boyfriends. Her mother had to know every detail about each one; his parents, his interests, his cultural and religious background. "They're just dates, Mother," Rachel had said to her on a number of occasions, but her mother's response was always the same—"A date one day, a husband the next." It had been Jake's idea to use his name as her universal date. To her mother's Sunday afternoon telephone question, "What did you do this weekend?" Rachel began to say, "Jake and I went to a concert," or "Jake and I had dinner at a Chinese restaurant," neatly substituting his name for her actual date's. No questions asked. Jake was as familiar, as beloved to them as if he were a son. She heard them sigh with relief to hear her say his name week after week. Once Jake was gone, she eliminated all references to her social life. "I'm studying, mostly, Mother. The work's much harder this year."

One puzzling factor about her mother's reactions: though she had always wanted to know details of where Rachel stayed when she had dates at Yale, she never inquired as to those details when Rachel said she had spent the weekend with Jake. Did her parents' conservative, antisexual morality have a perverse streak that allowed premarital relations with Jake and Jake alone? Why? Because he was Jake, all fitted out with the Parental Seal of Approval? Or because premarital sex was all right if you limited it to one person, and one person you were planning to marry? (All right, she let them believe that too, so that when her mother said, "if you and Jake ever get married, and I'm just speculating, here . . . ," she never told her mother to cut it out and stop being loony. Rachel allowed her mother to decorate the fantasy with ever more strings of colored lights.) Or was it because they thought Jake was no possible sexual threat because they'd been friends since life itself began? ("You might as well have been brother and sister," their parents were fond of saying.) And was that why they used to try to get them to call each other brother and sister when they were kids? Why had they nicknamed her Rake, arbitrarily making her twin to Jake? Had Alice and Grace been deliberately concocting a recipe for the ultimate asexual relationship?

"Maybe we should get married," Ben said when Rachel repeated one of the conversations about summer at home that she'd had with her mother. Rachel giggled. "Why do you laugh at that idea?" he wanted to know. She was surprised to see how his eyebrows moved together to make their own statement of rage. "Don't you want me around at breakfast?"

"Of course I want you around," she said, and ran her hand gently over his brow, smoothing out his anger. "It's just a surprise to hear you suggest it. It's not that long that we know each other."

"We'll make meals together," he said. "We'll have a toaster and make cinnamon toast and when we come home late at night from the movies we can have our own little homemade feast and not have to go to dirty old Olivia's and have to buy our snack. We'll have a double bed and have room to roll around more. We'll eat the toast in bed. We'll eat all our meals in bed. Don't you like the way that sounds?"

"Yes. I love it for its special quality of degeneracy that only you could devise." She kissed him.

"So?"

"So it's a narrow view of marriage, that's all."

"You want something broader? I'll love you and make love to you all night long." He wove his hands deep into her curls and brought his lips to her forehead. "Call your parents and tell them we're getting married. Be firm. Parents go nuts when you tell them that, but they fall in line. My sister did it. It's the ultimate announcement of independence. You're saying, I'm making sexual choices, and so snap to, Mom and Dad. And they will, believe me."

"No," Rachel said, "you don't know my parents. If I tell them I want to get married they'll say, 'Wait, Rachel. Wait, wait, wait. Life begins at twenty-two, and you're not twenty-one yet. Sex drive springs full grown from your college diploma.' What the hell can you do with people who have beliefs like that, Ben?"

"All right, all right," he said to her. "We won't get married and we won't live together. We've eliminated those possibilities. Time to go on to another option. Before I met you, I'd been thinking of hitchhiking around Europe. Scandinavia, I thought. Maybe I should go back to that idea."

"Without me?" she moaned.

"Your mother doesn't want to let you spend the summer in New Haven. You think she'll let you travel with your boyfriend in Europe, Rachel?" She shook her head in misery. She saw girls in trains watching Ben pass in the corridors, girls in railroad stations and airports watching his slender body, seeing what she saw; the way his hips knew how to move, and her hand reached out to touch him, to see if he were still there, still stateside, next to her, and she put her fingers across his lips. Why should she give anyone else the chance for five minutes alone with him? "Don't go," she said, and he moved his palm across her cheek, over her mouth. She kissed his hand, then his lips, and her knees were shaky. They knelt on the floor together, each sliding the shirt off the other's shoulders, but when she reached for his belt, his hand closed tightly on hers. "Marry me," he said.

"Make love to me," she said. He traced patterns around her breasts with his finger tip; he seemed abstracted, perhaps even bored. "Do you love me?" she asked him.

"I love you."

"Don't you want to make love to me?"

"I want you to say you'll marry me," he told her. "And then you can tell your parents when it's an established fact. You say, 'We got married.' "

She felt his hand close tighter around her own, like one fist enclosing another. She tried to shake free, but he held firm. "I'll marry you," she said. And he let her have her way with his belt buckle.

Next morning, holding her hand over her heart, she said to him, "I want to get married, but I'm not sure it's an entirely rational thing to do."

Ben shook his head in wonderment at her. "Don't separate yourself into little packages of rational and irrational like they were good and evil, Rachel. Act on what you feel. The world is dominated by policymakers and long-range planners. Whatever happened to gut reaction, the stuff that morality is made from? It's all this damn overrationalized policy that's driving us, as individuals and as a nation, down paths we should never have trod." He sounded like Jake when he talked that way. He told her he never read over his exam answers. First impulse, he said, was always the best choice. Would they be together now if she hadn't acted impulsively, and he as well?

"I guess not."

"I'm only waiting for you, Love," he said and it sounded to Rachel just a bit like a gauntlet, a catch-me-if-you-can of years gone by. I can so beat you. I can too catch up. Get him. Hang on. She had a need to gasp for air, then she wanted to scold him: Don't you leave me, you hear? She couldn't make it through a summer without him and, double whammy, without Jake as well. Ben was ready to go: "If we can't be together without being married, shouldn't we be getting married?" he asked her.

"Where?"

"We'll drive south till we find a place we can get married quickly."

They grabbed a few things and got in the car.

Just outside Newark, Delaware, she began to feel jumpy. They had lost Dylan and WBAI airwaves. She ran the radio dial back and forth but found no familiar voices with calming powers.

Sentences with formalized beginnings began to surface in her mind. She couldn't shake off Marriage is a commitment, or Forever is a long time. She fought each phrase back down, knowing how Ben would scoff at them; wrestled with each till it grew weary and meaningless. The silences in the car grew hot, and she had to fight with that, too. "How long," she asked him, her words garbled like a child's request of a stranger, "do you figure we'll be married?"

"Nothing's forever anymore," he said. "We like each other today. We want to sleep together today. We want to get married today. So we do." He took both hands off the wheel in a gesture of exuberance. "They're blowing forever up in a

Southeast Asian jungle. Our parents were the last generation who could think in such terms. We're married today, tomorrow, next week. Whatever."

"Hell," she said, "then let's get married already. Onward, down the highway. South Carolina, here we come." She stroked his thigh and his foot moved hard into the accelerator pedal. Maybe they were going too fast, but as Ben said, risk was its own pleasure.

There was a man at city hall taking pictures. He had a camera set up on a tripod just inside the clerk's office. You took one of his cards with a number on it if you wanted your picture taken. You could have it taken during the ceremony or just after. All the other couples there held their numbers. One of the brides, a young, pregnant girl, fanned herself with her card. Ben said no thanks to the photographer, and to Rachel he said he wasn't going to stage an event for an image on paper, he wanted to participate in the event itself. And it wasn't exactly a bargain price, either, that the guy wanted. They had forgotten a bouquet, so Ben said try to catch one of the others, for some of the brides tossed them after the ceremony, but the bride just before Rachel left city hall still holding her flowers. The clerk offered them the use of an artificial bouquet which turned out to be plastic, not even silk, and Rachel declined. What she said to Ben was, you didn't know what other marriages it had been in and she'd never been superstitious, but she thought it was better to play it safe and go with no flowers at all. She was the only bride who wore red, but that wasn't surprising, given how people are so bound by tradition, bound unto death sometimes.

Rachel was surprised by the brevity of the ceremony. She had thought there would be more pausing around the vows, perhaps some individualized moment when they were asked one deep question about the other, but the words breezed past, leaving barely any time for either of them to say "I do." "That's it?" she said to the official when he told Ben he could kiss the bride, for this was the first wedding she'd ever attended. "That's the difference between married and unmarried?"

"That's all it is," the clerk said and smiled.

After the ceremony they walked across the town green. Ben knelt beside a bed of daffodils and snapped one, then two more, low, near the ground, and handed them up to Rachel. An elderly woman walking her dog rushed toward them. "Mustn't, mustn't," she said to Ben. She pulled up hard on her dog's lead as she admonished him. "This is a park," she said. "Those flowers belong to everyone."

"That's why I picked them," he explained. "We're part of The Great Everyone." He took Rachel's hand and began to walk away. The old woman followed.

"To look at," she said from behind them. "If you,"—they heard her hesitate as she cast about for her next word—"hippies go and pick them all, they won't be here for anyone else's enjoyment." Ben and Rachel shot glances at one another, then burst into amused laughter at the same moment.

"Sorry," Rachel said over her shoulder to the woman. "We've just gotten married, you see." She was glad for a chance to tell someone. She would have liked to be able to say, "and we sleep together," to this woman, and to everyone. The woman slowed, but didn't entirely stop her pursuit. "Well," she said, and Rachel, though she faced forward now, sensed the woman had stopped. "Still . . . ," she heard the voice try to continue.

"Maybe I should offer her a joint and teach her to relax," Ben suggested and reached into his vest pocket. Rachel grabbed his hand away from his cache. "Hey," he said, "I was only kidding." By the time they reached the car, the woman had left them and gone back to circling the green with her dog.

They ordered ice cream sodas in the drugstore at the other side of the green. The soda fountain sported gold-colored taps and a black marble countertop. They pushed each other around on leather-covered stools as they sipped their way through their nuptial repast. After a while Ben was able to engage the owner in a discussion of the demographics of the town, affecting a slight drawl, or so Rachel thought, for the purpose. While Rachel sipped her soda, Ben tucked a daffodil behind her ear and tried to tie it in place with her pale curls.

When they left, the owner came out to the car and helped them attach, just below the license, a menu, whose blank back he'd emblazoned with letters announcing their so very recent wedding. The pharmacist dug up two empty cans for them which they hung, also, from the marker. But it all fell off somewhere, cans and menu, before they reached the highway.

It was much better that there were no photographs. Her parents would expect a white leather album, and they would expect to see a bouquet. They would not expect to see a groom wearing a royal blue shirt, a red leather vest, jeans, hiking boots, and shoulder length hair held back with a leather head band. Nor would they be amused to see the Mickey Mouse pin on her dress. Her mother would have asked, "Couldn't you have worn shoes, this one time? It's sandals or boots always, sandals or boots with you, Rachel." She had talked Ben out of wearing his buttons—the omega symbol of Resistance, the Hell No We Won't Go one, and the assorted variations on the peace symbol that he owned—over his breast pocket, as he had wanted. "It's so ironic looking, Rachel," he had argued. "It looks just like a bunch of goddamn military medals," but she had said, "Not in the Deep South, it won't." Most of all what her parents would expect was that the groom would be Jake. Well, hell, it was time they figured out they couldn't get their fingers into every damn part of her life. They weren't going to get to lie in her marriage bed with her.

She'd say, Jake knows all about him. I wrote to him about Ben—and she would, as soon as she could. That would have to be the antidote for their anxiety.

It took Rachel nearly a month to tell her parents that she was married. Twice she dialed their number and counted rings till she heard her mother's voice, jarringly eager, like a too hearty innkeeper wishing a resounding good morning to her unbreakfasted, sleepy guests. Once, too, in the intervening month, her parents had initiated a call and she heard her father, more distant-sounding, on the hall extension as well. Each time she intended to explain how it was she'd decided to get married without consulting them first. If they'd asked about him, it would have given her an opening; a beginning. But they didn't ask, because they didn't know about him. She'd never mentioned his name.

The morning after the Big Step, as Ben had taken to calling the city hall ceremony, they had bacon and eggs in a diner. Ben had passed all his change across the table and Rachel had started off for the pay phone, though she'd ended up in the tiny ladies' room instead, locked the door, and perched on the radiator to think about her call. "Mom, I'm down in South Carolina," was one of her projected beginnings. "Bet you can't guess what I'm doing." But her mother wouldn't have played the game. "What is it Rachel?" she would have asked, her voice gone brittle and frightened. "Why aren't you at school?" And then when she explained, that inevitable: "What did Jake say?"

Mother, it isn't up to Jake, you know. Jake's gone, remember?

That's really the point, Rachel, don't you see? Your judgment is hardly the best in the world, you know. Her mother would probably hand the phone to her husband and then Rachel would have to start all over again, because her mother would only shake her head, unable to explain it to him. How long have you known this young man? he'd ask. She'd say I met my husband two months ago (which was only a slight exaggeration of six weeks) and he'd see it was really true, with her saying *my husband* like that, and he'd understand he couldn't do anything about it, that she meant to stay married. He might say "impulsive," or "bull-headed," or another of those phrases he tossed around sometimes. But mostly, there'd be more passing of the phone back and forth or they'd each be on an extension, diluting the clarity of the connection by half—how she hated when they did that—the two of them finally talking to one another, not to her at all.

Rachel pushed herself down off the radiator, thinking, perhaps a letter would be better. Or at least a private phone somewhere so she didn't have to hear their accusations alternated with the operator's demands for more dimes. She opened the door to the toilet. It had been left unflushed. She heard her mother sigh and turn away in disgust. Her mother would have climbed back in the car and driven another twenty miles rather than use these facilities. She wouldn't have slid into the restaurant booth as she and Ben had and brushed the crumbs to the floor, nor wiped the table with napkins pulled from the table dispenser. She would have gone somewhere else. Rachel pushed each stall open, one after the other, letting each of them slam shut. The toilets were filthy, yes, but she selected among them, chose one that made her only nearly gag, used it, and made a brave, but futile attempt to flush it with a foot applied to the appropriate lever.

"So big deal," Ben said when she sat down across from him. "You can call them tomorrow." He wasn't rushing to tell his parents, he reminded her. "This is our thing, you know, not theirs." He tilted his glass of orange juice slightly in her direction. "To the bride and groom and the Kama Sutra," he said. "May they live happily ever after for a long time." They clinked glasses.

Married, they lived together part-time in his dorm room. The rest of the time she was back in New London attending classes. The enforced separation made her long to be with him again by the end of the week.

I have two lives now, she thought. Two lives, kept like secrets from one another. Weekdays she was at her college, working at being a scholar, in a world of narrow gray corridors and underheated college classrooms and art galleries. She studied reproductions of artwork whose surfaces gleamed hard and sharp from too much camera light. There were corridors with roughened stone wherever you dared to place a hand and the clang and clatter of cafeteria stainless. And weekends: the light taste of salt on Ben's shoulder, warmth in an unanticipated spot in an unexpected moment, feasts on sweet doughnuts or spicy pizza late at night, combined with the richness of grass. No harsh edges there. "We are each other's landscapes; each other's architecture," Ben said. They never worked on weekends. They had no time for it. In her parents' minds, she was the weekday person. Let them keep thinking that way, she said to Ben.

In time, though, she couldn't put off telling them any longer. The end of the academic year was approaching. Her parents were making plans to drive to New London and pack her belongings into their car and drive it all to their home. Ben will drive me home, she told them. They protested, no, it's our job, why should he have to and who is he, isn't he one of Jake's friends? And she laughed and said, no, my friend. And she said to Ben when she'd hung up the phone, I guess I have to tell them now. So they'd piled her things into a car he borrowed and drove it all to New Haven where they carried it up two flights and somehow stuffed everything into a corner of his dorm room. Soon they'd rent an apartment and move all those things into their own place, Rachel said. Too soon, Ben said. "We'll be up to our ears in leases and contracts and bills from Macy's," and she said, "Forget Macy's. Forget shopping. Forget possessions. Just remember me." He talked about crashing with friends for the summer. She was disappointed, for she'd imagined—though she knew it wildly impossible—a cottage someplace like Guilford, right on the shore. The two of them snuggled against one another in a bed that nearly filled the whole second floor of the house. "Just don't use the word crash in front of my mother," she advised him. "It'll blow her mind."

Rachel panicked on the drive to her parents' house. "Turn the car around," she begged Ben.

"I really want to meet your parents," he told her. "I want to see where you come from. It's part of who you are."

"Only part," she said. "You won't confuse me with them, will you?"

"Relax," he said, "and just live it. It'll be cool," Ben assured her. "Surprises are good for people. They bring out their real emotions and it's always good stuff that's in there inside good people. We arrive, surprise! And it's done. It's real and spontaneous. They stare at me. They're satisfied. Everybody hugs and kisses and we're officially married," he said.

"Ta-dah," she sang out.

"Raz mataz and ta-dah ta-dah," he amended.

Once they were there, though, walking up the path, her mother waving manically from the front steps, it seemed more complicated.

"Ben," Rachel's father said as he extended his hand to him, careful to show he had politely retained his name from phone conversations with his daughter. Alice clutched Rachel against her while she offered her hand to Ben. "Thought you might want to know," Ben said, "I'm you're brand new son-in-law." Rachel laughed, choked, then burst into tears and reached for Ben's arm. "So fast?" she whispered in his ear, but he seemed not to have heard. Her parents did not accuse or lecture, as Rachel had at first feared, nor did they hug and kiss either of them anymore as Ben had promised. (It seemed to Rachel that he had promised it.) Rachel thought perhaps her parents staggered as they went back into the house and that they grabbed onto the arms of the living room chairs for support as they eased themselves down to sit, but she wasn't sure, for she'd looked away at the crucial moment to wipe her face of tears. And certainly they hadn't needed to be so histrionic, it would have all been done for effect; for her, for Ben. "Well," her father said, and then her mother said, "Does Jake know?" and Rachel said, "Not yet, Mother." Alice stacked and unstacked a dozen yellow and blue Mexican coasters that lay on the coffee table while Ben described the wedding. "Have you met Jake?" her mother asked him when he was finished and Rachel said, "Mother, Jake's been gone since the winter and I didn't meet Ben till March. I told you that."

Her father asked if Ben's parents knew about the marriage, and he said, "No, Sir, we're planning to call them this evening. Rachel wanted you to know first." Rachel was surprised, but pleased, that Ben had addressed her father as "sir," though she did wonder if it sounded deliberately put on or even a touch mocking.

"You'll finish school, I assume, Rachel," her father said.

"Yes, Daddy."

"Where are you living?" Ed asked.

"In the dorm until they close it down for summer." Ben wrote down his telephone number and handed it to Rachel's father. "Eventually we're getting an apartment," he said.

"I'll need to take my summer things," Rachel told her mother.

"Of course. You'll need some shopping bags," her mother said. The two of them went up the stairs together and her mother held open a bag while Rachel dropped her sundresses, shorts, and tee shirts into it. "Rachel," she said, "there's a lot to talk about. Everything's different this year with Jake gone. Grace is a wreck, of course. And I didn't pick up any dresses for you yet. I wanted to talk about the party, first. About whether to have one at all. Do you think having the party would offend Grace and Manny? We'll have to talk after he leaves, I suppose."

"I'm going with him," Rachel said, "he's my husband, remember?" and she laughed.

"Of course." Her mother pulled open a drawer. "I've got a lot to get used to suddenly. It's a month, already?" her mother asked and Rachel nodded. "A whole month that I didn't know you were married. I didn't think about you during that time as a married woman." Rachel wished her mother wouldn't use such labels so freely. She was still Ben's girl, not A Married Woman. She'd never been called Mrs. Goodman, except once by Jennifer, and that had been in jest, and she still signed all her college documents under her maiden name because it avoided unnecessary confusion.

Her mother closed the closet and handed the bag to Rachel. "Are you enjoying married life?" she asked. Rachel said, yes, she was, and was going to ask her if maybe she could borrow a cookbook, one that had basics in it, but her mother said, "And Jake can't even come down to meet him."

"We'll visit him sometime," Rachel told her. "But I want to tell him about Ben myself," she added, "so don't mention it to Grace yet."

"He wouldn't even be able to come down if we had a party. Though I suppose that's just as well now, with you married."

"Don't you think Ben's coloring is like Jake's?" Rachel asked her.

"Something like it," her mother said. Rachel waited for her to comment further about Ben, but she said nothing more. They carried clothes from the closet to the bed, making wide circles round each other as they passed. Her mother pushed the line of dresses and blouses to one end of the closet, then to the other, then back again as she said, "First Jake, now you."

"I got married, Mom. I didn't go to Canada."

Her mother said, "You know your father and I never wanted to pry into your life," and left her sentence trailing, pulling implications and questions like colored kite tails behind it, as though she really did want to have it all straight; wanted to make clear and final sense of her daughter and this marriage. Rachel waited for a direct question. The older woman turned and faced into the room. "All these shopping bags are silly, Rachel." She reached into the closet and drew out a suitcase, then emptied the nearly filled shopping bags onto the bed and consumed more minutes transferring the clothes.

Rachel and Ben stayed for dinner. "A quiet little supper," as her mother described it. "If I'd known about you," she said and held her open hand out toward Ben, "I'd have had something more festive." She apologized for her steak and baked potatoes. During the melon course, her father told a joke about the blind leading the blind and Rachel thought Ben might have really thought it was funny (she thought it was moderately amusing), because he laughed, and he probably wouldn't have done so just to please her father. Her mother paraphrased all Jake's recent letters, as reported by Grace, and said she got the impression Jake had begun painting again, what had he written to Rachel about that? "Jake's doing just fine," Rachel told her mother. "You've got to stop worrying yourself to death over him." Her father opened champagne, and they clinked glasses, reaching across the table, and her mother said, "Happiness . . ." as though it were the beginning of a longer toast, but it seemed to drift off from her, and she smiled. Rachel's father lifted his glass to his lips and then they all sipped from their tulip crystal. "Where are you from?" Ed asked his new son-in-law after a silence, and Ben told him about growing up in Akron and about his father's law practice, but then her father got up from the table (it wasn't something Ben said, Rachel was sure of it) and said, "Alice, where is my date book? I want to check tomorrow's appointments," and they both disappeared for a while into his study, shuffling books and papers in there.

"Damn them," Rachel said to Ben. "They're behaving like morons."

"What the hell," Ben said. "Do we care?" She shook her head, though she would have preferred to shake her parents by the shoulders, each in turn.

At the door they kissed her and shook Ben's hand. "Such a lot to absorb," her mother said, and Rachel laughed again, surprising herself by the loud and raucous sound of her voice. "Won't you consider staying over?" Alice asked, and Rachel thought it sounded as if she addressed vague acquaintances and did so only out of obligatory constraints of etiquette.

"Another time, perhaps," Ben said.

"That really wasn't too bad," he said when they'd pulled away from the house. "They didn't give us any real grief.

Though if we'd stayed, they'd have wanted us in separate beds, I'm sure. Other than that, they were cool enough."

"Of course they didn't say much of anything," she pointed out. "They never said what they thought."

" 'Such a lot to absorb,' " Ben said imitating, accurately, her mother's slow rhythms, then laughing.

"I shouldn't have laughed at her. And I laughed so loudly, too." She covered her eyes, graying over the memory.

"Everything is Jake this, Jake that, like he's their son, not their neighbor. When she said that bit about 'Have you met Jake,' I thought she was talking about somebody invisible and that maybe she was totally loony tunes."

"Well he's just gone away permanently, you know." She felt the edge in her voice. "What do you expect? They thought I was going to marry him. It might have been nice if you made some effort to understand their position, to see they didn't need this, this marriage, sprung on them this way."

"Hey," he shouted back at her. "You never said you almost married him. What the hell do you expect of me?" and she saw his hands grip and pull at the steering wheel. "Maybe you should have married him, you know. Why the hell d'you change your plans, anyway?"

"I hadn't planned to marry him," she said, flinging the words out at him. "Jake and I were never like that. They"— and she pointed back behind them—"thought we were."

"Are you sure?"

"I'm sure." She tried to speak quietly—they had never raised their voices to each other before. "Forgive me for shouting," she said. The words stayed in the air between them. They waited for them to dissipate.

"I forgive you," he said at last, but his words were fierce, not at all consoling. He passed the car ahead of him and picked up ten miles per hour. She remembered her mother running to meet them when they first arrived and then her mother so unfocused, when they left, and suddenly Rachel was crying and she said to him, jaggedly, with little bits of stolen breath, "We shouldn't have done it."

Ben pulled the car over to the side of the road. He reached an arm across her shoulder and tried to pull her toward him, but she squirmed away, sliding deep into her corner of the car. "They hate me now. We should have told them first, before we got married." Why had she listened to Ben about her parents? She could have predicted their reactions. She was the one who'd spent twenty years with them, not he. And she should have told Jake, too.

"Don't get too maudlin," he said, "they can't expect us to lead their lives, and to do everything the way they would. This is grown-up time for you and me."

"They hate me," she moaned.

"Listen to me. We've gone beyond them. Anyway, *I* love you. They're just angry because you acted on your own. They're angry because you're not them. Wait till they have a chance to call up their friends and bitch about us, and that'll be it. They'll start pestering us about a party. They'll want to dress you up in one of those dresses you told me about. They'll try to make the cake look like a wedding cake, bride and groom and all. They'll try to convince their friends you're a virgin."

Rachel laughed at Ben's suggestion. "Maybe she'll want me to wear white this year."

"They just want it on their terms, Rachel. So it can be their wedding. They'll give us a big wedding gift, cash-dough, and suddenly it'll seem that even the idea of getting married was really their idea. I'll be approved *ex post facto.*"

He put his hand on her blonde hair, and she allowed it to stay. His tongue grazed her earlobe once, then twice, then sketched a path down her neck. With one hand on her chin, he turned her face toward him, but she averted her eyes. He kissed her face, his lips trying to meet her lips with little kisses, and she turned (she had thought she wouldn't give in, but it just happened as though someone else were in control, as it so often did with Ben) and she kissed him back, and he put his arms around her.

When they got back to New Haven, they sat down on the bed and he pulled the blankets up over their heads, and said, "see, our own little house, we don't need anything or anyone else," and they made love, but she kept seeing her mother the whole time, standing inside the closet but facing out, her hands brimming with summer clothes. "Everything'll be fine," he said to her. After he fell asleep, she thought about how when she and her mother were upstairs she could have said something about Ben, like, what do you think of him, or about how when they got an apartment she was going to make curtains, or maybe tried to explain why they didn't tell her before, but she hadn't been sure her mother wanted to know anything else. Did her parents think that if they didn't ask questions and didn't know much about Ben that he and the marriage would go away? That the fairy tale would end with Jake pardoned, returned home and married to their only daughter? What ostriches they were about human relations. About the war. About the way the world worked! Damn you, Jake, for going away. You'd have figured out what to do with them.

She cried again, but very softly. She didn't want Ben to wake up.

CHAPTER THREE

*T*HE ABSOLUTELY hardest thing to do was write to Jake about the marriage. It wasn't the sort of thing, no matter how well you phrased it, that should be in a letter at all. That was why she hadn't been able to tell her parents, either, till she was face to face with them. If she could have called him, it would have been better. It would be a while yet, though, he said, before he got a phone.

"Remember Ben?" she wrote. "I told you about him. He's the one I said looks like you. Longer hair, I suppose, since you've had to become a member of the shorn establishment. Or has yours grown back, with all those scrumptious curls? Don't you think it's funny that your hair was longer than mine? But back to Ben. We got married. Surprise, surprise!!!!!" The exclamation points were a mistake, she thought as she looked the page over. She'd wanted it to look funny and lighthearted, but instead, they lent emphasis to the deed. She wasn't going to toss the paper out, though. She'd done enough of that already. This letter was going into the mail. Next she wrote in the date and place of their marriage. This sidestep into the more formal aspects of her news made it easier to continue. "Not exactly your long white gown, catered affair, but you'd have loved it, Jake. I wore red." As soon as she began to give details of her wedding day (the pregnant bride, the woman who cried the entire time she waited for her turn at the nuptial vows), the telling became easier. She wrote of how she and Ben had forgotten to get either rings or flowers ("though we don't need symbols to ratify our commitment"). "It was so simple, this getting married," she told him. "The ceremony (if you can describe a wheezy Justice of the Peace's dozen mumbled words with such an elegant term) was about thirty seconds long. I can't believe anything so short that you could miss it if you sneezed could possibly have any legal significance. Ben says he bets people just walk away from each other rather than divorcing if they've married this way because it doesn't feel like a marriage. Unless you bring witnesses, that is. Some people did. We just used their official city hall types (a drunk and a deaf-mute, or so it appeared). I think that's partly why we didn't rush to tell everyone, either—as long as no one knew, it wasn't entirely real. It was our own private delicious fantasy.

"Ben's a junior, so he's got at least another year before he gets drafted, unless Johnson really flips out. After that, though, I suspect we'll be joining you up there and I'll be planting your garden for you. Anyway, here I am married to him, and I'm sure you'll like him. We're trying to find an apartment now, and Dear Jake, I wish you were here to tell me what you think and to tell me if you like the apartment we picked, which we haven't picked yet, haven't even started to look for yet, but will this weekend, I think. I am not different, you will be pleased to hear, at least I hope you will be pleased to hear that. My mother asked me how I like married life, which Ben says means how do I like sex, and I suppose it does in her mind." She drew a twisty arrow leading away from the word sex over to the margin and turning the page sideways squeezed in the words, "I married him for sex. Is that an admirable motivation? Do I care whether it is or not? Say it's all right, Dear Jake."

At the top of the last page she wrote "We're going to visit you this summer and I know *you will like him.*" And if he didn't? What would she do? What if theirs was a friendship that would die now because Jake and Ben disliked one another? Wasn't that unlikely, though? Hadn't she been drawn to Ben because of how much like Jake he was, how much the two men shared interests and concerns? "You're probably angry that I didn't write about this sooner, but it was hard to tell you, though I tried in several other letters. Perhaps this one isn't right either, but I am determined to mail it, for better or for worse, as I have so recently learned to say. I took a very long time to tell Alice and Ed as well. They weren't thrilled, which shouldn't surprise you, and then I did ask them not to tell your P's, because I knew once Grace and Manny knew, they would be sending you telegrams, and I wanted to tell you myself. Chances are, though, Alice was too horrified to mention it to Grace and she still doesn't know. For them the news isn't that I married Ben, but that I didn't marry you. Poor things, they'll have to reconstruct their reality now—and so late in life! I love you, I love you. We will visit soon. Love, Rachel.

"P.S.," she wrote, "we have no official wedding photos, but I will have somebody take a picture of us and you can see what Ben looks like.

"P.P.S. I am not pregnant.

"P.P.P.S.—or whatever—Ben is a history major.

"P.P.P.P.S. Jake: tell me truth when you answer. And forgive me. Love again, R."

On paper her words looked stretched out and attenuated. They billowed up high where they ought to have been straight and firm. And anyway, half the thoughts had run off before she got them out the end of her pen. In one of her letters the words had looked broodingly dark (a broad-point pen—she wouldn't use that again) and in the next, downright frail. Would he see special meaning in such change? Would a shaky hand, copied out on a bus ride, reveal some utterly false view of her psyche? (Please excuse my wobbling hand, I write in transit to New Haven.) Did he find her pedantic and egocentric in these scribblings? Do I bore you now, Jake? Please, stop me if I do. Have I lost your attention forever? She wanted spontaneity; give and take, not description and statement. When she needed Jake's reaction, she needed it right away. On the spot. Now. She despised waiting out the time till answers came.

She stayed close to home that week, waiting to catch the mail as soon as it arrived. She hoped, too, that Jake's response would come when Ben wasn't home. Ben had said they should read all their correspondence aloud to each other. So far, that had meant she read her letters because he hadn't gotten any. Usually she didn't mind all that much, unless he got critical (which had happened only once) and said stuff like, "The guy is just garden variety horny up there, Rachel." And probably, she had to admit when pressed by Ben, that was not an altogether incorrect analysis. Still, she did relish having the words first, alone. She wanted to take them slowly, to hear his voice, rhythms, and intonations across the miles, as she could only if she read his words silently to herself.

He answered right away. Still, that meant over a week of waiting. When the letter did arrive, she opened it immediately, standing on the front steps by the mailbox. If she was to be chastised, there was no point in putting it off. She ripped the letter open, unfolded his pages, and read what he had written: "Good luck, congratulations, or whatever it is you're supposed to say to the bride." Relief flushed through her, warming her face and hands. She refolded the letter, hanging onto just those few words of support for a while longer. She would walk to the park, she thought, and indulge herself by reading slowly through the letter there.

Stretched out on her bench twenty minutes later, she

glanced over the whole of his first page. His words were printed, much too neatly formed to have been spontaneous. She was afraid to read on, yet did: "I'm glad for you. And of course I will like him. I'm selfishly glad, too, that Ben may be a resister and bring you here, though sad that you two will be in anguish for that." Still his printing marched onward, all uniform, even, and careful. Not his thoughts, but the necessary business of polite exchange, she knew. She imagined him consulting an etiquette book, reading the paragraphs headed: Acknowledgment of Marriage Announcement.

The letters his black ink had traced out grew larger and broader: "Resistance is a serious business, Rachel. There isn't a one of us here who gave up U.S. citizenship lightly. So I advise Ben to consider, even in these terrible times, all that he surrenders in becoming an expatriate. Remind Ben if he doesn't already know, that I'm a janitor in an elementary school and lucky to have any job, but certainly no longer a painter. The Historian must beware." Why such tones of lecture? Rachel wondered with annoyance. He was distancing himself from her as though he were a draft counselor now. His letter went on to suggest that Ben apply to graduate school early so that he'd be all set when the time came to leave. He recommended a specific counselor at Yale, which really irritated Rachel because she knew all the counselors too, in fact knew more about the center than Jake possibly could because she still went over there all the time and he was a million miles away. Jake's harangue continued: "Remember, too, that all the counselors are in the States. None are veterans of expatriation. Tell him to think long and hard and to talk to a lot of people." This was such obvious stuff, why did he bother? Why was he talking all around her marriage?

She turned the page to see his printing disappear and the hand that she knew as his to surface: "How can I ethically counsel anyone when I'm still not sure, myself, what's right? Besides," he wrote, "if I were to counsel Ben to emigrate, part of my motivation would undoubtedly be to ease my own pain and despair by bringing you closer.

"Damn, Rachel, I'm having trouble catching my breath. You want some Truth, as you put it? I was shocked. I couldn't read your letter beyond the word *married*. I envisioned the ceremony: ushers in cutaways, heads all turning back to catch a glimpse of you (The Bride) on your father's arm. White velvet carpet, guests rising. I thought, OK, I am dead. They gave up on me and sat shiva when I crossed the border. I thought maybe somewhere between Quebec and Toronto I really did crash the car and that this pit of emptiness was, after all, eternal afterlife. 'No point inviting him anymore, Alice,' I heard my mother say, 'he can't come anyway.' I could see everything: the bride (you, Rachel) and groom lifted high on chairs to the music of the hora. And there I was, alternately trying to bang the door down or hovering like the bloodied spirit of the dead, just above the altar. At that point I threw the letter across the room (forgive me). The pages flew out, separated, then drifted so slowly down, they seemed caught out of time in slow motion. I tried ignoring them for a while, then gathered them up and went on. Once I read your description of the city hall event, my rage seemed foolish. You'd made me laugh. I gave up my fantastic notions of what it means that you are a married women. I think you're right, you aren't any different, which is all that matters to me." It was all right then. This was Jake's voice, judgmental, yet forgiving. She put his letter down across her chest and played the words of his last sentence over and over to herself. "You aren't any different, which is all that matters to me." The sun was warm on her face. It was going to be all right with Jake.

She read on: "I know you've mentioned Ben (I almost wrote

'this guy,' but caught myself), but I didn't realize this was SERIOUS, the REAL STUFF and all that, Rachel. I'm either high on the naivete scale or you're damn crafty at keeping secrets. I will like him, don't worry. So write more about him. Sex is an absolutely fine motivation. And to hell with ethics. Come to Canada. And bring my memory with you."

And his signature. But then more, barely legible, and in blue ink, a last minute note: "Elizabeth is anxious to meet you. I've told her that we are Old Friends. At least your revelation will lend more credibility to this description. She tolerates my dependency on the mail from home to a degree I can only marvel at. Did I tell you she has red hair? Very long, very soft. We will both love Ben, I'm sure. Tell him, though, to think long and hard. I love you—still. J."

Why this afterthought of Elizabeth? And *We* will love Ben? Why that emphasis? Had she missed something in his letters (as he had clearly missed in hers) about the importance of this other person? Was he telling her that her marriage freed him in some way? This was a positive side effect of marriage she hadn't anticipated. But this Elizabeth, whoever she was, had better take damn good care of him.

CHAPTER FOUR

RACE, Jake's mother, sent a note of congratulations that was short, sweet, and full of blessings. Grace's cards were always entirely correct. They arrived exactly on time to mark birthdays, holidays, or special achievements. That she had signed this one, "May you and Benjamin know great joy together in the years to come," didn't mean she actually nourished sincere good wishes: these words only confirmed Grace's ease with a felicitous phrase.

Oddly, though, Grace continued to write after her obligatory letter recognizing Rachel's marriage. Rachel had never received a letter from her unconnected to a specific event, but now the letters arrived several times a week.

They were a maudlin lot, these letters, though only quietly sentimental, lacking broad weeping gestures. They were letters patched together out of wishful, fabricated memories. "You and Jake never fought," she wrote. If she meant they had never done each other irreversible or fatal injury, yes, that was true. They had survived well enough, and lived to tell about it.

"You were such special children." It amused Rachel how Grace glossed over the evils they had done to one another. Certainly every injury that had occurred had been reported in glorious exaggeration to her as well as to Alice, Rachel's mother. Grace knew about the time Jake had left her adrift in a rowboat without oars. How he had slipped them from her oarlocks into his canoe. Because he needed to check their condition, he'd told Rachel, and then he'd paddled back to shore, pulled his canoe up, and gone back into the house. She shouted and called after him, screaming death threats, but he walked away as though he couldn't hear her, right up onto his back porch and into the house. When she finally worked her way back and entered the kitchen she couldn't believe it. Jake was sitting at the table drinking a chocolate ice cream soda and smirking. His mother was standing at the counter marinating the steak which was to be their dinner. Rachel had sobbed out her tale of mistreatment to Grace with a lot of emphasis on how totally exhausted she was from thrashing around for hours with her hands and she heard Jake slurp up the last of his soda through the straw. He stood up to clear his place and started pontificating about how he'd done it for her sake, to give her a survival lesson because she was so otherwise incompetent and then he had the nerve to compliment her, to say he thought she'd done remarkably well with it. Grace, by that time, was covering the steak and putting it in the refrigerator, seeming not to be listening, which really infuriated Rachel, and when she glanced up she saw Jake starting to leave the kitchen all free and easy. So she took a push-kind of swing at him that knocked him into the door frame. He pushed back—hard—and then Grace finally did walk between them, but it was as if she were strolling in a park, and somewhat preoccupied at that, not really trying to separate them at all. She remembered how his mother'd made Jake call Alice and apologize—not apologize to Rachel, but to her mother, to say, "I'm sorry, Mrs. Rothstein, I won't do it again."

Rachel had been much more subtle in her attacks: she destroyed his books by leaving them at the edge of the pond, or threw out his papers because "they looked like trash, Jake. Any normal person would think papers left like that down by the pond were trash. And you know how your father hates us to leave litter down there. It's not my fault. I was just cleaning up," she'd say. He pinned her against the wall at times like that and held a fistful of her curly hair in his hand and tugged. She'd once hidden behind the steps to watch him scrounge through garbage cans for his crushed and mutilated sheaf of drawings.

As they grew older, she could count on him not to tell on her—once it became clear that neither set of parents meted out punishments for their actions against one another. The adults were as removed from their scenes as though they'd accidentally wandered onto the set of a play rehearsal and needed to be steered back toward the wings.

Once they were both in college, he'd occasionally mentioned his past misdeeds against her. Often they were acts she'd forgotten till he spoke of them. He apologized for tying her to the tree that time. For locking her out of the house in the dark when they'd been left home alone together for the first time while their parents had gone out to dinner. "I can't believe I did that to you," he'd say. "I can't believe that was me." Jake carried all his errors around with him, slung round his neck like a weighty albatross. "Forget it," she'd say to him. "That wasn't you. That was a little kid I once knew."

Grace sent a card with a reproduction of a Jessie Wilcox Smith painting of two children playing together with building blocks. A boy and a girl, little chubby-cheeked darlings, who smiled up at Rachel from the shiny surface of the greeting card. "A boy and girl who can be best friends is very unusual, don't you think?" she wrote to Rachel. It had been one of those childhood friendships born of necessity. There was no neighborhood to ride your bike through, no doorbells to ring and ask if any little girls lived there. The pond they lived on was a mile off the main road. There were only two other homes on the body of water, both owned by retired couples. Sometimes a family would rent the little cottage behind the Delling house for part of the summer and then there might be children around for a few weeks, but other than that, Rachel and Jake faced off across the water from one another, set there to do childhood battle.

There was a photograph that hung in each of their homes. In Jake's house, the photograph had been framed and hung on his bedroom wall. It was a photo of two very small children, a boy and a girl, with light-colored curls tumbling over their foreheads. They sat in an enormous brass bed, propped against three or four large lace-trimmed pillows, their legs under the covers. A book lay across their knees, and the girl, the smaller of the two, was pointing at something on the page. A twin to this picture was displayed upon an end table in the Rothsteins' den. The photograph was taken when Rachel was two, and Jake, not quite three and a half. It was a candid shot, taken by her father, though she had heard her mother say often enough that it was of professional quality. "Young Marrieds," her mother said as she pointed it out to guests. When Jake was in sixth grade he'd gotten into a fist fight with a kid from school who apparently made some off-color comments about the photo. Jake had tried to get his mother to put it away, but she completely ignored his request. "They're crazy to have those pictures," he said to Rachel.

"Why?" she wanted to know.

"Two people in bed?" he said to her. "You know what people do in bed? Our Parents want it to look sexual, and that's obscene," he hissed with dramatic emphasis. By the time he was leaving for college, though, he told Rachel he planned to take the photograph with him. He said he would hang it in his room at school (over a fireplace, preferably), as a provocative piece of imagery; a place to begin a conversation. She knew, of course, that he meant a very specific kind of conversation:

conversation with a girl. Grace protested when Jake tried to take it from his wall. It was hers, she told him, and she would miss it if he took it. She promised to have it copied at one of those heirloom photography places. She never got around to it, though. The only two copies were still in their parents' homes.

Grace began to write about the very early days when hers was the only house on the small lake. She said that with Jake now out there in the middle of Lake Ontario (she exaggerated from a lack of geographical perspective with which Rachel could identify), she was reminded of those times and filled pages with repetitious musings of long ago. These were not new stories to Rachel: she'd heard Grace tell them to dinner guests, to workmen and deliverymen, to any and all captive audiences. In one letter Grace recalled being "filled with joy" when she saw what would become the Rothstein house starting to be built across the lake from her. Then, increasingly, Grace's imagery took on peculiar religious overtones. She referred to the arrival of her new neighbors as "a heavenly gift," and said that Alice Rothstein ("your dear, dear mother") had been "sent from God" to save her from her loneliness. Her own parents were not particularly religious, nor did Rachel believe Grace was on any other subject, so when she lapsed into conceits involving the spiritual, Rachel suffered acute embarrassment for her: she saw the woman was in pain, and that in choosing Ben, she was the cause.

Rachel remembered very little of those early days, so it was The Parents' recollections which served as memory for those times. She knew it was unlikely that she could actually remember the metal stroller which her mother had pushed along the narrow path that went round the pond to the Marshes', yet she could picture that stroller perfectly. It was painted white and had a series of colored beads across the front. The one Jake sat in was identical, except that it was pale green in color. But perhaps those were strollers she'd seen on the street, and not theirs at all. She thought she could remember identical stuffed bears that they held as they were pushed side by side down Main Street and a store where they were taken which sold ice cream sandwiches made from a scoop of ice cream and two giant-sized cookies. She had seen photographs of them in matching outfits, done up like twins.

Those details mattered to his mother and to her mother, but not to her. What she could remember was that eventually she divided her time between the two houses. Some days she was told to go to the Marsh house after school, and some days Jake was told to go to her house. It was the accepted pattern of their lives. Once a week or so, she slept at the other house where she had a room of her own and a dresser in that room with some of her clothing, just as he had a room and bureau in her house. Such an arrangement made sense in those houses that would otherwise have been too large for one-child families. Lately this had begun to strike her as an odd detail; one difficult to fit into the pattern of her parents' otherwise traditional world view. Rachel and Jacob were raised by four parents, not two. "But that hardly makes it a hippy commune, Rachel," her father was quick to remind her.

"No, but it's distinctly odd, Daddy." When her father frowned, she'd amended her words: "It's unusual. You can admit that, at least, can't you?" She took his shrug to signify concession.

CHAPTER FIVE

*W*HAT RACHEL liked best about their new apartment was the way the kitchen floor rolled and waved like the floor of a funhouse. Ben said it had speed bumps for a tricyclist. And it reminded Rachel of the blue and red linoleum floor that had been in the playhouse in her backyard when she was growing up. She wondered if they ripped this floor up whether they would find old newspapers as they had when the playhouse had finally been dismantled. She had gathered all those old papers and straightened and smoothed them, then piled them in a corner of the basement to explore like treasure maps on another day, but they were gone when she next went down to the basement; taken up by her mother to line the garbage pail.

The other rooms of the apartment had wide wooden floorboards, not asphalt tiles or flea-ridden carpets the way so many other old places had. The floors had been painted a dozen times already by the long stream of changing tenants, but she had plans for painting the dreary gray floors over yet again, this time in deep colors; red in the living room and blue in their bedroom, then spatter painting in multi-colors on top of that. She had a Jackson Pollock rather than a colonial effect in mind. She thought about blue window shades for the bedroom. One window was bare and Ben had thumbtacked the afghan over the other one, the one that looked directly into the next house.

They were subletting the apartment for the summer from

Alex, a friend of Ben's. Alex had moved off campus during the winter so he and his girlfriend Sylvie could have some privacy. Sylvie and Alex were very on-again, off-again, and as Alex phrased it, they were currently in their off cycle. Alex left the flat in their care and extracted only half the real rent from them. "In case I want to come back for a night or two," he explained. Though he didn't think that likely, he added. He was going to visit his parents for the summer. "A real money saver, living at home is," he told them.

At half-price rent, the equation was obvious. Their money would last twice as long. "This is terrific because we don't have much money coming in," Rachel told Alex when they wrote out their rent check.

"Much," Ben said and laughed. "I think she means none."

"There might be more wedding gifts," Rachel said, for his parents had sent two hundred and fifty dollars and just the day before she'd gotten twenty dollars from one aunt and uncle and thirty-five from another, checks that just showed up in the morning mail like an unanticipated shower of rose petals.

"I'm not holding my breath," Ben said to Alex.

The only real disappointment about the apartment was that it had no shower. "We'll take baths together," Ben said, and their first night together alone in the apartment, Ben took a poodle-shaped pink plastic bottle of bubble soap he'd picked up at the drugstore and pretended to crack it over the edge of the tub, like champagne across the prow of a ship.

Rachel's mother began to send packages through the mail. When the first one arrived, Rachel was taken by surprise. "They've finally sent a present," she said as she placed it on the bed for Ben to view. It was a large box, wrapped up in brown supermarket bags turned inside out.

Ben, still lying sleepily in the bed, pulled himself up to look the package over. "Well, roota-toot-toot," he said by way of fanfare. "It's probably a blender or a Mixmaster. Just what we don't need."

"No, it's too light for that," Rachel said, hefting it high to demonstrate its trivial weight.

"Money, maybe?" Ben suggested. "A box full of money would be a thoughtful gift. I'll take you out to breakfast to celebrate if it's a box full of money."

"And to dinner, too?" Rachel asked as she tried to work the broad, overlapping bands of tape off the package.

"If it's really money, I'll take you out for lunch as well. And we'll bring in pizza tonight at midnight." They laughed together. She kissed him over the top of the box. "It isn't money, you know that, don't you?" he asked.

"Of course I know that. It's hardly the custom, you know. And if it isn't the custom, you can be sure my parents wouldn't do it." Ben picked up his key ring from the floor next to the bed and ran the sharp point of a key across the tape.

"I can't believe this," Rachel groaned when she had pulled back the flaps of the box, "it's just some old stuff of mine." She pulled a sweater and several blouses from the box and tossed them onto the bed. "These are things I wore in junior high school."

"That's not exactly my idea of the customary wedding gift, either," Ben said. He shook the contents of the box out onto the bed. A few books tumbled out, some papers, and a pair of shoes. "These wouldn't even fit me anymore," Rachel said, holding up the shoes.

"What's all this?" Ben asked, sliding the pile of paper along the bed toward her.

"Old school papers. Grade school things," she added as she lifted a few pages off to examine them.

"Is there a letter with a fat check hidden inside?" he asked.

They sorted through the papers, but found no sign of communication from her mother. Rachel put the carton on the floor and pushed everything off the bed and back into the box. "This is creepy," she said, "her sending me all this." She closed the box up, alternating the flaps over and under one another.

"Maybe she was spring cleaning or something," Ben said, "and she didn't want to throw anything out without your permission."

"She should have sent a note," Rachel said.

"Maybe she wanted to save first class postage. The post office charges if you enclose a letter in a package." He stroked her arm. "Why don't you come back to bed, Rachel?"

"It's too weird," she said, not looking at him. "They haven't even given us a present."

"Forget it," he said. "They'll send a present. Maybe it's been raining a lot and she hasn't had a chance to get to the store yet. You should forget it and come back to bed."

"Maybe I should call her. Maybe the note got lost. Maybe there's a reason she did it this way."

"Give up on her," Ben said. Rachel had reopened the box, and was going through it once more, digging through the strange assemblage of her own past. "Screw them, Rachel," he said as he watched her. He lay back down and pulled the covers up over his head. He was asleep before she finished her unsuccessful search.

More packages came from Rachel's mother over the next few days. Old ski boots, hair ribbons, purses, and scarves. A mug with her name on it. Scrapbooks and a photograph album. "She's cleaning me out of her house," Rachel said when the photographs arrived. She put the album under the mattress, but closed the box up just as she had done all the others.

"So she's overreacting," Ben said.

"And she never sends a note," Rachel moaned. After that

Rachel's bedspread and curtains arrived and then four stuffed animals that had sat on her bookshelves when she was a little girl. "I can't use this," Rachel said and poked a finger at the yellow chenille spread as it lay in the box. "It's for a single bed."

"She forgot you sleep with someone," Ben said. He laughed loudly and reached out to touch Rachel but she turned away.

Then one more box arrived, much smaller than the others, and stuffed full with perfume samples and a porcelain jar Rachel had kept on her bureau at home. The jar was wrapped in tissue, though the bottles had only been tossed in, unwrapped, around it. There was a note this time. "I'm glad you finally have a place of your own for all this paraphernalia. Daddy is going to use your room as a study. He's always wanted a room on the lake side of the house for his work. We brought the big roll-top up from the basement and we're looking at wallpaper samples this week."

"She makes it sound like a normal thing to send this stuff to me," Rachel complained.

"Maybe it is normal," Ben said. "It's all your stuff and you can't have your room forever, you know."

"I don't want my room forever," Rachel protested, but she was furious with him for slipping over to their side. "They never sent a present," she shouted at him.

"It's not my fault," he said, his voice rising.

"It is your fault. You wanted to get married." She thought of rushing at him and shaking him.

"You married me and I have to assume it was of your own free will," he accused.

"Don't be so naive," she railed at him. "Nothing is done of free will, Benjamin."

"What the hell does that mean?"

"What somebody wants or thinks or does has to do with what other people think and want and do. It's all connected.

You wanted to get married, so that altered what I thought. It's a very simple concept, don't you think?"

"No. I don't at all. We're separate beings, Rachel." He cocked his thumb first toward her and then toward himself. "Don't give me any crap about coercion or anything. Don't go weeping to me about it being my fault. Listen to what your parents are saying. They're saying, 'Grow up.' Are we married or not, Rachel?"

"Married." She said the word to be done, to leave her mind to go over other things, and she saw saying that one word seemed to settle him. She wondered, does that paper, that marriage certificate, have any real legal standing? And besides, where the hell had they put it? Was it still in the glove compartment of the car they had borrowed?

"Why don't we go out for lunch?" he suggested.

"Why didn't they take over Jake's room?" she asked him. "He's the one who can't come back." Ben didn't answer. He was already at the front door. And she knew what her mother's answer would have been: "That little room? You can't even see the lake from it."

"Come on," he said. She had to run to catch up to him outside on the street.

That afternoon she took the chenille spread and pushed it back into one of the boxes. She carried that carton, and all the others that she'd piled up in the bedroom, down the stairs and left them at the curb. When the garbagemen came, their truck clanging and grinding at five-thirty in the morning, she went to the window to watch. There was enough light to see them toss the cartons into the mouth of the truck one and two at a time, and to see the flat edge of the compactor fold down over them. She felt for the photograph album as she climbed back into bed. It was there, tucked between floor and mattress.

CHAPTER SIX

*I*T'S BETTER with Elizabeth here," Jake wrote to Rachel. "Nothing is quite so black when you have a friend to get you through. Walking down the street with a Canadian helps: if one Canadian will hold my hand, I tell myself, perhaps Canada, herself, will as well." Sometimes Rachel was tempted to skip through these over-observed sections of his letters, to turn to the last page, to find what he was thinking. She used restraint, though, and continued, page by page. "I survive by ritual," the letter read. "I always buy the same breakfast cereal and the same brand of tuna fish. If I were to deviate from these ritualistic patterns, I'd be admitting that I'm malleable and capable of becoming someone different than who I was. Even though I'm here because I renounce the policies of my homeland, my fingers itch to touch anything American: a pair of Levis or a box of cereal from good old Battle Creek. And at night, I ward off evil by drawing Elizabeth tight against me. I thrash away at the goblins and shout, as if in passion, at the forces that regulate my exile."

Ah, so Elizabeth was his shield against darkness. Had he taken her in solely for the purpose of self-protection? Was there no more to her?

"Elizabeth hopes, I think, to chase away my nightmares. She's patient to a fault. She means to take off the splintery edges with the soft, repeated strokes of her hand. And she does make it easier, so very much easier.

"I worry that she'll give up on me because I'm so secretive and moody, though I confess I almost enjoy the role. This scowling, unpredictable Mr. Rochester that I've become sometimes intrigues me as well, with his nineteenth-century air of mystery. Still, I know I've got to let her see my other life—if I might still be allowed to lay claim, *in absentia,* to what I was. Maybe you could send me a breezy note I could read to her so it wouldn't always seem I squirreled your letters away from her. Write something about you and Ben that I could read aloud. I did tell her about how we used to lie low in the canoes so they looked empty and then let them drift. Do you remember the name you gave that game—Mythological Ghost Bark? You always managed to add drama to everything, didn't you?

"Listen, ignore that stuff about writing breezy notes. Just keep writing what you have been. I want the real stuff."

Rachel wrote back: "Do you love her?" She'd grown tired of his strange descriptions of Elizabeth. He needed to clarify, for himself, to stop all the denials of his own emotion. It was clear to her that Elizabeth must be important to him. Elizabeth was not just a physical barrier against the cold, but his lover, his friend.

"Ah ha," he wrote back. "The big question: Do I love her? Little Rake, I don't know. Sometimes, especially late at night, when I hear a creaking noise in another room and I realize it's Elizabeth walking across the floor, not simply the rickety boards settling, I'm glad in a way that is something like love, I think. She uses the whole room when she moves through the house, going to the window, maybe, or reaching for a dust ball over in the corner. She brings more life to the house than I do as I move linearly from one room to the other. I like the way she piles the newspapers next to the chair because I think she takes pleasure in watching the pile grow larger day by day. Neither of us does anything to dispose of it. I like the way she seems perfectly at ease in my ratty old armchair, with her legs pulled up under her while she reads. She's not holding part of herself aloof from the chair, not merely biding her time till it metamorphoses into a brand new department store chair complete with end table and floor lamp.

"When she asks for changes, even simple ones, though, that's when I panic. She mentioned curtains for the front room and I put her off. I want to say to her, 'Not yet. I may not be staying. They might call me back and say it was all a mistake, that war.' Of course I never say that kind of thing to her because I'm afraid of scaring her off with my craziness. I say something insipid like, 'I can't quite picture it. Let's wait.' I'm certain she sees through me."

And at the bottom of his letter, there were questions for her. "Does this sound like love to you? Can there be love that has such tight limits to its scope? Do you have a definition of love that makes sense for you—i.e., are you able to answer a question I pose: Do you love Ben? And the question that most perplexes me: Should I be loving Elizabeth? Am I hurting her in consciously trying to care more about her?" He wrote, just above his signature: "How is Ben?" Under the signature, "I love you."

"How can anybody define love?" she wrote back. "Perhaps what you feel for Elizabeth isn't love yet, but will be soon. It's almost-love. I don't think there's anything wrong in TRYING to love. People are too passive about love, usually; too romantic. In reality, we make our relationships happen (Ben and I have to work at loving, too, you know). What you're doing is right. You're more settled, more relaxed, I think, since you met Elizabeth. That's good. You're the one who said it's better with Elizabeth . . . Try not calling it love if the label disturbs you.

"I long to meet her, to hear more about her; to know what your life is like, so I can imagine every detail of your existence."

Jake's descriptions of Elizabeth continued to be sketchy and non-specific: Elizabeth emerged as the typical girl-woman; the universal companion. "Hey," she wrote to him. "If you painted her she wouldn't be so vague."

"Maybe I should do a watercolor of her," he wrote, "and send that on to you. I don't have the right words for physical description. She's thinner than you and shorter, I'd say. Less substantial looking, on the whole. And your hair is very, very different. Hers is a deep red, though in direct sunlight single strands of hair catch the light and look golden. I think the color (not in light) is called auburn, but don't bet on it—if it doesn't come in a paint tube, I'm not likely to know much about it. Her hair is very long, about halfway down her back, and almost straight, though it has ripples that run sideways through it. Most redheads have blue eyes, but hers are brown. This last characteristic may be the direct result of chocolate addiction. She likes dark chocolate, and the thinner and crisper, the better. Her favorite is the kind that snaps when your teeth close down on it. She's beginning to make something of an addict of me, too."

Rachel stood before the bathroom mirror trying to imagine it. Long hair. Not the too tight curls that sat on top of her head. She tugged at one of them. Her hair had much more length than most people realized. If she pulled at the curls, she could stretch them down nearly to her shoulders. Once she let them go, though, they were right back up there, the quintessential curly clown head. Lately she'd begun to wonder if she should have it straightened. Just for the hell of it. To be able to see herself for a while without the omnipresent kinks that had become her trademark. She picked up his letter again. Less substantial, this Elizabeth was. What did that mean? Delicate? A tiny little feminine creature blowing in the wind? Or just not such a chunky creature as she was? She stared at herself in the full-length mirror. Was she chunky? Did it have to do with breasts? Were Elizabeth's the small, perfectly curved kind that flattened down and almost disappeared under clothing? What was wrong with full, substantial breasts, anyway? With good hips? She wasn't overweight. She stepped onto the blue bathroom scale that had come with the apartment. It told her she weighed a hundred and twenty-two. She stepped down off the scale and back up again. A hundred-thirty, this time. She tried several times more, till she got it to say one-seventeen. A good weight she thought. Not too substantial at all. But perhaps this substantial talk was metaphorical, only. "Do not fear, Rachel," he was saying, "you are deeper, by far."

Jake included a narrative of how he met Elizabeth. He'd been standing on the top step of University College, admiring the Romanesque details. "I've always liked those curves and towers set in dark sandstone and terra-cotta tiles. I'm an antimodernist at heart, I suppose." And then he'd seen Elizabeth pause in the doorway, touching the stone as she walked through, seeking, he conjectured, to escape the twentieth-century world, too. He'd spoken to her, and they'd laughed about their mutual admiration of times past. It was his first flirtation with a Canadian, he wrote. They'd strolled King's College Circle together, then had sandwiches at a restaurant she knew of around the corner. Above his signature he wrote: "How is Ben?" Under the signature, "I love you."

Several missives later, Jake surprised Rachel by telling her that Elizabeth had not moved in, but only visited him. "She likes to feel very needed," he said, "so I let her go for two or three days at a time, then when I'm desperate, I call her back." Rachel looked through the dates of his letters. There was a clear pattern to his correspondence: letters two or three days in a row, then none for two days. He wrote when he wasn't with her. She would know, then, when Elizabeth became a

more constant companion. She would judge by the space between his writings.

And then a very long letter arrived. A wedding present was
on the way, he said. "I can't tell you how many times I've paced
through stores picking things up and putting them down, not
being able to find something right for you. And of course I
wanted it to be right for Ben, and since I don't know him, that
was virtually an impossible task. Every time I saw something
I liked, I'd think, but if Ben's the type who . . . so there was
always some reason for eliminating every idea I got. Elizabeth
actually helped me reach a decision. I suppose it's a bit more
traditional than I'd ideally hoped, but marriage is traditional,
as Elizabeth says, so enjoy it. Or at least don't hate it."

Five days after that, the mailman delivered her package. She
pulled it just inside the door and ran for a knife to slash open
the strapping tape. It was addressed to Mr. and Mrs. Ben
Goodman and bore a return address from Simpsons in
Toronto. Ben would understand that she couldn't wait for him
to open it. Presents—"another object," he always said when
one arrived—weren't important to him anyway. Inside the
heavy cardboard and newspaper she found a package wrapped
in shiny white paper and tied up with silver ribbons. Inside that
package was a large, cut glass bowl. The sort her mother had
displayed fruit in as the centerpiece for large dinner gatherings.
For me? she thought to herself. When on earth would I use
such a thing? Ben would laugh at it. What do we need that
for? he'd ask. Was this Elizabeth's doing? She pulled the note
from its small envelope: "With all my love for the two of you.
Jake." Not Elizabeth. Jake. Had he forgotten her, then, so
soon? She would put it in a closet, save it for when she was
older. Grown-up. She wouldn't even tell Ben it had arrived.

She put off writing to him. She would need to thank him,
and to do it well, but she needed time to figure out how. She'd

nearly worked out a pleasant lie about how nicely the bowl reflected sunlight (she hadn't had it out of the box long enough to know if it did), when she got another letter from him. "Is it possible to take back that gift," he asked, "at least symbolically? That same night I had it sent out, I dreamed about you and suddenly knew what your gift ought to have been—a painting. I haven't painted much at all these last weeks, but I think it was because I must have been working on your painting in some preconscious state. I want to do a portrait of the two of you, you and Ben, and I've already started the sketches. I feel ridiculous for having sent such a foolish gift. I even thought about going down to the postal service and trying to grab it away from them. I know you won't like that bowl. I kept thinking wedding present, and I got all narrow and formal. Anyway, I want you to interpret that bowl as a symbol of a new beginning. As an extension of the same tradition as the goblet at the Jewish wedding. And because a city hall ceremony wouldn't have given Ben the opportunity to crush a goblet under his foot, let both of you raise that glass together and strike it down to mark this commencement.

"Rachel, I know exactly what I want to do with this portrait. As soon as I thought of it, I picked up a brush. I was testing the pliancy along my palm and it was as though the brush hit nerves connecting my brain and hand and I could see the whole, completed painting. I knew the colors: brighter tints than I've used. I'm definitely going to use cobalt, for instance. I was ready to go. I wanted that cold touch of the paint tube in my hand. I can't tell you what an incredible feeling it is to have an image forming again in my brain. Play your recording of the Hallelujah Chorus in my honor." This was a Jake she knew, the one she'd seen with a trembling hand, waiting to begin a new work.

"This all started from the dream I mentioned: I saw you

hanging one of my paintings on the wall while Ben stood off to the side telling you to move it a little this way and that till it was perfectly aligned. It was your room at home that was in the dream. Ben hammered the picture hook in and you hung it up. Then all of a sudden the walls were covered with pictures—all mine, I admit from the depths of my egotism. No space left. And in the dream, just as I woke up, you're moving your hand in broad gestures, talking about the pictures, explaining, the way I've sometimes heard you do, about the interconnection of technique and meaning, and he reaches for your hand. It was that image that I had when I woke up, of your hands coming together, that I wanted to paint. I saw you as husband and wife then, for the first time. You've told me enough about him so that I can begin to sketch it all out, but please, send me a picture of him when you can."

And she saw, too, how right his vision was; that it would allow Jake to cross the distance that lay between them. It was the wedding gift she'd longed for, without even knowing it.

CHAPTER SEVEN

*T*HE FIRST really hot day of summer, she started missing the lake. Or the canoes, really. And drifting out on the lake, calling to each other, trying to figure out where the other one was. A game of sonar hide and seek.

How did people survive summer away from the water? No matter how hot it got, if you went down by the lake, you got that breeze that cooled you off. If you stayed down there late enough, it did something to your skin temperature, cooling it off for the rest of the night; making you invulnerable to the heat. Drifting in a canoe had to be the exact polar opposite of walking hot city pavement.

The first year they'd had the canoes, she wasn't allowed out alone. Fourteen (almost fourteen, her mother corrected her) was considered too young. Jake had to take her out. Why they thought that was safer, she didn't know; he rocked the boat till water sloshed in over the sides. Rocked it once so hard, they went right over into the water.

Then Barbara and Danny came to stay while their parents were in Europe. Though they were Jake's cousins, Barbara stayed at the Rothstein house, Danny, at the Marsh's. It was a delicious treat for Rachel; she'd always wanted a sister. An older sister. Somebody who would let Jake know he couldn't push her around. Not that Barbara actually told Jake off, but he behaved better while she was there. He didn't call her

Toothpick Legs and Fuzz Head. Maybe that was because he had Danny to keep him amused. It didn't matter why, really, it only mattered that she was free of his taunts once the cousins arrived.

Rachel and Barbara stayed on their side of the lake. They strolled the beach arm in arm. They took the bus into town and walked the aisles of the Five and Ten, touching, and sometimes even buying, costume jewelry and cosmetics. They ordered cherry cokes at the lunch counter.

In a way, it was Rachel's father who spoiled it all. When Barbara and Rachel asked to be driven into town one evening to see *Village of the Damned,* he said if he drove, Danny and Jake had to be invited as well. Rachel kept her fingers crossed, but it did no good. Jake and Danny accepted the invitation.

The theater was crowded and there wouldn't have been a chance of four seats together, so Rachel was, blessedly, back with Barbara again. But after the movie when they were waiting for Mr. Rothstein to pick them up, Jake walked over next to Barbara and asked her what she thought of the movie. Rachel watched Barbara answer; watched how she looked down when she said, "It was a little scary, but I liked it," and especially the way she swayed a little toward Jake (with her hips, somehow, not her whole body) when she answered his next question. Rachel walked away so she wouldn't hear any more.

The next night, after it was dark, the boys appeared on the girls' side of the lake. Barbara and Rachel sat on the fence, swinging their legs. "Want to walk down to the water?" Jake asked Barbara.

Rachel readied herself to protest on her friend's behalf, but Barbara had already pushed herself down from the fence. "Sure," she said.

"You two stay there," Jake commanded Rachel and Danny

and he headed toward the water with Barbara following behind.

Rachel paced up and down on the patio, fuming, swearing half under her breath to kill Jacob Marsh and trying to come up with some concrete plan of revenge. Out of nowhere Danny said, "In some states, cousins can marry." And she hadn't really known anything about it not being OK to marry your cousin, and she asked him, "what about New York?" and he said, "no not New York. Southern states, I think, and hillbilly states." "Is it legal for them to date?" she asked him. "I don't think so," he informed her. And she thought, well, ha, ha, Jake, you are out there doing something very illegal, and she started wondering if maybe she could do something with that information and then Danny said, out of nowhere again, "Let's you and I walk, too. To hell with him telling us we should stay here." He started to leave the patio and she had to move fast to keep up with him. She tripped and nearly fell in the darkness. "Don't swear anymore," she said to him when she caught up, though she wondered if there were a way she could tell Jake that Danny had sworn against him, just easy as pie, he did, said, To hell with you. Rachel hardly ever heard swear words— though Jake had once or twice called her an ass—and they always took her by surprise, as though someone had slashed through the air with a long-bladed, shiny sword right in front of her face. She and Danny walked toward the pond, though she hung back a little, staying behind him in case Jake was down there, too. Danny said, "You're not scared to be here with me, are you?" and she said, "No, I'm scared of what Jake'll do," and he said, "To hell with him," and walked back up toward her and put an arm around her shoulders and they walked on down to the edge of the pond. It was awkward walking that way, with his arm bouncing up and down with every step she took. She thought she could see Barbara and Jake down toward the other end, down by the willow trees, but she wasn't sure. They might have gone to the playhouse.

Danny and Rachel sat on the narrow beach alongside the pond, not very close anymore. They let sand run through their fists and Danny told her a couple of jokes; clean, silly ones, that made her laugh, and then they walked back up to the house and Barbara and Jake were already there, holding hands. Swinging their arms, like they wanted Rachel and Danny to be sure to notice. Jake didn't say anything about Rachel disobeying his command.

After that, she still hung around with Barbara, and Jake hung around with Danny daytimes, but once it was dark, they'd go off on their walks in the other combination. One night Danny leaned closer to her and asked, "Can I kiss you?" and she nodded. He put his lips on hers but it didn't feel like much, just dry lips, and no noise, either, no click or smack, like she had thought there would be, more like they had brushed by each other. It reminded her of Eskimo nose-kissing. She'd thought kissing was wet. So she kissed him again, to see if she couldn't get it to come out more like it ought to be and he said, "I guess you really like me." And she said yes, though she wanted to ask him, were those normal kisses? Were they good kisses?

The Parents put the playhouse off limits. They said it was too dark. Everything's dark at night, Rachel said. It's not safe, they reiterated. She tried to catch Jake's expression. He was looking out the window like there was something real interesting out there. Like he didn't care what The Parents said. So they had seen them, then, how they paired off at night. Later she said to Jake, "if you weren't so stupid about playing with the flashlight when you were out there, they'd never have known."

Sometimes Rachel and Danny lay back on the beach and

looked up at the stars and he held her hand in a way she hadn't known people did, with their fingers alternating one with the other. The kisses stayed about the same, though she tried to vary them a little, tried to get them to last a little longer, thinking maybe that was what was wrong with them, but they still seemed too simple, somehow. The last night Danny was there he leaned over her while she was looking up at the stars, and kissed her a lot of times in a row, little kisses. Then he started running one hand across her skin just where it showed between tee shirt and shorts when she was lying down. She didn't want him to work his way up and find out how flat she was, so she slithered back along the sand, out of his reach. They sat not talking for a while and he said, OK, we could just kiss a little for our last night together, couldn't we? and she came back and they did some more of the little kisses that went together nicely, all soft like something you wanted to curl up with and keep nearby. She had wondered if they liked each other enough to cry when they parted, but neither of them did, not then or even the next day when they really said their final goodbyes. He couldn't kiss her then in front of all their parents, and especially Jake and Barbara couldn't kiss because of it being illegal between cousins, but not being able to kiss made her sad and gave her a little pulling feeling right down there, like she'd felt sometimes watching romantic movies, and she figured that meant she probably did love him.

The next evening when there was still some light left in the sky, Jake asked her if she wanted to go out in a canoe with him. She was going to say, "No, thanks, I'm not in the mood for being tipped into the water, thank you," but before she had a chance, he said, "I want to talk to you about something important. I mean it, Rake." He sounded very serious. So she went, though she did say to him, "Don't you dare tip me out, Jacob Marsh," but he held the canoe very steady when she stepped into it.

For a long time he didn't say anything. Not till they were way out in the middle of the lake and then he pulled in the paddle, so she did, too, and they drifted. He leaned back and dragged his hand in the water.

After a while she did the same. "It's nice out," he said. She wasn't used to conversation with him. She wasn't sure what to say in response. "Do you miss Danny?" he asked, and she heard his hand splash in the water.

"I guess so."

"I miss Barbara," he said, and she heard more splashing. She leaned left a little and saw his fist punching up the surface of the water. "Too bad you can't marry a cousin," he said after a while. "You and Danny can get married. You're not cousins." She imagined being dressed in white lace, standing next to Danny in tails and top hat. She tried to stretch him taller in her mind. He seemed too short to be a groom. "If you marry him and I marry Barbara, I suppose we'd finally really be related. Would you want to marry him?" he asked her.

"I don't know. Not now. Not yet."

"I meant someday," he said. "We're too young now."

"Yes," she said. The more she agreed with him, the more he talked. It was like a game, keeping the conversation going.

"We might never see them again, you know."

So what. Or too bad for you, were the handiest responses. It was difficult to push them back down into some damp portion of the bow of the canoe. "I know," she said.

"In some states you can get married," he said.

"Danny told me."

"We could move, maybe."

She agreed. "They'd have to want to, too," she pointed out.

"Barbara would."

"I didn't ask Danny." Then they drifted again, all in silence.

"You didn't do anything with Danny, did you?" he asked and she felt her face redden. But dusk had settled over them already and she knew he wouldn't notice. "I mean besides kissing," he said. "I know you kissed him because I saw you one night." And he hadn't done anything about it, she thought.

"Just the kissing," she said.

"Barbara and I are older," he said.

"Like what did you do?" she asked him, then regretted she had, for a laugh was his only response. Perhaps that was all the talking she was to get from him.

"We're older," he said. They stayed on the pond till it was fully dark. Till the light on her parents' porch came on and lit a path from the water to house for them.

She had heard about brothers who threatened to beat up their sister's boyfriends. She thought of telling Jake how Danny had touched her skin that last night and she wondered if such information would have any impact. With all this talk of him being a brother to her—just how far would he go with it? "I like drifting in the dark," she said to him when they'd got the canoe pulled up into its rack.

"We could do it again," he said. He didn't take her hand as they walked up to the house, though for a minute she'd thought he was going to—like he'd forgotten and thought he was back with Barbara. "One thing we did do," he said as they approached the house, "we smoked cigarettes. You and I could do that sometime. We can sit in the dark in the playhouse. I've got it all swept out and clean now."

"We won't get caught?"

"No, it's safe."

She wished Barbara were there again, just for a minute, so she could tell her: He didn't tip the canoe.

Rachel told Ben she was ready to concentrate on the new. That was what this marriage was all about, right? New life. Fresh start. Bye, bye other life.

He was right about this being their life and only theirs.

What would her mother say if she were to see Ben toss his clothes this way and that when he came to bed at night or see him eating right out of a pot of soup on the stove? Everything had been so well regulated in her mother's life. There was no room for the spontaneity, or call it what it really was, sexuality, of someone like Ben. She watched him while he read the newspaper, sometimes reading over his shoulder, so she would know what made him laugh or what enraged him. She was "learning him," she thought, locating and memorizing his every gesture and reaction. She was carefully incorporating him into her consciousness. She looked forward to their trips to the supermarket, to pushing the cart down the aisles, gathering food for the two of them, thinking how other people in the store must envy them. She was sure others could read the sexual intensity between them, and sure they guessed that they would be making love again as soon as the groceries were put away. She slipped her arm across his waist and kissed him. Right when they were standing in the peanut butter-jelly-jam aisle. Anyone could see. Mother, we don't hide ourselves away.

Mornings they slept late. They'd make love when they woke up, then go back to sleep. They'd concoct a meal, once they were up, from whatever they had on hand. That's real eating, Ben would say; creating, not following recipes—the same sort of thing Jake might have said if he were into cooking.

Ben always had ideas about what they should do, crazy things like borrowing a car and driving up to Boston to go to the aquarium, or down to New York to Chinatown, or up to the Cape just to get lobster. They were always exhausted the next day, but there were no pressures or commitments to meet, so what did it matter? They slept it off and started over when they felt like it.

She tried to write as much as she could about them. She told about Rockport, Massachusetts, where she and Ben had day-tripped. She didn't tell him that she and Ben had argued about the wisdom of spending a lot of money to get up to Toronto. She wrote only this: "We might not be able to get up there before school starts again. Maybe in the fall, though. I imagine Toronto will be exquisite then." He seemed to ignore most of the content of the letter. He gave no indication as to whether it made good material for reading at the dinner table to his friend. He wrote only this: "Reconsider. Come, visit. Now. You don't need to stay long. I promise I will let you go."

When the two hundred and fifty dollars of wedding money had noticeably dwindled, Ben got a job driving an ice-cream truck for the summer. His commission started at ten cents a confection. "Confection is a wonderful word," Rachel said when he began to tell her about the job. "It's such an elegant and pretentious way to say ice-cream pop."

"They're not ice-cream pops," he explained to her with mock seriousness. "Some are Candy-Treat Surprises and some are Fudge Delights and some are Whammies while still others are Rainbow Treats."

"And kids call them that?" she asked. "Don't they just say, 'Hey Mistah, gimme one a them vanilla and chocklet things?' "

"That's what kids say, sure, but the company," and here he did a brief soft-shoe routine for her, "says 'confection.' "

"My goodness," she said. "And they put you in a uniform, too. A lifelong goal finally realized, right?" She grabbed his white cap from his hand, put it on, and saluted him.

"No salutes," he said and whisked the hat off her head. "Don't make jokes about salutes."

"It was an anti-salute," she said, demonstrating again, her hand held backward and upside down over her nose.

His hours would be late, the company said. Most ice cream was sold between seven-thirty and nine-thirty in the evening so they wouldn't be able to go anyplace too far, except on his day off.

He felt really good about getting this kind of job instead of some desk-type, paper shuffling thing, he said. He remembered how when he was a kid everybody really loved the Good Humor Man and how he and all the other kids had followed him around, running out of the house as soon as they heard his bell. "The modern world pied piper equivalent," Ben said. Ben had what the company considered a "less desirable route." "Isn't that real white, middle-class talk?" he asked her. "They won't even go near the ghetto since the riots, and they think an integrated working-class neighborhood is tough stuff." He saw it as potentially a really beautiful thing—wasn't it a perfect way to do some basic social work, and to help kids? He was going to ride around first, see what the pattern of the area was, where the kids hung out, who the leaders were. Then he was going to start by parking across from one of the hangouts, maybe cultivate a core group of kids, then go down their streets in the evenings, later, and meet their friends, their older siblings, and their parents. He'd talk to them about strategies for neighborhood change. The streets are the key to change, he told Rachel. Leave the psychiatrist's office to the middle class.

Ben thought Rachel should get involved in helping kids, too, so she called six or seven psycho-social agencies that dealt with children but none of them was hiring summer workers and all but one of them closed down entirely for the month of August. The ice cream company didn't hire females, otherwise she might have tried that. "We'll get by," Ben counselled. "Why don't you paint the living room or something." Rachel visited a couple of hardware stores and brought home paint chips and color charts. She made a list of the work she would do in the apartment.

If they'd had a little more money she could have bought

fresh acrylics, started working on canvas board, gotten back into shape a little, working the eye and hand back to some semblance of vision. And pastels were so expensive, how could she justify that? It would have been fun to send stuff to Jake, let him critique it (laugh at it, at this point), but it might be pushy. He was the one who was the artist, she was the art historian. And to send him her stuff when he was having trouble would be like a slap in the face: Look, I'm not even an artist and I can work, what's wrong with you buddy? Then she thought of sketching Ben, since there was no way he was going to let her take a photograph of him, and she tried that, but he said he didn't like her peering at him the way she did when she was sketching, and besides, what made her think a drawing was any better than a photograph? She did sketch one of Alex's cats (the mean one, the one that tried to scratch her when she put food out for it) when it was asleep, and she did it only when Ben wasn't there in case he thought cats shouldn't have portraits either, and she worked and reworked it, getting every little hair exactly the way it fell, till it made her sleepy (The New Drug, she called it), and then just as she was putting that into an envelope to send to Jake she thought, now why am I doing this? Jake hates cats and the whole thing looks like over-worked, bedraggled, junior high school artwork for the cover of a report called "My Pet." He'll look at it and think, I know it's not art, but what is it? What was it she intended to say by sending me this? So why'd you stop giving me drawing lessons, Mr. Artist? she could say to him. Or on second thought, forget the whole thing. She'd send him something else and put the sketch away, or so she thought, till she remembered all the drawers were Alex's. "Ah well," she said aloud, "such is life," and she ripped the drawing into small pieces.

Jake wrote that he thought Elizabeth was bored hanging around watching him paint. "I'm so involved with this portrait," he said, "that I end up neglecting her. She's very naive—or perhaps candid is the better word, for I mean it in an entirely positive way. Either she likes something or she doesn't. Fortunately," he added, "she likes everything of mine she's seen so far. Even the way a painter paints is new to her. It fascinates her that I work for so long at one single painting. And she was shocked the first time she saw me paint over an area. I told her that not everyone works the way I do, but she wanted me to take her to a gallery to see if she could detect overpainting in other people's work. I could work on this painting all weekend, every weekend, but I'm afraid I'll end up driving her away. It's so damn hard to find time. Sometimes I can get an hour in late in the afternoon, but you know how I've never liked that light. My color sense gets all jumbled together at dusk.

"Graduate school, by the way, has probably become a non-option. Amex sees the tide turning for fellowships. With the first wave of expatriates, the universities seemed almost anxious to get us and pay us, besides. Now it seems they've had enough of foreigners. Good, qualified people are getting turned down all over the place. The money's gone. I don't really want academics for myself, I want painting, and as you said, I've got to concentrate on getting finished products to show for myself. Still, it's hard to accept yet another barrier. I want them to want me. I want them to want Americans deeply, truly, from their hearts.

"I have been to the Ontario Gallery of Art (and back) to see about a job. I thought that might make a neat compromise, but the place was crawling with Amexers and Amex wives. And they're all horribly overeducated with three advanced degrees. There are Ph.d.'s in art history there doing clerical work. What use have they for a palette holder with a BA? They were polite, of course. We'll call you and all that.

"Elizabeth is a realist. She wants to know how a painter can make it in this modern world. She's right, isn't she—artists have gone the way of the fairy tale."

Jake had asked again for a photograph of Ben. He said that he was getting her image very clear in the sketches, but that Ben could only be a vague suggestion. He'd toyed with the idea of making both of them less focused so they became more equal images ("which is, obviously essential," he wrote), but he thought that that would be less satisfying in the end.

She didn't want to tell him that Ben had refused to have his picture taken. When she explained how Jake needed the photo to get on with the painting, Ben had blown up at her. "I don't want a goddamn painting of me, either, Rachel. Why do you think a painting would be any better?"

She began, in perfect earnestness, to explain exactly how, when she realized by his headlong dash for the door that his question was rhetorical. "Ben," she said, calling after him as he went down the staircase, but he took the steps at a run, flirting, or so it appeared, with the possibility of flying to the bottom, and was gone.

CHAPTER EIGHT

*E*VEN AFTER Jake had gone to college, telling The Parents he was leaving and not coming back, they pursued him as a group. Despite vehement protests, two mothers and two fathers, accompanied by Rachel, came to visit him on Parents' Weekend in October of his first semester at Yale. "Can't you come up one family at a time?" he protested.

"But we all miss you," Grace had insisted.

There were jokes made by roommates and friends, particularly about Rachel. They were all sure she was his sister, pointing to the blond curls as proof, despite his claims otherwise. "Just a neighbor," he said.

"Good looking," one of them said. "Damn good looking," another added. These were comments made almost against the will of these freshmen: Rachel knew this. They had arrived at Yale with higher social hopes than high school girls. Jake had told her how they had dressed themselves up as Yale freshmen on successive Saturday nights and presented themselves at mixers. But such a crowd of others like themselves they met at the door, and such swarms of girls, eyes looking everywhere but at them, counselling them to go home to solitary sleep, made them weary of their fantasies. "Invite your sister back," he told her his roommates had urged.

"Neighbor," he'd corrected.

"Please," one friend said, "whoever she is, invite her back.

This cloistered life is killing me."

The following Saturday, Alice and Grace drove Rachel back to New Haven, walked her all the way to Jake's entryway and up the stairs, and stood by while she knocked on the door. The two women planned to have lunch, go shopping and to the art gallery, then come back late in the afternoon to retrieve Rachel.

Jake and three of his friends walked her to Freshman Commons for lunch. The three friends fussed over her; guiding her choices from the cafeteria counters, carrying her tray, and fetching her seconds of soda and dessert so she wouldn't have to get out of her chair. They fought quietly among themselves as to who would sit next to her, nudging each other gently out of the way. Like children at odds over who would get to hold the teacher's hand at the head of the line, they agreed they would take turns. They made her promise to come back, to make a next time for each of them. Jake stayed off on the sidelines, casting glances, winks, and smiles at her. She and Jake understood these boys. It was just one of the secrets they shared.

"What do you think?" she said to Jake as they waited for their mothers to return. "Should I come back some other time?"

"Sure," he said. "Why not? It's a lot better than studying perception for Psych 10." And when they sat alone in the room that last half hour, he said it was nice that they didn't have to do anything special the way they would have if they'd been each other's date. Every other Saturday after that one of the parents, Rothstein or Marsh, drove her to the station so she could catch a train to New Haven.

They moved together in the same social group, each paired with someone else, yet always near one another. He kept her well supplied with boyfriends. "The more the merrier," she said to him. "I am a true advocate of the whirlwind social life."

"Which means exactly what?" he asked.

She knew he wanted details, so she chose to tease him. "What business is it of yours?"

"I'm supposed to be in charge of you." The Parents had lectured him—in her presence—that he had to make sure she was back in his room by midnight ("She's only in high school, don't forget, Jake").

"Do I make a fuss about you having a girl stay in your bed?" she asked him.

"No."

"Do you send them weekly reports or something on me?"

"No." He shouted his response, and threw an arm out in a gesture of frustration. "I'm sorry I asked," he said, his syllables brittle bits of torn pages from an ancient, discarded book. "Whatever Our Parents' intention might have been, it was never mine that I should be your keeper."

"OK, then," she said with belligerence, but she saw how stricken he was and she couldn't help but tell him, "I haven't slept with any of them, you know." He nodded, and she saw he had the answer he'd sought.

Keeper? No. He wasn't her keeper, nor she his. Yet she homed, certainly, as though he'd trained her, like one of those gray and white birds, to turn around, to come back. A pallet on his floor was roost and lodging place. His existence gave her power; power to say to an aggressive, boring, or obnoxious date, thank you very much, but I must be getting back to Jake's room.

When it was just the two of them, they read aloud, made up stupid jokes, or turned songs into parodies, while they lay together on the floor, her head on his chest, maybe. Touching was easy between them: they held hands as they walked, put arms around each other when they stood side by side. Not keepers at all. Friends.

And if there were three of them? That got tough, sometimes, she had to admit. She always figured he didn't want to be a third wheel so she tried staying clear of him as long as she was dating someone. And he liked his privacy when he was in a relationship. He'd lost his temper with her once or twice, over just that. One time he said to her, "Your timing stinks, you're always breaking up with someone, you always *need to talk*" (she'd been infuriated by that imitative emphasis) "when I'm trying to get things going with someone."

"Well, sor-ree," she'd said, picking up her book bag and slinging it over her back. "I don't plan it, you know, I don't say, hey, I'll think I'll break up this week because Jake has a girlfriend now."

"No?" he retorted. "You could've fooled me."

That had been a bad blowup. Most times, he was just annoyed, not vicious. But even that time, he'd eased up pretty quickly. There was always the "I don't care what you do" introductory portion of the sentences, but she knew, if she stood her ground, the words would always turn at least partially conciliatory. "OK, sleep here if you want to." "So come with us to dinner." And in the end, he'd take the time to talk to her. He'd explain to his new girlfriend: "I've got to go do my big brother thing."

"Thanks a lot," she said, her words steamy with sarcasm, when she'd heard him say that. "It isn't exactly complimentary to be cast in baby sister role, you know." But it was all just harmless patter, and she knew that. It was the way in which they chose to mark out their individual territory; their selves. Once all the insulting preliminaries were out of the way, they'd talk. They'd work it out. The harsh edges, those not so pretty un-friend moments didn't last.

The guys she dated? Bright, always bright, those Yalies, and always sexually eager. For them, a glance, or a touch of a finger, was the pistol shot at the start of the race. Not that she didn't like her share of hot, frantic kissing and stroking, but it was the headlong nature of it she disliked, the sense that she couldn't turn back, that the *he* of the relationship, once aroused, controlled the pace, and the itinerary. She didn't relish losing control of a situation. So she said goodbye a lot. Much more than Jake did, who always told her she was too capricious; never gave anything or anyone enough time. So I'm crazy, she said to him. So you are, he agreed.

There was one time, her freshman year, April, she thought it was, when she was out late, half the night probably, and she came back to his room. He'd gone to bed, but the door was ajar, and the soft light of a candle showed along its open edge. His own girlfriend had begged off for the weekend, saying she needed space, time, room; all the things that are mentioned when a break is imminent. She moved the door gently, saw he lay with his eyes open and asked if she could come in to talk. He nodded and she sat on the floor beside his mattress.

"Are you all right?" she asked him and he said, yes, just angry as hell. He'd gone with a couple of friends to Linsly-Chit to see *Potemkin*, and Sally, his space-seeking girlfriend, had been there, waiting on line, with somebody else.

"What'd you do?" she wanted to know.

"I left."

"You didn't say anything to her?"

"No," he said, shaking his head. "I was just incredibly pissed and I wanted to get out of there. I felt like a fool with everybody else knowing more than I did about my life."

"What a bitch," Rachel declared.

"The funny part is, I'm actually more upset that I didn't

confront her than that she was with someone else. Everybody else was foaming at the mouth and telling me to tear the guy apart."

"That's not your style, Jacob." She touched his cheek lightly.

"No, I suppose not," he said and she saw the hard set of his mouth begin to soften.

"For what it's worth, I never liked her," Rachel said, "I didn't like the way she laughed and talked at the same time. You couldn't be sure she wasn't laughing at you."

"I think I'm sure now: she was." He grimaced and closed his eyes. "So you don't think I should go beat up her new boy-friend?" He made a growling noise and slashed comically at the air with a clawlike hand.

"No, I don't." Her growl was gentler than his.

"I guess I don't either. And I don't want to think about it anymore tonight. Tell me how you are."

"I'm all right." She twisted one of the curls from the nape of her neck around a finger. "Do you have any idea how many of the so-called great philosophers wrote cogent arguments in favor of pre-marital sex?"

"No, how many?" She was pleased to hear his laughter. "Has Mark been reading these treatises to you deep into the night?"

She smiled. "No, just quoting them wildly out of context and moaning about the existential condition. And then we shout at each other for a while—I can be oh so very intellectual, too, when I want to, you know. What it all comes down to, though, is that we've reached a sexual impasse. He wants to do it, and I keep getting scared at the last minute." Jake nodded solemnly. "What do you think of Mark, anyway?" she asked.

"I like him well enough. He seems intelligent."

"Over-analytical, I think."

"It sounds it."

"But why should that matter?" she asked him. Jake shrugged as response. "I think he's sexy and good looking and smart and not really pushy exactly . . ." she'd begun to tick off his traits along her fingers.

"If he's not pushy, what's the fuss about?"

"Well I guess he is pushy. I mean he says he's not. He's not really. I think he likes arguing. He's in it for the sport, you might say." Jake laughed. "Please don't laugh at me," she said.

He put his hand to her blond curls and stroked them back from her face. "You made it seem funny, Rachel. You always do, you know."

"But I mean to be serious, Jake. I want to understand my fear so I know what to do with it. I don't want to fear decisions. I don't want to be afraid to govern my own life."

"What is it that you're scared of?" he asked. "What goes through your mind just before you back off?" He sat up, leaning against the side of his desk that served as headboard.

"I don't really know. Pain, maybe. That it's the wrong thing to do at the wrong time. We're not thinking about getting married or anything. I don't suppose we even love each other, though he likes to say we do for the purposes of bolstering his argument. Or maybe it's just the traditional Fear of the Great Unknown." She clasped her hands in front of her chest and put on what she thought of as her look of utter terror. He wasn't laughing. "Oh Jake, I don't know what it is. What do you think I'm afraid of?"

He leaned toward her and kissed her lips. She drew away, surprised, breathless, but then there was something about the way the candle made his face first clear and then distant, that made her move toward him to catch him before he disappeared into darkness. They kissed once more, tentatively, gently, and their fingertips met and intertwined. And in this lighting that belonged to dreams, she remembered that she had actually dreamed this dream, exactly like this.

She slipped her arm around his neck. "Remember when we practiced kissing?" she whispered. "We had that blanket we kept out in the playhouse. Remember how you taught me?" And the fear was there again, but she saw its shape more clearly now, felt it in her throat and her limbs. His fingers traced her lips and lingered, as though in contemplation, on her cheek-bone. She felt the shape of the terror soften, saw that, after all, its real name was desire. He held her close. "We could prac-tice," she said in a halting, whispered request of her friend. "Like we used to." And he drew her into his bed and made love to her.

It was a brief coupling, a coming together just long enough for the act to be called intercourse, and then a drawing back, a thinking twice, no, three times, or more, a statement of regret, a turning away. She felt it in him, that rethinking that could be called disappointment, and she cried. She tasted loss, cold and dark, in her own tears. She saw it in the shape of his body, its slight curve inward toward itself, and away. She saw it in his slumber. Every gesture and movement now called up a question. What are you thinking? What are you feeling? Every nuance and every breath must henceforth be interpre-ted. How had she led him, and herself, to such a narrow blind alley?

"Jake?" she whispered, but he slept soundly, like a child worn out by his game; escaping her.

She had played this trick upon him, calling him teacher. And penance was this: she would put them back together as they had been. In going away, she might be able to call him back.

She wouldn't wake him. She'd take a walk in the early light and have a cup of coffee by herself at the Copper Kettle, then meet Mark for breakfast, just as they'd planned.

When she had dressed, she took paper and pen from his desk and wrote a note: "Thank you, R." She left it on the mantle for him. When she did return, late in the day, Jake was raging. "Where have you been?" he shouted at her.

"With Mark. You must have known that's where I was."

"Did you tell him?"

"Tell him what?" She'd begun to shake.

"About us."

"No," she said. She looked away, afraid of his darkened eyes.

"I suppose you slept with him then, between breakfast and lunch."

"Yes."

"Bitch," he said. "I don't want you in here anymore. Get out and stay out."

Her tears came sudden and hard. "Why are you doing this to me?"

He threw back his head and laughed. "We were lovers last night," he said, spitting his words at her. "And now what are we?"

"We tried to be lovers because of other things, other people," she said, "not because of us. Because of Mark, because of Sally."

"Excuse me for misunderstanding, then," he shouted and turned away from her.

She pursued him to the other side of the room. "You did misunderstand. We both did."

"Just get out, Rachel," he still insisted.

"Don't do this to me, Jacob," she implored, but by then he had left the room, slamming the door as he did so.

She sent him a letter. "Don't be cruel," she wrote. "We made a mistake. We both were needful, hurting, that night. There were other people in our lives. It had to do with them, not us. You and I were never boyfriend-girlfriend. I love you, but I love you differently. I'll take the blame because I did the asking. I'm sorry. But please forgive me, I can't stand to lose you."

Jake did not write back. Rachel stayed in Mark's room after that. When a few weeks had passed, she knocked on his door. "Jacob," she said to him as she stood in the doorway, "I want to be your friend again. I miss you." He motioned for her to come into the room.

"Brother and sister reunited?" he asked, and she felt the edge in his words that was meant to wound her.

"Something like that, I guess." After a pause, she spoke again. "Don't you want to be my friend?"

"Yes," he said. And then more quietly: "I want you to keep coming here." He didn't hold out his hand or open his arms.

She began to cry. "Good," she managed to say. And they were friends again, but never lovers.

CHAPTER NINE

FRIDAY AFTERNOONS, Rachel still went to the Resistance office. Ben had come with her once and hung around while she answered the telephone, but he said the place made him nervous. He had enough reminders of the frailty of his existence already, he said.

Lately there'd been a series of bomb threats against the center. After the third one, the police had suggested they close down. After the fourth, they had implied they might have to close them down. Though opinion among the resisters was that the police couldn't legally put them out of business, they also knew they had few friends and things were not going to get easier. The anger was deep on all sides. The storefront might turn out to be just another dream, among so many others.

Dreams and plans had transformed, for too many people she knew, into nightmares and escape routes. Jake, for instance. Fresco was what he'd always talked about doing. He was a wonderful anachronism: a man who would put art, not graffiti, on the walls of public buildings. He talked of mentors and patrons. "Like the olden days," she used to say to him. "When kings were kings and artists were treasures." As the military advisors in South East Asia turned into soldiers, and "involvement" became "conflict," Jake learned to scale down. Instead of a mentor, he'd have an advisor in a graduate school, he said. Instead of plaster, he'd have canvas. So he'd teach and paint in his free time. Everybody makes compromises, he said.

When the conflict became a war, and he was called for a pre-induction physical, he had to scratch the option of graduate school. He learned that unless you are blind, deaf, lame, or gay, the only occupation possible in war is that of soldier. It was then, when the army confirmed his fitness for service, that he had cried out—to her, to the Resistance—for other choices. He still needed to have plans that were his own.

Tom Berson, Jake's roommate and a lifelong Quaker, filed for Conscientious Objector status and won it. His alternative service was to be served in a mental hospital in Boston. Ethan Tuthill, half-Catholic, half-Jew (and neither half Bar Mitzvah, Ethan would add), applied for CO and was rejected. He had decided on the emigration option. "I'd like to see if I could make it somewhere in northern Ontario without electricity for a year," he told Jake.

"You can't come back," Jake said to him.

"What is there to come back to? Shame and filth in government? Would you want to come back to that?"

"To policies, no. To some people, yes, maybe," Jake said.

"I'll meet other people," Ethan said.

Jake had let the idea of jail play through his head—at least that was circumscribed and definite, he told Rachel. You served your time and came out again. "Sodomized and beaten punch drunk," Ethan said, "and with the label ex-con, to boot."

"They can't put us all into jail," Jake said.

"You pays your money, you takes your chances," Ethan said and laughed.

"Maybe you could paint in jail," Rachel suggested. But they had guffawed impolitely at her idea.

"And write novels and have Lady Bird Johnson in for tea," Ethan offered as a counterproposal.

Through the Resistance organization, they had met guys

who were trying to get into Canadian graduate schools. They knew of others who were getting married, because some draft boards, but only some, were taking single men first.

Jake decided to send out letters inquiring about teaching jobs in major urban centers. There was a shortage of soldiers, but there was also purported to be a shortage of teachers. Most draft boards let you go if you were willing to do time in the inner city. The way he explained it to Rachel, teaching was only till three o'clock or so in the afternoon so there would be time left for painting. There was always the possibility that draft policy might change—in or against his favor—but for now, teaching was an alternative which didn't put his life or his rights into jeopardy.

So if there was a teacher shortage, where were the jobs? He had thought the half dozen letters he sent out would produce five or six job offers. He was going to be a graduate of Yale College. What better credentials could he have? Four of his inquiries went unanswered. Two of the systems he wrote to sent applications. He called the other four and talked two of them into sending him applications, though both told him they were full up. "Every Harvard, Yale, and Dartmouth man who wants to save his skin has applied to us," one personnel director told him. "We've got guys with masters and doctorates applying." The Boston school system was the only one which would interview him. No places, though, for art teachers. The openings were all junior high school positions in math and science and though they liked his ideas and his theoretical approach to the classroom, his background was weak in those areas (how many math courses do I need to teach Algebra I? he asked). "You've got to remember," the Boston administrator told him, "we've got the M.I.T. draft dodgers here, too."

"I can't kill anyone," he told Rachel. "They can't make me kill."

July slipped by. August. He checked each morning's mail for a reclassification notice, but none arrived. He and Rachel drove up to New Haven so he could talk to a Resistance counselor. He went over each option every night, sitting by the side of the pond with Rachel, passing a joint back and forth. "No brave acts," she told him. "Please, no heroics, Jake. You pack your stuff and you go to Canada. That's the only choice." He went through the list he'd arranged in his head like a litany, he couldn't let it go: enlist in the navy, join the reserves, cut off a toe, get drafted then desert if Vietnam orders come through, go to jail. He added new ones from time to time: he'd heard of drugs which would produce an irregular heartbeat, drugs that made you temporarily act psychotic (though he'd also heard the sharper doctors sometimes kept you till such drugs wore off), and he'd heard of one guy who'd shot up with heroin before he reported for his induction physical. One shot of heroin wasn't supposed to be addicting and it showed up clearly in a urine specimen. That was the option he most liked, though he didn't precisely know how he'd get hold of the stuff. He knew of one guy who'd been so nervous at the final physical that his heart rate had gotten him off, but he could hardly count on that working for him. Rachel made jokes, said they ought to market a board game, sell the rights to Milton Bradley, with game cards you turn over that had all those options. Even as she spoke, she imagined him picking a card off the top of the pile and reading it aloud to other players. "It wouldn't sell," he told her. "It's a game of chance. There's no skill involved. Gambling games don't have a broad appeal." She saw the yellow playing card become his draft card, saw the flames begin to form along its edge, saw his hand engulfed in the growing flames and she had to close her eyes.

Each night the evening news had a casualties scoreboard,

right up there in the upper left-hand corner. Each night they watched more men fall on battlefields, filmed by cameramen who penetrated the jungle side by side with the soldiers. "Turn it off," he shouted at her. "I won't watch us die anymore in someone else's civil war." She wore a button now that read, "Bring the Boys Home."

Jake began to work on percentages. What are the chances they'll draft me if I do nothing? What are the chances I'll get sent to Vietnam if they do draft me? "If they're high enough, maybe it's worth some small self-mutilation," he suggested to her.

"I want to come to a decision," he shouted out at the lake one night, then tossed a rock high over the water. The splash was muffled, distant-sounding.

"Go to Canada," Rachel said. "I'll come with you."

Jake pantomimed lifting another card from their imaginary game board. He read the invisible words aloud to her: "You must emigrate to Canada. You may not come back."

In the last week in August, when he'd begun to have nightmares of a draft exam in which he was asked to fire rifles at cats and dogs while men in full dress military uniform had rifles trained on him, he got a call again from Boston. There was the possibility of a position. Not a permanent position. One of the elementary school art teachers had been in an accident and his car had accordioned right into him. He'd be in the hospital two months, recovering at home for at least two months after that. If Jake didn't mind a temporary position, one that was dependent on when the teacher returned, well, he could have it. They had been very impressed with him at the interview.

"It's just a permanent substitute position. The pay is lousy, strictly on an hourly basis," he told Rachel.

"Who cares?" she said.

"No benefits, either."

"Jacob, I'll pay you, if you want more money. You have to take this job."

"I did," he said. "I was probably much too eager. I wasn't cool at all."

"Ah, Jake," she said and started jumping around the room, shouting, "We did it, we did it." She stopped and smiled at him. "You've turned over a decent game card at last: 'Teach deprived kids. Collect a salary. Evade the draft. Pass Go.' "

"Boston," he said in a reverential tone. "Everybody's up in Boston. I can move in with Tom. I can breathe." They hugged. They danced. They had an enormous Chinese food feast. She helped him pack.

At the end of the first week of teaching, Rachel took the train to Boston. He was exhausted, he told her, mostly because he'd been so nervous about starting, but it had gone really well. The kids had seemed anxious to do what he had for them. "Anything's better than those ditto sheets they give us," one of them told him. He showed Rachel a collection of drawings a class of fourth graders had done of their neighborhoods. There were monsters, people big as houses, houses big as skyscrapers, and cars as souped up as planes.

"All this is in their neighborhoods?" she asked him.

"I guess so," he said. "The neighborhood of the mind, anyway. Isn't it wild? I love them."

Supplies were tight, but he'd expected that. He'd buy some things himself as his way of donating back to the font that had saved him. And artists, as he'd told his kids, make do with odd things. Found things. Look around, he told them. Everybody come back next week with something you can use in art that isn't a crayon, paint, pencil, or pen. He was exhausted, yes, but that was crazy strung-out energy hitting through the top of his head. He was doing this, he was going with it, and he was safe, man, safe. He told Rachel he loved her. He loved the kids. He loved art. He loved Boston. And most of all, he said, he loved being alive.

Fairly soon after that he began to go out with a friend of Tom's girlfriend. Theresa was dark and slender, younger looking than she actually was. Very politically aware. Her hair was cut short, and not altogether evenly because she'd done it herself, staring into a mirror. "I always get confused about which way the scissors' really going when I do that," she explained to Rachel, running her hands against the natural fall of her hair. Her self-administered trim gave her a boyish, waif-like look. Jake said it was a face that went with a tweed touring cap and he'd bought her one.

At first, he talked of taking some pieces around to the galleries, but by late October, with daylight savings time nearly over, he wrote to Rachel about what he said was "the quickening center of fear" that came with "fewer hours of light, fewer hours to paint." He was seeing certain things differently, he told her. Autumn for instance. He'd always thought of autumn as yellow and orange. But now he saw how there was a range from pink through maroon, from sage to lime drifting across every hillside around. "And I can't hold the landscape in my mind," he told her. "It's too changeable, too volatile. I'm forever taking another look, checking its newest phase. I can bear witness to changes that take place between morning and late afternoon: I can see that there's more red in that tree, fewer leaves on another. The transience of it is astounding." In a letter to her he wrote, "Has fall always been like this, or is it the Boston climate (further north, yet down by the sea) that makes it so much more dramatic a landscape? Tell me, did it look this way on the pond? And are you aware of how black the trees appear beneath all that color? Those rigid trunks and branches become more visible with each passing day, more dominant as the leaves strip themselves away."

It was the first week in November that the letter arrived from his draft board changing his classification from the 2-S of his student days to 1-A. He had not been exempted for his teaching. He called Rachel. "File for an appeal and get a Ouija board," she said. His laugh sounded horribly forced.

"What you need to do next," the Resistance told him, "is to ask for a clarification. Ask why you didn't get a 2-A because you're employed full-time in the inner city as a teacher. That takes up time," they advised him. "They can't draft you during that time. Then you file for an appeal. They can't draft you then, either."

Rachel told him it was very important that he not stop painting, but he said November light was very sharp, the little that there was by the time he got home from school—what, maybe a half hour?—and it distorted colors. He was planning a picture, he said, she shouldn't worry.

"How about using morning light?" Theresa asked him one time when the three of them were having lunch and he banged his fist on the table. "Get off my back," he said. Rachel saw Theresa's eyes fill.

Later, he apologized to both of them. "This war," he said. They understood, they told him.

The clarification letter explained that a substitute could not be considered a permanent position, despite the use of the word permanent in the letter from the Boston school system. Without a permanent appointment, there could be no exemption. He appealed to the assistant superintendent of schools for a permanent position. "There is none," the man told him as he dipped a lighted match in and out of the bowl of his pipe. "Then just a letter," Jake asked, "saying I hold such a position." The superintendent laughed. "I can't do that," he said. "Listen, I'm as opposed to this war as you are. But I'm sure you can appreciate my situation." Jake pushed him harder, said he couldn't possibly be opposed to the war and not take an active stance, couldn't just leave it to others all the time, and the man said, "I don't believe we should be discussing my politics right now." He leaned into his intercom and asked his secretary to send Mr. Burke in, please.

Jake wrote that he'd asked Theresa to go to Canada with him but that she was driving him mad by hedging the issue. "It's a big move," Rachel reminded him. "You don't know each other very long."

"She keeps saying we've got to take it one step at a time."

"She's right, Jake," Rachel said. "There's no point in worrying about things that might never happen. And don't forget: Appeals can drag on and on. And wars do end, sometimes." He filed for his appeal.

The men on his appeal board were old. He'd expected that. But they seemed softer than he'd expected, gentle, almost. "Maybe they care," he said to Rachel that night on the telephone. He told her how one of them had called him "Son," and that Jake had found that comforting, not insulting. "We're not out to get anyone," they'd told him. "We'd like to let you work up there in Boston. We believe you're doing a service there. We have some discretion on these matters, too, you know. Though we have quotas, we also can choose between candidates." When he left, he felt reassured, though the only definite thing they'd told him was that he was still 1-A. What did Rachel think? Did she think their discretion and wisdom would protect or sacrifice him? Had their fatherliness been merely a way for them to incorporate him into the ever expanding pool of "Our Boys?"

Three weeks later he received his induction physical notice. "Ah," he said to Tom. "The sweet men just didn't want me to blow in their office. They lied."

"They lie all the time," said Tom.

"Now," he said to Theresa, "come to Canada."

"There's no rush, is there?" Theresa asked, and Rachel heard the nervousness in her little girl laugh. "You're not even sure they'll take you."

"I have to make plans," he said. Rachel saw his eyes darken and narrow. She saw a large map of the Northern Hemisphere in her head, with heavy black arrows, all pointing north. She thought of tunnels; of snow and ice.

"When you know," Theresa said, "we'll decide."

He unfolded his letter, held it out to her. "I know," he said. "I can't."

"Theresa," he whispered, and held out his hand.

"Hey," Rachel said. "Tom and I are going for a walk, aren't we Tom?"

"Absolutely and definitely," Tom said and they both headed for the door.

Theresa decided not to go. Her home was in Boston, she told Jake. The U.S. She had a job in Boston, no job in Canada. "It's the same with me," he'd said to her. "No," she said. "You have to go, I don't. Anyway, what would I do there?" she asked him. It was then, he told Rachel, that he had a vision of himself foraging in snowdrifts for objects to be used in art. He said it was a frighteningly vivid image: he could feel the glare of sun strike sharply off the glazed snow, and he could see the blackened trees stretching high above him. He saw a landscape that had permanence. Sameness. He saw himself in black silhouette against that white.

He called Rachel at dawn on the morning of his physical. He said he'd been up for two days and he hoped that would be enough to change his vital signs, but he knew it probably wasn't. He'd been eating ice cream and doughnuts and hadn't done any dope since the day before because he wanted anything that showed up funny to seem perfectly normal, not drug induced. Still, he felt really high. From the sugar, maybe, he thought. What he was really worried about, he said, was what would happen at that moment when he refused induction? What if there were some wacko types there who knocked him to the ground and beat him to death out of some need to make an example of him?

"Don't go," she said. "Call in sick." She managed to get him to laugh.

She cut her classes that day, sitting by the phone, waiting for his call. It was mid-afternoon before his ring sounded. "I'm OK," he said. "And technically, I'm now a full-fledged criminal. I've refused to be inducted into the United States Army. It's only a matter of time till there's a warrant out for my arrest."

"Are you all right?" she asked him. He said he was. He was going to try to sleep, and then he'd pack up, drive down to see The Parents, then come say goodbye to her.

"The worst part," he told her when he arrived, "was standing there in my shorts, with my pulse thumping so madly I could see it on my wrists and ankles. It hurt like hell, like I had miniature jackhammer operators all along my insides. And I was terrified that I might step forward accidentally, or that somebody would push me forward." When the actual time came, though, he said, his feet wouldn't move. "All the other guys stepped forward and turned around to look at me. The guy who administered the charge asked me if I'd understood it, and I said I did. He said, 'Don't try to be a hero before you're a soldier,' and some guy behind me was snickering. Then they read the charge again. Everything they said had a horrible metallic sound, like knives scraping against each other, but no one touched me. I could tell they were being very careful about that. One of the officers explained about how I was in violation of the law. I just stood there nodding. Then I thought, Hey, what am I doing here? Waiting around for arrest? So I went and got dressed and left."

They took a walk then, heading out toward the barber shop. He had his hair cut short, his beard shaved off. Rachel gathered the longer pieces of his hair and put them in her pockets. From there they went out for lunch. She made him order a roast beef sandwich, though he had trouble concentrating long enough to eat it. He bought her an ice cream sundae, and he ate the whipped cream off it. He told her that he kept thinking about the other men who had stood with him, a bunch of naked bodies, who'd be lining up two weeks from then to be clothed in khaki. To board planes bound, to where? "They might all die," he said. He bought her a dozen ribbons for her hair. Twelve yards of color. She twisted them together in bunches, mixing them in different color combinations. "Like when you were little," he said, when she tied one, then another, round a clump of her blond curls. "I'll come with you," she said, while she leaned into the window of the car and then she kissed him goodbye.

CHAPTER TEN

*B*EN STARTED having some trouble with his job. Lots of kids hung around him, but they seemed to be different kids all the time. He got some good conversations going once in a while and he thought he did some decent interventions, but he sure as hell wasn't making much money given the heat out on those streets. He was frying his brain out there. He missed being home with her, he said, missed going places—that's what summer vacation should be, right? And he asked her to describe every little thing she did all day. He was jealous of her leisure, Rachel knew, and she couldn't really blame him. They talked about him maybe quitting, but reality was reality and they needed some kind of money. She stopped sleeping late and started painting some of the nicked-up baseboards and really cleaning the place up. She bought a set of curtains at Goodwill for seventy-five cents— amusing ones with funny little green and yellow roosters all over them. She washed and shortened them for the living room. Whenever she described her day to Ben, she tended to exaggerate the difficulties of cleaning the brushes or of mixing plaster patch in hot humid weather. She did read sometimes, and she tried to stick to the dense stuff, materials she needed for her thesis. She told him that it wasn't exactly a barrel of laughs to do that kind of stuff, either.

Kids were always trying to talk Ben into free ice cream. "Give us a break," they'd beg, but he really couldn't, not with the ridiculous commission he got. If he took a nickel off, he was left with almost zilch for himself. A couple of times kids pulled the freezer open when he wasn't right next to it, stuck their hands in and grabbed and ran. They never got much that way, but they got some of his take, that was for sure. He got to thinking maybe he'd talk to them about how he was really in the same bad scene they were, having to get the nickels and dimes to be able to eat and thought he might really get somewhere with them that way, but one of them said, "Man, we don't want to hear no complainin.' You hear us complainin'?" Some streets he stopped on, they were waiting for him. Not as he had originally envisioned it, but waiting with diversionary tactics, faking injuries on the other side of the street so he'd run over and the others could get into the freezer. He started skipping some streets. As it got hotter, as July boiled up, the kids got jumpier, poked him with a finger now and then, leaned on or pushed at him. One of them jumped on the hood of the truck once, then up to the roof, executing a wild dance before jumping back down to hood and finally to street. Rachel tried to soothe Ben by suggesting the heat would eventually quiet the kids down. Slow the pace.

One morning he said he couldn't do it anymore. Couldn't let little grade school kids make a monkey out of him. He'd just forget about it and hide under the covers he said.

Rachel wasn't sure what to do with him, or about him. She was frightened by his sullenness, a mood she hadn't yet seen. Do we have enough money for you to quit? she asked him, though she knew the money could last two, perhaps three weeks at most. "Of course we don't have enough goddamn money," he shouted at her. He got out of bed, dressed, and left the apartment without eating. He refused to take the sandwich and peach she'd packed for him for later. "I could try again to get a job," she said to him as he went out the door. "Sounds good," he said from the hallway. "Sounds real good."

She went to the library to read the want ads—it saved the cost of a newspaper. She called any ad that sounded possible, then opened the Yellow Pages and called all the department stores, the fabric stores, the book stores and eight restaurants, but no one wanted college girl help. They needed full-time, lifetime, workers. She painted one wall of the kitchen royal blue.

"Why do you tell them you're going back to school in September?" Ben bellowed at her when she described the difficulties of her job search.

"Because they ask me. Because it's the truth," she told him.

"Think about it, Rachel, what's more important, truth or food?"

The smell of the paint (cheap paint, so it probably smelled even worse than good stuff), hung, thick as pudding, in the super-heated air of their stuffy attic apartment. As soon as he left for work each day, she began heading for someplace that was air-conditioned and free: the Yale Art Gallery, Sterling Library, or Macy's.

On one of her wanderings through the department store she selected a black cotton bikini from a long rack of bathing suits. She didn't try it on, for she didn't want time to think it over. The instant she'd handed over her money to the salesgirl, it was hers, pure and absolute, for bathing suits are nonreturnable.

There was no full-length mirror in the apartment. She had to stand on the edge of the tub to see the bottom half of the bikini, on the floor to see the top. If she jumped, she could see herself briefly, nearly naked, plummeting through the air.

The racks of marked-downs had reminded her of her annual excursion to buy two new bathing suits. Like all seasonal events, it was difficult to resist the pull of familiar cues. She remembered how she'd stood in front of the mirror each summer, turning sideways, seeing the changes in herself; her image (and her mother's behind her), reflecting off its own reflection in the multiple mirrors. And how she had always thought to herself, This year, Jake'll say something. This year it'll happen.

She stepped back up to the edge of the tub, then jumped down once more. Even with a bifurcated view she could see that the fabric had too much give and so stood away from her breasts at the sides. She stood up taller and arched backward a little to try to take up the slack, but then the fabric hung forward, rather than to the side. When she had taken it off, she saw that the stitching on the bottom edge was pulled out for a run of about four inches.

It had been a mad gesture to make such a worthless purchase when they had no money, when there was no place to swim and she had perfectly good suits sitting in her drawer. She cut off the tags, ripped them into small pieces and flushed them down the toilet. She opened a drawer and dumped the bikini in, then lifted and turned the other clothes around so it seemed more mixed in; just another old piece of clothing. Ben would never notice. But she'd been an idiot to spend the money. This was hardly the year that Jake was going to take notice.

That evening she longed for the cool of the movie theater, but she knew she couldn't spend any money: The days of ice-cream vending were definitely numbered.

On a real scorcher, when the barefoot kids hopped and skipped along the sidewalk like Mexican jumping beans and Rachel saw a small child pour water out of a plastic bucket onto the pavement before she dared step on it, a ten-year-old pulled a knife on Ben and pressed it to his belly while two friends emptied the freezer. Later he told her how in just those few seconds, time slowed slower than when you smoked pot, slower than when you tripped, till he imagined the knife passing through each thread of his white apron, into the fibers of his button-down oxford cloth shirt (required dress by the company) and then beyond the borders of his being through the layers of his flesh (organized quite neatly like a diagram in a biology textbook), into his nerves, and on into his guts. He wanted to shout to the kids with their heads stuck in the freezer, hurry up already, get the goddamn stuff and get out of here. He wanted to reach in and pile it into shopping bags for ease of carrying. His head began to throb. He imagined the blade poking at his brain, teasing one layer of gray matter away from the rest. They dropped some Whammies as they ran away. He said he felt melted and filthy with sweat as he watched them run; watched the whole neighborhood of kids appear from doorways and alleys, following the real pied pipers—the kids with their arms loaded with ice cream. A small child darted into the street to capture the dropped booty. Ben wiped his face as they ran off to be sure it wasn't blood that ran down his temples. He tried to drive to the warehouse, but he could barely see. He pulled over to be sure his brains, turned liquid from terror, hadn't oozed out through his ears.

"Yeah," the route manager said to him, "that sometimes happens. You have to stand firm, or you'll lose your stock over and over." What did he mean, stand firm? Take the knife in the gut? The manager handed him a bill for the ice cream and Ben protested that it wasn't his fault, but the company policy, according to this guy, was that the confections were Ben's responsibility and could he prove he was robbed? He owed them. Ben walked out then, tossed his hat and apron on the floor by the door, and he figured they'd come after him, shake the money out of him, imagined even they'd pull him into an alley and rough him up a bit, and the same knife, the ten-year old's black-handled knife, was there, held razor sharp to his neck.

He walked to the bus stop, turning back, doing little spiral turns round some invisible center, looking to see when they would come after him, but the bus came to take him home before anyone stepped toward him again.

"What's a human life worth?" he said to Rachel.
"I'm sorry," she said to him. "I've been trying to find a job."
"It's not your fault," he said. "Don't act like it's your fault. It's society that's completely screwed up. We're all caught up in it. Why do I have to be miserable in order to have a few dollars? Why should anyone have to be miserable?"

"We could ask our parents for money," she suggested, though the thought of her stony-faced parents made her nearly choke.

"My father won't give us any money to live on. He already told me that. Tuition is all I get. He wants us to learn to be independent." Ben paced and laughed in short starts and stops. "Do you think he ever had to live this way?" he asked Rachel.

"I don't know." She wished she hadn't cut off his options, forced him indirectly, in becoming his wife, to have that job. To be mugged. She thought of an enormous crowd of people, grown people, not small children, jumping on Ben, stomping all over him. She burst into tears and reached out for him, one last touch before he died.

"It's not your fault," he said and shut himself away into the bedroom.

Ben said he needed more time to think now. Seeing a knife had altered him. He sat in the bedroom and thought. "We should talk about it," she urged him. He shook his head. Rachel suggested they take a ride or go for a picnic, like they had been doing. Couldn't he think of it as a kind of blessing in disguise that now that they both were out of work they had the time for that stuff? But he said no, he couldn't. "Don't worry so much about the money, if that's what it is. We can always take out a loan," she said, though she suspected banks didn't give out money for people to buy groceries.

"It's not money," he said.

"It's summer," she reminded him. "You should sit on the beach and close your eyes and relax. We've only been swimming once all summer. I always used to go swimming every day in the summer. Swimming's free lots of places. We could find a lake where they have canoes and go out and just float around. I used to do that with my friend Jake," she said. "The motion calms you down."

"So go do it with your friend Jake," he said. "Go get calmed down with him."

"It's just that water . . ." she tried to explain, but he said, "The hell with water. The hell with oceans and lakes and rivers. The sun on the water would glint like the knife," he said. The sun would catch on the blade, shine into his eyes, pierce them, so they ran bloody down his face.

"You need to think about something else," she said to him. She would have stroked his chest, his cheek, whatever she could reach, but he was always stepping away from her, slipping out of reach.

Since the knife episode he slept on his side of the bed, she on hers. He said it was important for him not to be touched for a while. He'd been violated. Raped. "You need to think about something else," she said. He didn't need to think about something else, he said, he needed to think about this. About the meaning of human life. About violence. About what people mean to each other. About wars.

"Maybe you smoke too much dope," she said to him, and he said, "If I didn't smoke I'd have to kill myself at this point. Which do you prefer, smoking or suicide?" he shouted at her.

"Smoking," she shouted back and slammed the door.

In some ways he reminded her more of Jake now, that brooding way he had. Though Jake never got quite so edgy as all that. He didn't yell the way Ben did. He just got quiet.

Evenings, she sat on the front stoop and watched people walking by, listened to children shouting their rhymes and playing chicken with the cars that whizzed down their busy street. When it finally grew dark, she made lists in her mind of what she would tell Jake about this summer. She turned the phrases over in her mind, but they came out too well turned, too polished and stiff. "Come get me," she said one night to the dark which still rang with summer voices, still rattled with cars and trucks.

Ben wouldn't open the bedroom windows. "I can't stay in here," she told him after two nights. "I can't breathe." She kicked the sheet off the end of the bed.

"The world is crumbling around us, Rachel, and you worry about open windows. We're killing each other on the streets. We're killing each other in the jungles. What hope is there? What reason to open the windows?"

"Ben, you're getting crazy," she said and she got out of the bed. He pushed her book off the night table and turned toward the wall.

He refused to come to meals at the kitchen table, so she brought their meals to the bedroom. Then he said he wanted to eat alone. He said she should leave a tray for him at the door of the room. At dinner she made him an egg salad sandwich and a tall glass of iced tea. She folded two sheets of origami paper, one yellow, one red, into little birds and placed them side by side on his tray. "Listen," he said to her when he passed the tray back out through the door, the birds still on the tray, fallen onto their sides, "Don't try to make me happy. I don't want to be happy right now. You have to respect that. Give me room. You understand that I don't want you cheering me up?" She nodded.

When it rained, she stayed inside and watched TV. "Will the Real Ben Goodman please stand up," she said to him from the doorway of their room one night.

"There are no absolutes. There is no truth," he said to her. "There is no reality. Explain truth, explain reality, and I'll try to tell you who I am. How I fit in." She watched him sitting on their bare mattress (he wouldn't let her give him clean sheets), knees pulled up to his chest, his beard getting denser every day, and it made her cry rich, wet tears of self-pity. "What's next?" she said to him. He didn't answer.

CHAPTER ELEVEN

RACHEL PACKED a few things into a knapsack while Ben watched. He slept lightly now, when he slept at all, so even though she had waited till the middle of night, he woke when she turned on the high-intensity desk lamp (hers). She had not chosen this bleak hour so as to conceal her actions. She had not, she thought, chosen at all, but had merely reached some end point, suddenly, brutally, and turned the light on as another person might open her mouth and scream.

Once she realized she was going to leave, she tried to move quickly, tossing whatever came to hand into the pack, but with him watching, gradually pushing himself taller in the bed, she found herself slowed down, her hands lingering over her dresses and batik skirts, folding the few objects which she had room to layer into her pack into smaller and smaller squares, composing unspoken explanations as she worked.

He blinked his eyes in the light but didn't speak. When the pack was filled and she could do no more folding and stuffing, she swung it onto her back. "Well," she said, and tried to smile, though her chin shook and kept her mouth from turning up properly. "I'm off for a while, I guess."

She thought he would ask what men were reputed to ask in such circumstances: What will you do for money? Going home to mother, are you? or just, Where can I reach you? But he asked nothing. She felt in her pocket for the fresh new bills she'd been handed at the bank in exchange for the last of the wedding present checks, and she headed for the door.

He followed. It was the first time he'd left the bed, except to use the bathroom, in days. "Where will you go?" he asked her. She was relieved to hear his voice mixing about with hers again.

"I don't know," she said. "I'll call you when I know. I need a change of pace for a couple of days." When the lamp had first come on, she had thought her leaving would be forever— the light and the dark had seemed so definite, so extreme— now she was less sure. He gripped the edge of the door and it shook in his hand. Was that from some emotion? What could she call it? Rage? Sorrow? She wanted to shout at him: What do you think? She wanted him to shout back. He slid a bare foot forward, his toes breaking invisible barriers stretched across the door jamb and she thought for a moment he was going to keep walking beside her; follow her down the stairs in his white Jockey underwear, delivering explanations bit by bit each time his foot lowered to a new step, but he stopped just outside the door, though she continued. As she went down the stairs, she heard his voice, level, slow, "I divorce you, I divorce you," and then a pause. She had reached the landing before she heard him begin again: "I divorce you."

City buses didn't run in the middle of the night in New Haven. And even had she enough money for a taxi, no cabbies cruised through East Rock that time of night, nor any time of night, for that matter. The day's heat still hung in the air, and the nylon pack stuck to her, as though her tee shirt weren't there at all. She reached behind her to raise the pack a few inches off her back from time to time. She stopped once, when she was nearly downtown, to take it off and shift the contents around before putting it back on, though that didn't help either. From a distance, she could see people outside the bus station. A busy night. Everybody moving about. As she walked closer, however, she saw the figures were derelicts, the pack of hangers-on who could always be found on that corner. One of them asked her for money as she approached, another, a woman in a baseball cap, reached out to touch Rachel's white-blond hair. "Like an angel," the woman said, as Rachel ducked out of range and escaped into the station.

It was a small bus station, but thank goodness, air conditioned, though that was obviously what had attracted another crew of wanderers into it. Snoring indigents lay like piles of rags on the benches. A man traversed the length of the station, his feet following the lines of the worn linoleum, and a woman argued volubly with an unseen companion. No one, save herself, Rachel thought, had the look of a potential passenger. As she stood at the window waiting for the agent who carried on a telephone conversation punctuated with sly and greedy belly laughs, a toothless drunk kept smiling at her and saying, "carry your bag for you, girlie?" Sometimes he reached out to touch her backpack, and once he gave it a slow caress before she was able to spin around and get it away from him. If that damned agent would only get off the phone and get me on a bus, already, she thought, but whenever she tried to get his attention, dodging away from the still undaunted bus station loony, the agent held up one finger, between laughs, to indicate he would be hanging up soon. His minutes stretched on, and she wanted to shout at him, Who the hell can you be talking to in the middle of the night? "Hey," was what she finally said, partly to him, partly to the wino who continued to smile and bob beside her. The agent gave gruff warning as he finally approached the window: "Leave her alone, Tommy, or I'll toss you right out the door." Tommy hung his head and shuffled back toward the benches. He took up a seat on the floor and leaned his head back against the bench.

"What can I do for you?" the agent asked and swung that no-longer laughing belly fully around for her to view.

"A ticket to Toronto."

"That's a big wait," he told her. He ran his hand down a schedule. "Ten-twenty-two A.M. Comes up from New York, bound for Buffalo."

"There's nothing earlier?"

"It's the middle of the night, sweetheart. If you want to go to New York, you can go to New York in twenty minutes. Toronto is another story. Go back home, come back in the morning, then go to Toronto maybe." What home? Give me directions to there, she ought to have said to him. When she hesitated, he added. "Tommy won't bother you anymore."

She watched an old woman lift a brown bag-encased bottle to her lips. Why did it have to smell so bad in there?

"So what'll it be, dear?" he asked. He tapped a book of matches on the counter.

"Toronto," she said, and he punched a ticket through his machine. He wanted six dollars more than she had. "That'll get you as far as Buffalo," he said after he had watched her count it out. "I wish you hadn't had me run this through if you didn't have the money. I'm not supposed to do that. I'll change it to Buffalo, but I'm not supposed to do that. When you get to Buffalo, you call whoever it is and let them come get you."

"He can't come get me," she said. "They won't let him." She wanted to stamp her feet and scream at him, at them all: every last damn one of those sick drunks.

"Sounds like this person you're trying to meet's in with a tough crowd. Won't let him do things." He pulled a cigarette from a pack, tapped it on the counter a few times, and placed it between his lips. Behind her, one of the residents began a sustained pattern of alternating coughing and retching, though he seemed to Rachel to be asleep. "Jesus," the agent said and shook his head. "I can't stand it when they do that. Tommy," he shouted, "get him to stop will you?" Rachel hoped the man wouldn't vomit, for she was certain her reflexes would imitate his. Tommy walked to the bench and shook the man by the shoulder. The sleeper sat up suddenly, stared at Tommy, then slid back down to the bench, eyes slowly closing. He was quiet again. "It works every time," the agent said. He lit his cigarette. "I'd offer you one, but the bums would all come crying to me, then. Favoritism or something. You want Buffalo or not?" He had begun to glance back toward the phone. She was keeping him from something, obviously.

"New York," she said and held out the money, all of it.

"You're lucky I'm not a cheat," he said after he had counted out the appropriate amount and given her back the rest. When he had punched out her ticket he handed it over with advice: "Sleep on the bus. You'll feel much better when you've gotten some shut-eye." She took up a post at the door, ready to escape if Tommy pursued again. But the agent, the overweight protector of lost souls, had been right: Tommy left her alone after that one warning. The smell and the snoring, snorting, gagging noises, still pervaded, but no more hands reached for her.

So she'd taken a detour, she explained to herself on the bus. That's all it was. She'd call her friend Jennifer when she got to New York. Jennifer had written that her summer sublet was "indescribably teeny," but it wasn't as though she needed a whole room to herself. A six-foot by two-and-a-half-foot spot on the floor would be perfectly sufficient. Then she'd figure out some way to get more money. She'd borrow it if she had to, though not from Jennifer because Jennifer never had any money. And then she supposed she ought to call Jake before she set off for Canada, anyway, because he might not even be home; he might be travelling himself. And maybe she could say something like, I'm not sure how long I'll be able to stay, perhaps for a couple of weeks, and he might start to get the idea without her having to say it outright, that the marriage was rapidly fading.

She tried to stay awake on the bus because there was a crazy person on it who was shouting "Hallelujah," and "God be praised, yes, sir," (though at least he didn't get out of his seat) but she couldn't help it, her eyes closed somewhere around Stamford and she woke up only when the bus stopped in the Port Authority and the driver shouted, "Last stop," with his face practically flush against hers. The nap refreshed her (damn the fat Trailways agent for knowing anything, even something that simple and obvious, about her), and she decided not to call Jennifer, but to walk over and surprise her, and feel the city come alive as the sun came up.

Jennifer didn't care that Rachel had wakened her. She was absolutely ecstatic, she said, to see Rachel, and she couldn't wait for her to meet Stefan, the new Great Love of her life, as soon as he woke up. Stefan lay sprawled (not naked, Jennifer assured Rachel) across the fold-down bed, beneath a pale blue sheet, at the other end of the studio flat. Jennifer led Rachel to the kitchen area, which had been delineated by a screen fashioned from cardboard and held together with yarn. Jennifer pointed to the screen. "I made that," she said. "And I ask you, is that clever, or is that clever? I mean abracadabra and suddenly there's a kitchen in this apartment. Not just a kitchen area."

"It's very clever," Rachel said. Jennifer had painted each panel of the screen a different color. The blue had proved a bit pale so that Rachel could still see the letters beneath, revealing the screen's origins as a refrigerator carton.

Jennifer pulled out a chair at what she called "The world's absolutely teeniest table" and made Rachel sit down. She took some eggs from the refrigerator and broke them one by one into a cracked red bowl. "You can stay as long as you want," she told her friend. "Rent free," she added. "Provided, of course, that you let me in on all the pertinent gory details of what's been going on in your life." Jennifer lifted a wire whisk from where it hung on the pegboard. "Start talking," Jennifer demanded as she held the mixing bowl across her abdomen and beat her yolks and whites into scrambled eggs.

Jennifer had a certain point of view about marriage that began to emerge over the next few days. She thought people could always work things out if they tried hard enough.

"Not always," Rachel said the first time Jennifer stated her position.

"I know you're angry, Rachel, but you can't just walk away from it like you can from a lousy date. You've made a commitment." Rachel decided not to tell her that she had been trying to get to Toronto. That New York was only a rest stop.

Jennifer wanted Rachel to call Ben. "I want it to work out for you two," she said. "You owe it to yourself. To Ben. To your parents," Jennifer catalogued. She had a long list of people to whom Rachel owed a good marriage. It included Jennifer herself. She was thinking of marrying Stefan, she said, and she needed good role models, not quitters, to look up to.

"But we're not good role models," Rachel tried to explain. "We shouldn't have gotten married."

"Come on, Rachel," Jennifer admonished. "Everybody has moods."

"Don't marry Stefan," Rachel advised. "Don't marry anybody."

"Of course I'm not planning to rush into it the way you did," Jennifer countered.

A few days later, in order to prove to Jennifer that Ben was done with her, Rachel called him. His voice sounded clear and firm, the way it used to. Rachel had pulled the phone into the closet to attain some semblance of privacy. The clothes which hung down around her face muffled and softened their words to one another. Ben said he was so glad she had called, he thought he had lost her, and what she had done, walking out on him, was the ultimate act of love, she had such fine instincts, he said. She was such a beautiful person. She had done the right thing. He was whole again. He understood it. He understood that most of all people needed each other. And he'd realized that he'd been hard on himself. He'd undergone such rough stuff, and that he couldn't take the blame for the whole world, could he, he'd been punished enough, that's how he saw it, he said. Alex had come back because the job he'd had proofreading telephone books in Des Moines had been horrible and boring and they'd had a really good talk about it, they'd gotten really stoned, and you know how it was, he told her, sometimes you have to touch bottom before you came back up and the grass—Acapulco Gold, he was sorry she hadn't been there because she would have really appreciated it—gave him that little push to the nadir of himself, turned him nearly inside out but got him going again, did she know what he meant? Hello Life, he'd said, here I am back again. And things were probably back on again with Sylvie and Alex. Oh and he was so glad she called him, because he'd been worried not hearing from her for so many days and he was missing her and he whispered low into the phone, then, that he had serious plans to undress her very, very slowly and to pretend they'd never made love before. To begin all over from a new day. And she felt a sudden disappointment, oh, not disappointment, probably, so much as surprise, because she hadn't expected to hear the same old Ben ever again and she felt like there'd already been a decision, yet here she was, right back in the middle of it all again. But one thing was for sure: she wasn't about to pretend that nothing had happened. She wanted him to know she wouldn't tolerate any reruns. "No more locking doors on me, Benjamin Goodman," she said. And he said, "Rachel, I love you," direct and simple. And needing, too, Rachel thought, and she realized she would have to be totally selfish not to meet him, in Jennifer's hackneyed, proverbial terms, halfway. Still, when she envisioned herself walking the two flights up to their apartment, she didn't see herself flying to his arms. It had been so tight and hot up there. Had they been able to take regular-sized breaths of air?

"Give me—give us—a few more days, Ben. To make sure we should get back together." She had, after all, been on her way to Toronto.

"Rachel," he moaned into the phone.

"To make sure, Ben." This was accompanied by groaning, but he did agree.

Ben called every few hours. He began to talk about the spiritual aspects of marriage, as he called it. "Do not give up on the spiritual side of us, Rachel."

"I'm not giving up on anything, Ben," she said. She had promised Jennifer that she would go back to Ben, though Rachel thought that promise had been extracted as much for Stefan's sake as any other. "How can we make love with her here all the time?" he whispered to Jennifer in the dark. It was a small apartment. You heard whispers.

"Let no man tear asunder what God has joined together and all that," Ben proclaimed.

"It was a civil ceremony, Ben."

"I hear a spiritual inner voice telling us to stay together. Do you hear it, Rachel?"

At first she thought it might be a joke. "Are you stoned?" she asked him, but he told her cynicism was self-destructive. "Do you not believe in a directing spirit?" he asked her.

"God, you mean?"

"Call it what you will. Call it God for simplicity's sake. It is part of us. It is part of how we make decisions and choices. Part of how we chose each other. It is outside us but inside us. We need to listen to its voice."

Was this religion? she wondered. Was this Ben? "What about real voices?" she asked him.

"What do you mean?"

"I mean talking, Ben. You didn't talk to me for almost two weeks."

"Rachel, you are not following this." No, I'm not, she thought to herself. "I was wrong in not talking. I admit that to you. Do you have the capacity to forgive?"

"Yes," she said, "but since when did you become an evangelist? And for that matter, when did you become a believer?"

"I do not think of it as religious. I think of it as intellectual inquiry. Respect for the mind. For my mind, for your mind, for the mind of mankind, and especially for the force, be it divine or not, which inspires and motivates those minds."

She felt a strong urge to say something silly and make him laugh. He sounded like a preacher. Next he would begin to roll his "r's" and build mild crescendos and decrescendos into his speech. "I don't think this'll get you a C.O., Ben," she said. She wondered if he would greet her at the door in a black robe, his hands folded over a Bible.

Excuse me, she would say, I thought you were somebody else. You looked so familiar, just superficially, of course. I was reminded of an old friend. Excuse me. Just let me get the rest of my things, if you don't mind, and she'd take down Jake's pictures and leave.

"Come back, Rachel. Come back and leave cynicism behind."

"I'll try."

"We must try," he said. "We are married. Joined. Come back to me and celebrate that union. I am lost without you."

"I'll see you tomorrow," she said. She wished he would start using contractions again.

He didn't, at least, affect the black robe. He was still in jeans and a work shirt. Still blonde. Still looking disturbingly like what he had always looked like. He did go down on his knees, though, when she sat on the bed, and she had wanted to set a few more things right, and even had a vague idea that they might outline something on paper (His Responsibilities, Her Responsibilities), but he started asking her forgiveness and he put his head on her lap, and forgiving got mixed up in touching and unbuttoning shirts (and he had new jeans, ones with a button fly) and she forgave him.

That was her first night back. After that, he began to argue for cycles of abstinence. Rachel made a face. "Is that what they do in Zen?" she asked. He had a volume entitled *Zen Philosophy* in his hands. He was reading it as part of his research for his Conscientious Objector application. "It has nothing to do with Zen," he said. "It's coincidence that I mentioned it while I was holding this." He tossed the book to the floor.

"Then why?" she asked.

"Because it was so good when we didn't do it for three weeks, wasn't it?"

"Yes," she said. "Haven't you liked it other times?"

"It's not the same. Last night something went off in my head, something explosive, and made it phenomenal. It wasn't just a physical thing, I don't think. Look," he said, "it's a question of saving up moments. You can dilute or you can intensify any experience. Little kids like certain foods, chocolate, for instance, but if they eat it every day, it's no longer so special. They no longer are totally engaged by it."

"I like chocolate every day," she said. "I could eat it every day."

"Sure, eat it, but not be engaged by it. Not have your senses tantalized and then overwhelmed by it." He pantomimed sniffing some chocolate and collapsing into an ecstatic state. "If it's every day, you just eat it. Have it. Digest it. That's not how chocolate should be experienced. Certainly not how love should be experienced." She frowned. "Abstinence is a rite of purification," he said. "Last night we came back together with more love because of that purification."

"That wasn't just love, was it?" She hesitated, seeing him look puzzled, but she would push him. She wasn't going to let him get away with periodic convenient memory lapses. "Wasn't there anger there, too? All the anger for the last three weeks?"

"I wasn't angry. That was a rite of forgiveness, I thought."

Rites, now? He was getting into primitive rites? If that physical act had been a rite, it had not been one of forgiveness on her part. The verbal forgiveness had been there, yes, offered to get by the barriers that kept her from meeting him physically, naked body to naked body, in an ancient form of combat. I forgive you, now take off your clothes and let's get on to business. And that business? Perhaps that was a rite. A catharsis of anger. She had fought her way into and out of his embrace, thrust and jabbed at him, meeting his aggression with her own, treading very close to primal violence; a first taste of blood. And then calm. It had been a heated wrestling match which no one won and in which no one was hurt. And she had thought: now that's done. Now I'm ready for a next time, a future moment when she could think of their coming together as an act of love.

"If purifying is what you're after, sex is what does that, Ben. Not abstinence. Abstinence is arbitrary and manipulative. I think it'll make us crazy and angry and impatient with each other."

"Sometimes you're so narrow, Rachel. So inflexible. How can you be so negative about a new idea?"

"Sometimes, Ben," she said with precision, "I think you're a flaming maniac." She watched a fine spray of her saliva carry her words toward him. He didn't wipe it from his face.

"I love you, and your cynicism only causes me pain." Again he pantomimed: one hand on top of the other upon his chest, his eyes raised upward, short, rapid breaths, like one in pain.

"Cut it out," she said. He picked up his book and went back to the chair. He flipped through the pages till he found his place and began reading again.

So in August, they didn't make love.

She shouted nearly everything she had to say to him, as though he were at the other end of a long, fog-filled corridor. And though at first she had entertained ideas of seducing Ben and showing him just how absurd he had been (and laughing at him, maybe, but then, finally, passing through some narrow passage, then emerging at a spot where they would both start over again), he was impervious. He lectured her whenever she tried to kiss him. When she stood up in the middle of the living room one hot evening and pulled her tee shirt over her head and threw it at him, he left the room. "I think I'm going to have an affair," she shouted at him one night. "Why aren't you worried that I might have an affair?"

"Because you're my wife. Because you took vows," he said, curving his mouth around the final word as though it were a cat's snarl—but quietly. Ben had said he was never going to raise his voice again.

"I never agreed to this," she bellowed at him. "I never took a vow of chastity, Ben Goodman."

He started requesting special things for dinner. "Cook something Chinese," he instructed her. Or, "Make that macaroni casserole with the Swiss cheese in it." She banged pots and pans around the kitchen, brought meals to the table in their cooking vessels, and one night poured his favorite, vanilla pudding, down the sink while he watched, because, she said, it had burned. "It was hardly scorched," he said. "A little bit stuck to the bottom of the pan. We could have eaten the rest of it."

"No," she said, running the water hard and fast, pushing the still warm pudding with a bare hand toward the drain, "once it's burned, it's no good. I can't stand the smell. It's disgusting." She glanced over toward him. He looked like a small boy, his face all ready to cry over a broken balloon. Cry about it, she wanted to shout at him. Cry about something, damn it.

She left the apartment as much as possible. One time she lured him to the door, standing there with it half open and calling to him, so she could inform him of her intentions. "I'm going out," she said. "So you can feel really pure." Then she closed the door quickly, almost jumping across the jamb, as though she expected him to come after her, to lunge for her, though he made no such move. She walked down to Yale and sat on the Cross Campus for a while, thinking about things. On rainy days, she went into Sterling Library and sat under the lion gargoyle where she and Jake used to study.

Then the weather changed. It began to grow comfortable by four or so in the afternoon. By five, Rachel's mind no longer lingered over visions of ocean surf nor glided along the still, clear surface of an empty swimming pool. The winds were more in evidence, constantly, but gently, chasing clouds from west to east across the sky. The sunsets arrived earlier, but seemed to hang about, as though reluctant to depart. The heat in the apartment dissipated, slipping first under the bed and into the closet, tucking itself into the eaves on the south side of the house, in the hope, perhaps, that if it curled up small enough, it might go unnoticed and be allowed to stay on. Rachel swept the apartment with a stiff old corn broom she had found in the utility closet, and gave final warning to all lingering pockets of summer. She sympathized with the dust which swirled in the light as it struggled to escape the heat's grasp. August was ending, fall was approaching. Time is now, she said to herself one morning. We go to Toronto now, in the little breathing space between New Haven summer and Toronto winter, or we'll never go at all.

She would explain to Jake what she couldn't explain in letters. I am like you now, Jake, cut loose and floating somewhere. The people who had held on had let go. Or is it I who have let go of them? she wondered. Who is the responsible party, in the end? Will it go on forever? Who catches us, who jumps for those nearly invisible life lines that hang back down behind us? Please don't make it be Ben. I am frightened of time, Jake. Of how it stretches in front of me, while I am held by his hands.

She waited till the day was right, and the hour, as well, till Alex was out, till Ben had had his three servings of macaroni and ground beef casserole, enough grass to be a little stoned, till he even reached out for her and stroked her arm and she said, "Why don't we hitch to Toronto and take sleeping bags? It won't cost that much, not if we camp the whole way."

He laughed. "We'd have to be mad to hitch that far. It'd take weeks."

"Maybe we'd get a ride that went straight through."

"How likely is that? And you know, we haven't spent any time doing stuff with Alex and Sylvie this summer."

"They could go too."

"Why would they want to? People don't want to visit other people's friends."

"To see the sights and all that," she suggested. "There's a

good art museum. Jake lives on an island. It's supposed to be very beautiful."

"Listen," he said, "you don't just go crisscrossing the border when you've got long hair. They start following you wherever you go after that. Anyway, if we go anywhere at all this summer, we should go to Chicago. We should be out in the streets for the convention, Rachel."

"People are going to die in Chicago, Ben." He shook his head, stood up, and began to walk away from the table.

Perhaps the grass had been a mistake; she thought it had only highlighted his edginess, not mellowed him down at all. "What if I went by myself?" she suggested (then wondered, who is this I ask for permission?), and added, "I think I'll go myself."

"What am I going to do if you take off?" he asked, though she wasn't sure what that meant. Did he mean, how would he find the grocery store, cook the dinner, something like that? Or did he mean that the appeal of abstinence was wearing thin?

"You'd get by, I suppose," she told him. She worried whether she would. In her mind she saw a police car stop by the side of the highway, two tall cops emerge and the voice of one piercing the darkening evening: Don't you know hitchhiking's illegal, honey? And would they drive her home, return her, road-weary, hanging from their hands like a wet rat, to her husband? Caught her we did, sir, and brought her back. Or would she wait endlessly by roadsides, cars whirling past, and if a car stopped, flung its door open to her, and inside was rape and death incarnate leering at her, would she say, thank you very much, I didn't really want a ride or would she be unable to turn and run, unable, having come that far, to do anything but slip in next to any old Grim Reaper who came along? Would she be trading up or down to be irrevocably in a stranger's power, some worse power than she faced now across the kitchen, some power that took its pleasures in inflicting real, physical pain? "If we had money," she said to him, "I could take the bus," and instinctively, she reached a hand (she'd stopped doing that weeks ago) for his, and he laughed at her.

"But we haven't," he said.

"Go with me?" she whispered. He had moved his hand away.

"I told you I don't want to."

Rachel watched the Democratic convention on TV. Ben missed it; he was tripping most of the week with Alex. She saw heads battered, faces bloodied. She saw Jake drift close for a moment in Ribicoff's outrage and she wept for him as he was tossed further away with every fall of the nightstick. She saw the unwelcome twin Phoenixes, Humphrey and Nixon, rise from the ashes of the Chicago streets. She wept for Jake. She wept for Rachel.

In September Rachel took the bus back to school and registered for classes. There was no money for such luxury as a room off campus for the days she would be in New London, so she slept in a sleeping bag on the floor of Jennifer's dorm room. She skipped breakfasts and chose between lunch and dinner. She put up a sign in the college post office seeking a steady ride to New Haven for weekends. She called a girl who had advertised rides leaving late Thursday and coming back early Monday morning. It was cheaper than the bus.

When Jennifer's phone was installed, Rachel sent her parents a postcard with the number. Below it she had scribbled: "Weekday number, New London." She expected no response—they hadn't called the New Haven number once the entire summer—but after only a week had passed, they called her. Did she need any money? they asked her. "Well, maybe some for a meal plan ticket," she said.

"Oh, Rachel," her mother moaned, "what have you been eating without a meal plan?"

Her father was on the extension. "Tell me where to send the check," he said.

"Send it to her in New London," her mother insisted. "Do you need your room paid for?" her mother asked.

Did she get the tuition check? her father wanted to know. It was like stepping backward. She was careful not to mention Ben. As long as she was who she had been, a college student, nothing more, they seemed delighted to talk to her. When was she coming to visit? She didn't know, she said. "We could drive up to school and see you," they suggested.

"I'm not here much except during the week."

"During the week is difficult," her father said. They didn't suggest a meeting in New Haven. Nor did she.

Toward the end of September, Ben had forgotten abstinence. He was into what he called the combination platter: sex and grass. Suspension of time, extension of orgasm. Sometimes they did so much grass between Thursday and Monday, it took her nearly till Thursday again to straighten out. And once when they were really out of their minds, she looked up at him and he looked like Jake. First she tried to tell herself it was just the same coloring with them both being blond but it was as though his face had metamorphosed into Jake's face. She blinked her eyes and it went away, he was back to Ben again, but then it happened a second time when they had some hash and that time blinking didn't help, he stayed being Jake and she screamed and that made it go away, but after that she said no more hash, and for a long time she hardly inhaled at all when they smoked. She looked for another driver, one who defined weekends more conservatively, and found somebody who left for New Haven Friday afternoons and returned Sunday at three o'clock. She explained to Ben that now that she had a meal ticket in New London, it was a big savings for them if she stayed at school more. She thought of it as a way of getting straight.

CHAPTER TWELVE

M"Y VISION is that of the cubist," Jake wrote. "Distance and time have worked a strange conversion in me. I no longer have the whole of your face in my mind. I'll think I have the profile, then there's a shift, and I'll see the rise of your cheekbone, or the shape of your lips, but never the full face at once anymore. I can't hold your image long enough to bring paint to it.

"I've taken the wedding painting down from the easel for a while. I just turned the whole thing to the wall. Elizabeth thinks I need a break. She's always trying to find funny movies for us to go to because she thinks I need to laugh more. She's probably right."

Rachel could think of nothing to write. She knew she ought to address the problem of his art. What's so terrible about cubism? she might write. Listen to your unconscious, it wants to explore a new way of perceiving images. How is that bad? Or she would write: Put this particular painting aside, but not all painting, Jake. Pick up another canvas and deal with another subject. Don't stop painting.

What she wanted to write was: turn it back from the wall. Paint it. Paint me. Don't go to funny movies. Please, don't let me go. Not now. She put a hand to her face. It was true, her face was fractured, no longer whole. Was it because she hid so much from him now? Was it because she never spoke of her life with Ben anymore that he could no longer imagine her?

144 ...... *Painting on Glass*

She didn't want to write to him about failure. How different their lives had become. "Listen to Elizabeth," she wrote. "She seems to have good instincts about you."

She sent him photographs. Not pictures of Ben, as he would be expecting, but black and whites of herself, himself, and both of them together: children. Jake and Rake, like two sides of one coin, arms across each others' shoulders, leaning toward one another, heads just touching, no smile, but only that same quiet expression on each of their faces. "I've had these copied from prints in our old album which my mother sent me, along with everything else I ever owned, without my even requesting it. I think about coming to see you, but the practicalities of such a trip with my cash supply flirting with the subzero values is bleak, and so the photos. They're better than nothing, aren't they? We'd have a good time if I did come, I know, and just thinking that makes me feel good. I'll get there. Believe in it, Jacob, and pick up the brushes again."

"Thanks for the photographs," he wrote back. "Elizabeth got me to teach her how to cut mat board and construct frames, so I gave them to her to mount. They look very nice, I think. She says she's jealous that I get to use both hands and head in my profession. I tell her my profession right now is strictly hands-on, not mind at all, janitorial work. She says the only reason she got sucked into the whole university thing was because she grew up in a family where there were so many generations of scholars that it never occurred to her she could be anything else. She talks about dropping French literature, but I don't think she will. What would she do? Work in a frame shop?

"She's done the pictures in a three-color mat of primary colors to, as she put it, 'emphasize the childhood theme.' Elizabeth isn't big on aesthetic restraint, but it really doesn't look bad. The narrow, unfinished wood frame she used works quite well. We've hung it in my hallway.

"She's also framed up those small watercolors I brought with me from the States and hung those throughout the cottage. I'm touched by her interest in doing something connected to my art, even if she only dabbles at the edges of it. I confess, though, if she weren't here, I would have taken the photographs and stuck them away randomly in various books in the house so that I could come upon them unexpectedly, and with wonder, and only from time to time. You and I had so many secrets once—maybe I want to preserve who we were back then by keeping us a secret, as well. Still, I like the way the finished product looks hanging on my wall. Come take a look at it, soon, why don't you." She never opened the letters in the apartment anymore, only collected them and slipped them into her back pack. She saved them, though it meant waiting days, sometimes, till she was back in New London.

"I've passed through all seasons here," he wrote from out of one of his darker moods. "I know what to expect. I know the landscape in winter and in summer. I can feel the next phase coming. I know when the sun will rise. I read the daily local paper and have a grasp of its editorial stance. I know what issues will get the populace aroused. Elizabeth is familiar, available, and needed. I reach my hand up in darkness sometimes to catch at my old life—but I no longer know how to hold it, can no longer turn my fingers the right way to catch it in my grasp.

"I feel less and less pain, though, as time passes. But in that loss of ache, I feel a fiercer secondary anguish. Here is the realization I must face: Everything that was once so important I'm now learning to give up. I see my life before Canada shrinking, growing less significant, as though it didn't matter. As though it never had to happen. I could have started full grown from my first moment in Toronto. What is Elizabeth, if at the next crisis, I can give her up? What am I if I have no past? Sometimes I think, even if the war ends and there is amnesty, I'll stay here. And I'm ashamed to feel myself deny my past in those moments, yet I've begun to realize that I'll be likely to deny it more and more. You'll be memory. If enough time goes by, we'll order gifts from catalogues and have them sent, direct at Christmas, the gift cards filled in, at our instruction, right at the warehouse. With such knowledge of loss, now and forever into the future, Elizabeth's love for me, and my love for her, seem only expedients. Has anything that has ever happened had lasting import?

"I'm back to doing landscapes," he wrote. "I think I can lose myself more in large spaces than I can in portraiture. I wish there were another term, though, than landscape—that's always had such negative connotations in the art world. I'll call them abstractions and I'll put cryptic quotations about ice and snow on them for titles and they'll be taken for something more than 'mere landscapes.' I like working with these big planes of white, and the positive sounds of solitude they evoke. I know you remember me as the all-time, best-ever hater of snow and ice, but I confess I've begun to like the look of fresh snow falling. This is not to say that the sense of isolation and entrapment of this place doesn't still bother me, because it does. But I also welcome the snow: at least that's a natural cause that compels me to stay indoors or to stay on my island. If I must lose free choice, I'd rather relinquish it to the elements than to a government.

"You'd be amused to see my new beard: I believe it has a will all its own. It's bushy and wild toward the sides, and doesn't frame my face the way the beard you would remember did. I'm like those animals who grow thicker coats in colder climates, I suppose. Elizabeth likes to comb the beard back and the hair forward so they form a continuous ruff around my face. She bought me a red and black woodsman's jacket on the assumption that mixing one American with one lumber jacket will produce an instant Canadian. I've got some other superficial props that I've gathered about me as well: parka, watch cap, mittens, and thick-soled mountaineering boots that are a great improvement over anything I've ever seen in the U.S. for cold weather. When I go out in crowds now, I don't feel so much like a foreigner. Now I share something with those around me—if only a style of outdoor clothing. She calls me Mountain Man when I'm in my Canadian garb."

"Don't adapt," she would write. Or perhaps, just, "Wait."

"I've started a portrait of Elizabeth," one letter proclaimed. "She hasn't the patience to sit for me, so I paint her in the kitchen while she cooks. I think it's a good bridge for me to get back to your painting because it's a kind of crossover from landscape to portrait. The kitchen has the largest window in the cottage and it's filled with midday light. The window frames her face, and the light coming in is intensified by being reflected up off the snow. And of course, being a redhead, Elizabeth is very pale, so the subject becomes whiteness, and the different textures of the indoor and outdoor world." Rachel imagined the scene: Jake, Elizabeth, the oversized kitchen window with the homey print curtains. It was working out, then, and their lives were meshing. "Paint away," she'd write back. "Elizabeth sounds wonderful." She wouldn't write: let me come before it's too late, Jake. What could she say, anymore? I am fine, how are you? Regards to Elizabeth. Ben is well, or so I've heard.

"On Sunday I went to church with Elizabeth. I went to try to make amends for ignoring her so much lately, but I ended up liking it. I admit I didn't concentrate much on the God and Trinity and sin business, but I loved looking at the stonework, the arches, and the neat tricks of perspective that had been done to the altar area with some cleverly applied paint. I've said

I'd go again, and next time I really plan to listen to the sin stuff. I'm curious about how others have organized the hierarchy of misdeeds. I want to know which sins are bad, which are very bad, and which are heinous." Such was the passage of time, she thought. A new intellectual interest in Catholicism. What was next? A written agreement to raise the children Catholic? He was moving on, whether she was there or not, in directions she couldn't fathom.

"Elizabeth thinks I should move to Toronto," came next. "She thinks my isolation has its roots in this place, though I tell her my isolation comes from being here and not stateside. It's true that there aren't very many people out here ten months a year because it's basically a summer community, but that's exactly what I like about it. And I like the water. I need the water. She thinks I should get a place in Yorkville or the Annex, one of the neighborhoods out near the University, so I could be where things are going on; be where there are other people with long hair and beards so I can 'merge better.' Merge. Fit. Assimilate. Forget. Next week, maybe. Next year. I have a real hair trigger response to the subject and invariably blow up at her. The other night she was talking about how cosmopolitan Toronto is, how much it's like an American city. She hasn't ever been to Boston or Washington or New York. I keep telling her: Toronto isn't like an American city, believe me. It's clean. Somebody goes into the subway system every morning to scrub it clean, just so I'll be reminded that I'm not home.

"Here's the routine: I forgive her, I beg forgiveness. We get together again. When my canvas looks so white, so void of her image, that I have to make sure she still exists and hasn't gone up in smoke, I have to go find her and bring her back.

"Supposing we got an apartment and then things didn't work out with us? I don't feel that I'm reliable enough.

"I've had a number of dreams about mail lately, which I know has to do with my fear of moving. First I dreamed that everyone I knew—The Parents, you, my friends from Yale—had all moved, and none of you had bothered to tell me. I kept getting letters back unopened. And then I dreamed I lived in a house with no street address. I was sitting in an upstairs window and I saw the mailman approach the house, then throw up his hands in frustration, letting the letters scatter out over the snow. I rushed around to find my boots, pulling all kinds of unmatched shoes and boots out of the closet, playing Cinderella games where I couldn't find any that fit, so that by the time I got out the door, the letters had all disappeared. So remember the address, will you? And remember I love you."

A telephone didn't help. It was already too late, Rachel thought, at the point Jake had one installed. The few times they spoke, they had rapid, giggly exchanges. "What's the weather there?" "Remember that great Chinese restaurant, Shanghai Village? It moved to York Street." Because of the cost, they told each other, they had to be brief. And just as well, she thought. He might ask questions. She might have to answer. Better to write, they agreed. "Can't stand this pressure to perform," he quipped. The phone is too expensive, and, yes, we'll write.

Another pretty card from Grace: a Swedish artist, this time, a great airy kitchen done in blues and whites. And two children, again, boy and girl, seated opposite each other at the small kitchen table, eating a tempting looking dessert of chocolate and cherries. The light mood of the picture belied the news she had to tell. She'd been visited by federal agents: "men in gray suits, white shirts, and boring blue ties," was the cryptic way she referred to them. "I don't dare tell him about this," she wrote, carefully avoiding Jake's name, "because I now think the telephone lines are bugged and letters opened. I invited these men in, made them sit down on the love seat, and offered them coffee cake and tea. When they said no, I went and got the cake anyway, sliced it up, put it on plates, and handed it to them because I was so nervous, I didn't know what else to do. They ate it, though, I want you to know, and complimented me on it. It was obvious why they were here, of course. I said I'd had a falling out with him years ago, had no idea where he was, and that if it were true what they said about him, I certainly didn't approve. But I learned my lesson," she concluded her note, "I threw out the address book with his particulars, and I won't ever call him from home again. You should do the same. Don't put a return address on your letters to him. And please, destroy this letter, too."

Rachel, who didn't give a damn whether the government read her letters, told Jake of his mother's ordeal. He wrote back that he had noticed a change in her letters, and had been worried that something was wrong. Her post-federal agent letters omitted references to all things personal or specific about the family. Rather, they were filled with details of such hot topics as gutter estimates and the current cost of various items at the grocery store. Though it made him laugh to read her grocery lists, he played the game with her, comparison shopping at his Toronto market. He wrote back that tuna fish was, indeed, cheaper in the States, though marmalade was a better buy in Canada. She mentioned no one by name anymore, but referred only to *your father,* or *our neighbors,* so as to avoid incriminating anyone when the censors got hold of the letter. She warned him, too, to omit return addresses. It might have been amusing, he said, but for the very real terror that she obviously suffered because of him.

Rachel wanted to know one thing: Why was the world so hell bent on rendering Jake Marsh homeless?

CHAPTER THIRTEEN

*M*ORE OFTEN than not, Ben wasn't at the apartment anymore when she arrived. One weekend he and Alex went off to New York to hunt down some peyote. "You should have told me you were going," she said when he finally got back.

"Why?" he asked her. "You wouldn't have gone anyway. What would be the point?"

She stared at him. "Why don't you know the answer?"

"Listen, you wouldn't have come, would you? I'm right, aren't I?"

"Why do you phrase questions so that I'm always in the negative role, always looking bad?"

"I can't help it if you oppose so much of what I choose to do. Would you have come?"

"No."

"OK. Case closed."

"The case is not closed. There is no point in my hanging out here alone. I could have saved time and money by staying home in New London. I could have gotten some work done there."

"I think of this as your home, Rachel. I think of New London as being where you are when you can't be home. I don't have to be here every minute, do I?"

"Next time, would you have the courtesy to call me first and let me decide what I want to do?"

"Fine. I'll call you. But don't expect me to feel sorry for you.

It's not like it was hours and hours of driving for you. And I thought I'd be back sooner. I thought we'd be back last night." He slid his hand along the counter toward her. "No more arguing," he said. "I'm glad you are here." He touched her face, then tried to kiss her. She backed away. "Don't you love me?" he asked her. She had moved into the right angle of the kitchen counter. There were no obvious escape routes.

"Who went to New York and didn't leave a forwarding address?"

"I said, let's be done with that. Let's also do one question at a time. Do you love me?"

"I don't know."

"Forget love, then," he said and lurched backward dramatically. "How about if we're friends and you type my philosophy paper for me."

"No."

"Because you don't love me or because you're angry about New York?"

"Forget love, forget New York. Because I hate to type. You know that. It's bad enough I have to type my own papers."

"But you see, you're a good typist. I'm not. And you can be part of what I'm doing that way. Sharing. To each according to his need, from each according to her ability. It has a nice ring to it, don't you think? A kind of joint ownership."

"Yeah," she said. "I do the work, you get the credit."

"I'll make it up to you somehow." He was going through the kitchen cabinets, pulling out anything edible, forming a collection of bags of pretzels, coconut, crackers, and chocolate bits.

"We spent all our money on the stuff," he said, "so we didn't have anything left to buy food." He laughed. "We cleaned out Ernie's refrigerator. That was the guy we stayed with. Alex's friend. We even ate his moldy cottage cheese." Ben drew a handful of pretzels out of a bag, then arranged them on his hands, draping the rings over each finger. "Do you have any money?" She shook her head. He began to eat the pretzels from off his fingers.

"How can you have any papers to type if you're always stoned?"

"Oh come on, Rachel," he said, "that's the whole point. It's easier for me this way. The insights come like shock waves— but beautiful, sensual, shock waves." He stripped the few remaining pretzels from his fingers and reached for her hand and kissed it. "Why do you reject it all, Rachel? If you'd only come along." She watched him trace the lines in her skin, run his fingertips over her fingernails, and turn her ivory ring around. "I don't dread the papers the way I used to. It should be the same for you." His hand felt cold against her skin. He was getting visibly thinner.

"It isn't the same for me, Ben. I get depressed when I smoke. I get scared when I trip."

"Because you resist." He seemed to look around her, or past her, when he spoke to her, as though his line of focus fractured when it reached her face. She imagined the lines of sight converging again at a point somewhere behind her. "Just read the paper for me. Just look at it. I don't care if you type it. I just want you to tell me what you think. I want to share it with you." He left the room before she could protest, returning almost immediately with a yellow legal pad covered with his scrawls. He tossed it to her, though it only struck her open hand and slapped down onto the linoleum. She bent, slowly, very slowly, and retrieved it.

"Ben," she said, when she'd read a few lines, "this is the same paper I typed two or three weeks ago."

"No it's not."

"It is. I remember some of these phrases: 'internalized structures,' 'universalizing,' 'inevitable comprehension.' You used those same words in the last one."

"Yes, but it's not the same." He took the pad from her. "I'm going deeper."

"Ben, he's going to read it and think you just handed in another draft of the same paper."

"I don't make different drafts."

"That isn't the point. He's read this paper. He won't want it again."

"Rachel, you misunderstand philosophy. It's the ever deeper exploration of human thought. That's precisely what I'm doing here. Going deeper. Grumbach will love it. He loved the other paper. Anyway, he has readers. Somebody else will read it this time. Grumbach reads papers about once a term and probably never two papers in a row. He just glances over the papers and reads the reader's comments."

She held the legal pad out to him. "It's so patently dishonest, Ben. I can't type it."

"Christ, Rachel. I don't understand your rules. You belong to another time, another place. Your goddamn rules are so outdated, they've begun to smell. Like Ernie's old cottage cheese," he added and laughed.

She stood up. "I'm going to go back tonight. This is a waste for us. Maybe I should stay in New London all the time."

He stared at the papers in his hand. "Maybe it doesn't have to be typed. I could probably just hand it in like this," he said.

She kept having to take these big breaths. Bigger than it seemed her nose or throat or lungs could handle. It hurt on the way down. Pushed her chest out too hard.

State it as simply as possible, and get it over with already, she told herself, and she wrote: "Dear Jake, I haven't said much about Ben, I suppose, because he's not that easy to describe. He changes a lot. Or, maybe it's that his interests change a lot.

One day he says I'm flirting with Alex. (Alex lives with us, so we have something of a casual, friendly relationship.) The next day he asks me why I'm so nasty to Alex all the time and says I'm cruel because Alex really loves me. One week he wants to make a baby, the next he decides sex drains away vital energies. He's applying to Harvard Business school one day, deciding to do subsistence farming in North Dakota the next. He fixates on something and then he seems driven, almost immediately, to its natural opposite. (You should know he would be horrified to hear how negatively I put this—he would call it intellectual probing or flexible thinking.) Meat is impure, he tells me when I'm making hamburgers, but the next day he wants to go out for the one true food experience: Indian lamb curry. Chocolate kills. Chocolate saves. Love is the answer. Love is only a euphemism for selfishness, self-love, and egocentrism. Life with Ben isn't boring, anyway. It's the proverbial roller coaster ride with surprises at the end of every curve."

She read the letter over and laughed. How come I don't laugh when it's happening? she said aloud, and her laughter grew louder, heartier, till she couldn't stop, till her stomach muscles ached, but still she couldn't stop. When the tears began, the pain spread to her chest, to her cheekbones, till she had crumpled the letter and tossed it in the wastebasket. She put her head down on her arms and listened to her own sobs. How can I tell him what I've done? she asked herself.

"Just us today," Alex said when he opened the door to her the following Saturday. He bowed his lean body low, one hand on forehead, salaam-style, rolling out gestures of welcome. "Let me take you out to lunch."

"He's not here?"

"Nope." Bastard, she thought. Why did she bother coming here at all?

"Where is he?"

"He didn't say."

"When's he coming back?"

"Don't know that either. Lunch?" he asked once more and pushed his straight brown hair back off his forehead.

"I'm too angry to eat," she said. "I'm going to take a walk." She started back out the door.

"Dinner then?" he asked as she went through the hall.

"Maybe. Or I might go back to New London."

He followed her to the staircase. "I'll cook for you. Come back if you like. I'll be here anyway."

"Thanks," she said.

He was making spaghetti sauce when she got back. She offered to prepare the garlic bread. There were no greens for a salad. "So where's my errant husband? New York?"

He shrugged his shoulders, a little boy gesture, accompanied by a touch of melancholy in his eyes, as though he was pained by being so unhelpful. "I told you I didn't know. I wouldn't lie to you." He tasted a spoonful of sauce and declared it magnificent.

"He's getting into speed, isn't he."

"He's tried speed, I know that, but then, everybody has."

"I haven't."

Alex laughed. "Maybe you should." Alex drained the spaghetti into a colander in the sink, then turned it into a too-small bowl. Strands of spaghetti hung out over the sides.

"He's getting skinny. He looks like he's down to about one-twenty. Somebody ought to tell him to stop." Alex served the spaghetti onto their plates and pushed the garlic bread across the table to her. "He's into secrets, isn't he?"

"Maybe," Alex said and shrugged once more.

"Trapped by the baggage of a Too-Early Marriage, is he?" She thought of a humorous greeting card she had once seen with a weary, cartoon-figure man weighed down by a string of pots and pans that hung from around his neck.

"Maybe."

"Aw, you can tell me," Rachel puckered her mouth and tilted her head, "I'm just his wife."

"You can talk about it with him, OK?" Alex spoke quietly; without anger. She supposed it was unfair to encourage him to tell tales about his friend. Or whatever it was that was involved here. She did wish she knew what was involved.

"Sorry," she said.

"I'm not offended."

She passed him the red pepper flakes for want of anything else to say or do. "What's your considered opinion of marriage?"

"It's anachronistic."

"How so?"

"It's a holdover from the days when virginity was important and women had to be protected against pregnancy. Birth control makes marriage unnecessary."

"I wish I'd thought of that last spring. Any chance he's out getting a divorce?" she asked Alex. Another shrug. "OK, I give up on you. It's my problem, not yours, right?"

"Right."

"So. Onto spaghetti," she said, and twirled a quantity of it onto her fork.

They cleared the table, adding their dishes to the other dirty dishes overflowing the sink. "Why don't you guys ever do your dishes?" she asked him.

"We do, when all the clean ones are gone."

Why not take the dishes one by one, she thought, and break them over the edge of the sink like an experiment on Mr. Wizard: Now Rachel, do you think these will break on clean lines into two equal pieces, or do you think they'll shatter? Remember, before you answer, consider the properties of porcelain. "You don't do the dishes because you're hoping I will when I get here."

"Not exactly," he said. "We're hoping something magical will happen to them. But we don't assume that you're the fairy godmother."

"You mean I don't look the part?" She stretched her curls out on either side of her head. "I don't look like I just love the feel of dried-on food yuck? Why don't you get yourselves some paper plates?"

"Too expensive," he said.

"You're going to have to cope somehow. I might not be around much anymore."

"I'll miss you," he said.

"I'll bet. No one to wash the dishes."

"No," he said. "I'll miss you, Rachel. And I'm sorry about Ben. I'm sorry he goes off like this."

"Thanks, Alex." He had spoken without mockery in his voice. Without the edge of needing to be witty. "I'm glad for an ally." She pushed the dishes farther back on the counter. "The dishes, however, are still disgusting. They wait, silently plucking at my more lofty notions of cleanliness."

"I'll do them." Alex began to remove dishes from the sink and pile them onto the table. "If we have dish detergent," he added.

She scrounged for a few minutes behind the fabric skirt which hung down from the sink. "We do," she said, holding it, like a torch of victory, above her head.

"I'll dry," she offered. "Do we have any towels?" She searched again below the sink. "There were some," she said. "Where'd they go?"

"Into the wash probably."

"Which you haven't done." Rachel took her own clothes back to New London and washed them in the dormitory laundry room.

"Right."

"And which I'm not doing for you." She poked him in the back with a finger.

"Can't say I blame you," he said as he filled the sink with steaming hot water. "The idea of doing it makes me quite ill."

She disappeared for a few moments and returned with a pale blue terry cloth towel. "Wedding present from Aunt Elsa," she informed him. "Such a hideous tradition," she said, as she displayed it for him to see, "to put the groom's initial in the center."

Though she had planned to read Pevsner on Italian architecture after they'd cleaned up, and she had explained that to Alex, he caught up with her just outside her bedroom door and put his arms around her. Then he eased her up toward the wall and her feet felt not so much heavy as entirely disconnected from her brain. He kissed her and she put her hands up on his chest to let him know he should stop, but he kissed her again, and all she could think of was Ben coming through the door, maybe in some sort of moral outrage and beating up on Alex or her.

"Cut it out, Alex," she said, though he kept kissing, touching. "What about Ben?"

"What about him?"

"He could walk in."

"And? All we're doing is kissing," he said. "Just after-dinner cordials." He kissed her again and she slid her hands up onto his shoulders, thinking to gain leverage that way. "We hear his key in the lock," he explained in reaction to the increased resistance, "and we stop kissing and start talking." He put his hand over one of hers and his fingers slipped between her own.

"This is so bad, Alex," she said, but her lips went to his again, and felt how different his unbearded, unmoustached lips were from Ben's. Alex's were naked lips that tasted of flesh, not beard.

"Come over to the couch," he urged her, "unless you can give me three good reasons why you shouldn't. Start enumerating for me what you owe Ben."

"Just this minute," she said, allowing herself to be led to the other side of the room, "I don't feel I owe him a whole lot. He's the one who's disappeared."

"He's the bastard."

He lowered himself slowly to the couch, pulling her gently down till she lay beside him. He put his hands on her hips and drew her close and she felt his erection hard against her. "Just kissing," she reminded him and Alex nodded. "I am, after all, a married woman," she said in what she thought were very crusty, upper-class tones, which made them both laugh, and for a while he just kissed her, but then he lifted her shirt and brushed his lips across her skin. His mouth found her breasts, her nipples, her neck, and she said, "We can't make love," but he said, "this is just kissing, only kissing," and when he started to unbutton her jeans, she touched his hair, pushing it off his forehead, watching it fall back again. "If he comes in . . ." she said, as his hand slid jeans down past hipbones. He lifted his wrist to look at his watch. "We've got a half hour," he said.

It was accomplished in well under the deadline. Not all that many clothes had been removed. Alex moved fast, and, if truth be told, somewhat awkwardly, as a lover, the couch being too short for his long legs, too narrow for any subtle variations. When it was done, she watched him zip his pants, saw how careful he was not to catch hairs, for he wore nothing between skin and jeans.

Rachel straightened the cushions on the couch. Alex turned on a cowboy show on the TV and put an arm across her shoulder.

"We're in a royal mess now, Alex."

"We'll manage," he said, and kissed her.

"What'll we tell him?"

"Nothing. You can't tell Ben anything he doesn't want to hear, anyway, can you?"

"No." She heard Ben's key in the lock. Her heart rate speeded up. She moved away from Alex's arm. The door opened and Ben stood there, his hands stretched out to touch the door jamb on either side of him, his form illuminated from behind by the hall light. He laughed, but didn't step into the room. He was high, and he looked more scrawny than he had even a week ago. She stood up. "Where were you?" she asked him, and she felt the unease in her voice. Why had she thought Alex would stand too, perhaps rage at Ben for her? What was next for the three of them? She imagined for a moment, herself drifting back and forth between the two bedrooms. Alex stood up then, and she nearly said, See, he is doing something, but he had started walking toward the kitchen. "Close the door, Ben," Rachel said. He surprised her by stepping into the room, shutting the door behind him.

"Didn't he tell you?" Ben asked and cocked his head in the direction of the kitchen.

"He didn't tell me anything about you. He said he didn't know where you were."

Alex reappeared with a can of beer in his hand. He took a sip, tipping his head far back.

The great silent Alex, she thought. "What the hell's going on?" she said to Ben.

"He didn't tell you about Kathy?" She glared at him. She turned to Alex, but he drank his beer, eyes closed.

"Shit, Alex, you said you would." Alex lowered the beer from his mouth and, with his signature gesture, shrugged his shoulders.

Ben walked up to Rachel. "Kathy—she's only eighteen—but . . ."

"Benjamin, what the hell?" she interrupted him.

"We've been sleeping together. That's what he was supposed to tell you." She covered her eyes with both hands, but he pulled them back away from her face. "Don't get so pissed. I assume you two have done fine together, too." She started to walk away from him, but he grabbed her arm. "Come off it, Rachel. We've got an even score, don't we?" He looked from her to Alex.

She remembered Alex's words: we've got a half hour. "You two bastards set me up, didn't you?" she screamed at Ben. She saw Alex shrug yet again. If I had a baseball bat, she thought, I'd batter in both those shrugging shoulders of yours. "I'm getting out of here," she said.

"Rachel," Ben said, "calm down. Stay with me, talk to me." He tried to put an arm around her, but she thrust it away. She picked up her pack from where she'd left it by the door. "You're both bastards," she said.

"Look, Rachel, suppose I forgive you your trespass and you forgive me mine." Where the hell was she going to go, she thought, her whole body beginning to shake, the library closed at midnight, the restaurants all eventually closed down. She'd had it with the freaky bus station. She had nowhere to go till daylight. She sidestepped around him and ran to their shared bedroom and closed and locked the door. He banged unremittingly on the door. "Damn it, Rachel. Till death do us part, remember. Rachel Goodman, open the goddamn door." She stood in the middle of the room till he stopped shouting and pummeling, then she turned out the light and sat in the corner in the dark.

In the morning she had hoped to sneak through the living room and out the door without waking him, but he was already up, out in the kitchen, mixing something. She went straight to the door. "Hey," he said, "don't you want to meet Kathy? I invited her for breakfast."

"What did you have in mind? A threesome? A foursome?"

"OK. I made a mistake. I miscalculated your rage." He reached for her arm.

"Don't touch me," she said.

"Adulteress," he hissed at her.

"Adulterer," she sneered back.

"We're on equal footing now, Rachel. Isn't that a good starting point?"

"Say goodbye to your co-conspirator," she said, pointing toward Alex's room. "And tell him to go to hell."

"Watch your language Rachel. He screwed up. He was supposed to tell you about Kathy first. Sex after."

"And you too, Benjamin. Go to hell."

"Reconsider," he said. "Kathy will be disappointed. And I've already been to Cumberland Farms to get pancake ingredients. I'm making a special breakfast. I know you like pancakes and bacon and I'm going to slice apples into the pancakes the way you like. If we have some brandy I can put some brandy into the batter."

"Screw you," she said and slammed the door.

CHAPTER FOURTEEN

*I*T WAS STILL early, and it was Sunday, so the bus was
nearly empty. It was a dark morning, just warm enough
for the precipitation to be rain rather than snow. And
it was heavy, pounding rain of the sort that made people
say, Good thing this isn't snow, or we'd be up to our ears in
shovelling. She could see places where the water flowed all the
way across the highway. As they barreled along, water splashed
up onto the windows. It's like being in a boat, she thought.

The driver had turned on the lights, but they flickered for
a while, crackled once, and then shut off completely. The air
machine stopped, too, and the bus became suddenly stiller,
though the sounds of the splashing water seemed closer and
more palpable. Rachel pulled her feet up on the empty seat
next to her own. It was eerily dark for a morning. When she
was a child, she had loved dark days. Loved even more, though,
dark closets and the hideaway space beneath the staircase. In
darkness, you give away nothing. No one can read your
thoughts. Can't even poke around at the edges of them, the
way her mother always tried to: You're up to something now,
young lady, I can tell by the way you turned in your lips just
then. When you're a child, you can only own yourself fully in
the dark. Under the covers. In the closet. Out in the playhouse.
Even when she was older, when she and Jake used to sit out
there together, the darkness was refuge. They were escapees
from the outside world, their voices ripe with secret admissions.

Perhaps she ought to have hung around long enough to meet this Kathy. It would have given her pleasure to say something coarse to her—"Hi, oh, I thought you might have big tits. Ben's always looking out for the big round variety." Or if she were flat-chested, some show of surprise, "My goodness, I wouldn't think Ben would have chosen you at all, he's so fond of big-breasted women."

Oh, hell. What good would insults do? What she would much prefer would be to slap their faces. To take the bus back down there the following Saturday, walk into the apartment and slap first Ben and then Alex, hard across the face. She heard the sharp sound of it vibrating in her ears. Nineteenth century, yes, but wasn't that what was called for here?

What was so great about these times anyway?

To Jake, she wrote, "Send my letters to New London from now on." The less said, the better, she thought, for she knew he'd understand something was amiss (probably even exactly how bad it was) from those few words. There would be time, later, to explain how there'd been foolishness on both sides that added up to disaster. Right now, though, she wanted no lectures via mail about hasty actions, nor about the nature of love. He was falling in love with Elizabeth, so he would believe love easy and natural. He might use words like concession or even sacrifice. Let him come to it slowly, she thought. Let him ask questions one at a time. She imagined he might start with, "Are you in New London all the time now?" It would take a while to get to "Are you separated?" When he did, she would answer. And then it would be as if he had told her, not the other way round at all.

She added these words: "I've more chance of getting a letter in New London because I'm there weekdays, i.e., mail delivery days. And things are more orderly here. I have my own little mailbox, so the letters wait there till I release them. Back in New Haven, things can get misplaced or lost in the general chaos of the apartment."

These were not lies that she chose to write, though they were not precisely truths, either. She sealed the letter and mailed it without lingering. The important thing was that his letters get through, and that they weren't held hostage.

When a week had gone by, she only dropped Ben a note in lieu of a personal appearance. "Ben," it began. "Please forward my mail."

But he wouldn't forward her mail. He called her to tell her as much. "You live here," he said. "With me. In New Haven."

"Not anymore," she said.

"Why should I forward your things to goddamn Connecticut College for Women?" He said he was going to call the dean of her school and tell her Rachel was living illegally in someone else's dorm room. "You can come and get your mail if you want it so much."

One time she did. Ben was out, and she'd just had time to take Jake's paintings off the walls and pack them carefully into a box, and then he'd walked back in. She'd searched all over for the mail and hadn't found it. When she asked him for it, he opened a kitchen cabinet and pulled out several envelopes. He tossed the College Wine Shop bill and an advertisement for *Encyclopedia Britannica* at her. While she bent to pick them up, he waved two envelopes in front of her face. She could see Jake's handwriting, dark and large. The letters U.S.A. underlined three times. She reached for the white envelopes, but he held them over his head, well out of her reach. Then he put them in his back pocket, sat down in the living room chair, and said, "Come and get them if you want them so badly," and she wanted to kick him one in the shins and wrestle him to the floor (hah! fat chance of that), but she picked up her box of paintings, instead, and went out the door.

He followed her down the stairs, raving at her about how he was quitting school because he was failing anyway and it was her fault because she'd left him. She started running and he was shouting, "Listen for my number when it comes up in the body count on the evening news, and remember it'll be your fault." He didn't run after her.

There wasn't a bus for two more hours so she had to hang around the Green till it was time, and then she only ran for it at the last minute because she thought he might be waiting at the station to try to shout anew at her.

A few days later he showed up in the lobby of the dorm where she was staying. He held two bent and ragged letters out to her. She reached for them, just as she had back at the apartment, and she could see her hand was shaking. She was thinking, what tricks will he try in this public place? But she got the letters into her hand, though it was all she could do to keep from crumpling them into a tiny ball, making them invisible and invulnerable. She thanked him.

"Could we talk?" he asked her, and she led him into the public sitting room. "Can't we go upstairs?" he queried when he had seen the other couples playing bridge, and the three girls gathered around the piano singing old Broadway tunes. "There's only ten minutes left to visiting hours," she said. "It wouldn't be worth it. We'd get upstairs just in time to come down."

"Husbands have to follow those rules, too?" he asked her. She nodded. One of the girls had begun to play the music from Porgy and Bess. Rachel raised her voice slightly over their noise: "Fathers and brothers and husbands. No males allowed up after eight o'clock."

"Sneak me up there, then, Rachel, damn it. Take me up some back way. Let me stay with you." He put his hands on her arms, way up high by her shoulders. Like he's going to shake me, she thought. She felt herself grow narrow under his grip, and slide inward, toward herself, far away from him.

"No," she said.

"Then give me the goddamn letters," he barked and she heard the piano slow and soften, felt the bridge players' eyes turning toward them. "Go away, Ben," she said, and she ran out through the fire doors and up the stairs to Jennifer's room. She hid the letters under the rug, then waited for him to appear. The desk attendant downstairs wouldn't be able to stop him if he wanted to get by her.

Rachel listened for sounds of his storming the hall in pursuit, but she heard no such indications. Then she heard him shouting from down on the street. He bellowed her name over and over into the cold air. She sat on the floor near the window where he wouldn't be able to see her from the street. The shouting stopped for a while, then she heard her name again, though this time with less belligerence and with a hint of the interrogatory to it. "Rachel," he said, again. "Is this it? Is this going to be permanent?" She edged over to the window and she could see him in the light of the dormitory carriage lamps. He looked up toward her. She unlatched the window and raised it halfway.

"Yes," she shouted out.

"Permanent?" he repeated.

"Yes."

He raised his hands, shrugged, and said, "So be it." He walked briskly out toward the gate. She watched till she could no longer see him. Then another five minutes more, at least. Then she rolled back the rug and took out her letters.

One of the letters Ben had tried to keep from her contained three sketches. These were not new drawings, but ones which had yellowed edges and old wrinkles that had been pressed smooth, though Ben's rough treatment had introduced many new creases as well. "I found these when I went to read some D.H. Lawrence short stories last night," Jake wrote. "How earnest I was at sixteen. I had to get every line just so. I hadn't come to terms with the power of suggestion, I suppose. Don't laugh too hard at them. Or at least don't tell me you have. That boy is still somewhere in me. Keep these," his note concluded. "I have more."

These were his drawings of her as she lay out on the beach, sleeping. Stroked out by his hand, she lay on her back here, face downward there, and on her side in the last. He had sat in the sun while she turned and baked her body. Yes, she saw how there was too much striving. His eyes, and then his pencil, had felt along every curve. His hand had remade each turning on paper. She saw the tendrils of hairs which crept from beneath the bottom edge of her bathing suit and across the flesh of her inner thigh.

All this while she slept, consumed, by his all-seeing staring; captured by his so sure hand. She remembered that he always had sketches to show her on those warm afternoons: the lake or the houses. And one sketch, that she still had, hidden, as he had hidden his. It lay at the bottom of a box of stationery, yellowed, like these. Herself, reaching to take something from a shelf. Not even her face, only her back, her arm, her curls. But it was because of her arm that she'd kept it, the way he'd caught that arc, and held on to it, though her action had lasted, what—a few seconds, only. He had an eye that held and held. Did she still have shape in the artist's inner vision?

The summer he'd done that sketch, and probably these three others, was also the same summer he'd tried to give her art lessons. He'd been pushy about it. He'd ridiculed her and said she never did anything the whole summer except sleep.

He suggested they meet everyday for the lessons at two o'clock on the Marshes' beach or in the playhouse if it rained. At his instruction, she went into town and bought herself a sketchbook and pencils. And for a week—maybe it was two, she couldn't remember—they had met. She thought of him as the Drawing Master, an image she'd picked up from reading nineteenth-century novels. He was the young man her parents had hired to teach her to draw, but who would eventually fall madly in love with her. But the real situation was more nerve-racking than romantic: she drew and he leant over her, watching her every line. She said she needed privacy to draw. She told him to go away, to give her time. So he began to give her assignments that she could do on her own but which she was to bring to their meetings. And then what a critique he delivered! How much he found that she needed to "improve." And he wanted her to look through books at Dürer and Rembrandt and Van Gogh; to talk about them and even imitate their styles. "This is too much like school," she told him. "You're too much like a teacher. It's summertime, you know."

Then good old Richie had arrived. An Italian family had taken the little Delling cottage on the east side of the pond for two weeks. She made friends with the renters, as she always did, and she brought Richie—the oldest boy in the family— around at two the next afternoon. "He looks like a hood," Jake said to her when Richie had finally gone in for a swim. "And you can see his balls right through that flimsy red bathing suit."

"So what?" Rachel said.

"Why does he want to be here while we're drawing?" And she explained how she felt sorry for him, how he had nothing else to do.

So she quit the lessons. It seemed easiest at the time. She and Richie met at two, instead, and things got a little heated up between them. She remembered how scared she'd been that one time out behind his cottage when she caught sight of his erection through the flimsy suit Jake so abhorred. She'd had to avoid the playhouse with him, claiming her parents had put it off limits and that Jake was such an unrepentant spy he'd be sure to report them. And she did see him spying on them. She remembered how bold she'd felt, how excited and shameless, when she knew he did watch, to let Richie kiss her.

In the end, though, it was a bad summer. Richie's family packed up and left after their two weeks and Jake refused to have anything to do with her.

"Listen," she said to him, "I'm back."

"Too late," he said. "Too goddamn late. Your timing stinks."

He strapped the canoes up on Labor Day. Much too early. There could have been another month at least of canoeing.

She picked up his sketches that had come in this latest letter. She hadn't always been asleep. She'd known what he was doing, or at least suspected. Saw how his eyes lingered, how his hand had followed a shape in the air that was her breast. I will write and tell him his adolescent violation is forgiven, she thought. But she would not say, I thought about your body, too. I wasn't asleep at all. Nor that Richie was such an obvious ploy. That the adolescent mind is so convoluted, so married to indirection.

The other letter was short, a note only, detailing his newest project: "I'm doing the cottage, stylized, on glass. It's painted on the wrong side, so near things have to go in first. I'm used to starting with the central focus, but instead, I'm down in the lower front, putting in the steps of the cottage, then moving back and away. There's no repainting. Only a single touch will do, for the first-laid stroke is the one that counts; the one that's seen from the other side.

"I'm playing with the idea of doing something with the lake

172 ...... *Painting on Glass*

on glass. Making those two surfaces speak one for the other
interests me. Or something with an old mirror. I have seen
people etch out the silvering on mirrors and then paint in those
blanked out spaces. The juxtaposition you get of a real image
(is a reflection real?) and a painted image intrigues me."

She wondered as she read these words what would happen
if he were to scrape the silvering clean away. Through some
illusion of paint would he disappear altogether?

Rachel's friends found it difficult to give up on her marriage.
They had had such hopes that it would work.

She imagined that they secretly kept a book on their shelves:
Your Wedding; subtitled *The Story of Rachel and Benjamin.*
It would be like the baby book her mother used to bring out
on rainy days for Rachel to leaf through: *Baby's First Seven
Years.* She remembered the drawings of smiling, pink-cheeked
infants, and preprinted milestones: Baby rolls over for first
time, Baby's first word, Baby's favorite food, Baby's favorite
bedtime toy. Rachel's mother had only had to fill in the blanks;
no free descriptions were required. The tooth chart was already
there. She'd marked the dates when each tiny white tooth
popped through the gums. She had filled in the names of the
guests at baby's birthday party, the food that was served, and
the gifts that were given.

Though Rachel's friends appeared casual in their questioning (So what did you do this weekend? So married people really
make love, do they? What did you make for dinner Saturday
night?), Rachel sensed the information and statistics were important to them. They would have liked to set the answers
down neatly into the blanks of their book. All married people
argue about money the first year, they told her (First fight:
six weeks). They prodded gently when she was falling behind the developmental guidelines listed in the introduction.

Why Rachel, you haven't had a real dinner party yet, have you?

There were no blanks for first temper tantrum. None for *Coercion, Desertion* (mutual?), or *Distrust.* None for *Rethinking.*

Faults? Blame? Well, it's difficult, of course, with this living apart they would say. They were losing patience with her: Rachel, there just isn't anything in the index for *Separation,* or *Apart,* or *Split,* not one of those is listed. Please Rachel, try harder to stay within the bounds of accepted behavior.

She told them nothing of Alex, for she had no need to hear their judgments—she had imagined them often enough to suffice.

After a few weeks, she was able to hear them talk of reconciliation without going into a defensive rage. For a time, she thought it would be easier to let them think she was coming round; thinking of getting it all resolved. When they asked her, Do you love him? she said Yes, though often she couldn't keep from adding a conditional *but* or *except when.* They stopped listening, though, before she tagged on labored phrasing and took their satisfaction in her single affirmative word. That's all that's really important, they told her.

They told her that unpredictability was better than stasis. They always pointed out how things were better than they might be at worst. But even they never pretended things were good in and of themselves.

One evening Jennifer had taken up the cause yet again, assuring Rachel if only she went back to New Haven for one day she would "work it out."

"Why are you always on his side?" Rachel demanded to know.

"Not his side, Rachel," Jennifer said. "On the side of the marriage, that's all. On making it work."

"Give up. Haven't you figured it out by now? I don't love him."

"You do," Jennifer snapped. Rachel shook her head. "You did," Jennifer countered.

Rachel shrugged and felt her friend's disappointment—and her own failure—splash over her like cold sea foam.

"I'm sorry," she said. "I should tell you, Jennifer, he has a chicky. He went and got himself a girlfriend."

"Bastard," Jennifer hissed. Rachel nodded, reminding herself of the mechanical dolls in the windows of Lord and Taylor at Christmas time; endlessly, hopelessly bobbing.

Bastard was what they all said. Repeatedly. They put their arms around Rachel and held her. What a bastard, they said. (What! Nothing listed in the index under *Mistress, Unfaithful*, or *Fooling Around?*) This is where I absolutely draw the line, Jennifer said. Rachel was suddenly surrounded by mourners. They patted her on the back when they came into a room where she was. She'd see them coming, lugubrious as could be, and she'd cry. Stop acting like someone died, she railed at them through her tears. It just makes me cry. But they shook their heads. You're crying because you're sad, they said. Just give in to it and cry. She didn't want to cry over him. She just wanted to know how to get a divorce.

The crying, it turned out, was a side effect of the sudden rush of hormones that accompanies early pregnancy. Rachel's only knowledge of hormones came from a brief unit in high school biology. Pregnancy had not been specifically mentioned. Morning sickness she knew about, and didn't have, but loss of emotional control—nobody'd ever mentioned that. But then nobody with much authority had ever mentioned pregnancy to her. Unless you counted her mother's comment the day she took her to Connecticut College to begin her freshman year:

"Rachel, just remember, you can smoke a little, you can drink a little, but you can't get a little pregnant."

Though she and her friends had been trading information on sex for years, they never bothered with discussions of pregnancy except in the context of avoiding it.

The cause of Rachel's atypical weepiness would have been more obvious, had she had the regular periods which provide instant verification that something has gone wrong. But for Rachel, a period was an unusual event, occurring, at most, every other month. A perfectly normal pattern at your age, the college doctor had informed her at her yearly checkup. She had no other symptoms. She certainly didn't look pregnant, and when her breasts started to swell, she assumed her period was finally coming. It just seemed to be taking a very long time in getting there. No one had ever mentioned enlarged breasts as being associated with pregnancy, but when her blouses no longer buttoned easily across her chest, she grew concerned. Her belly was still as flat as ever.

She fought back as an intellectual. She picked up her books and notebooks and went off to the library. She found a copy of *Pregnancy and Childbirth* in the stacks and carried it to an isolated carrel. She read. If she were pregnant, she soon realized she had no way of knowing how pregnant. Nor, for that matter, who had been the cause. She turned the page and looked at the drawings of pregnant women, their shapes ballooning ever larger. On another page pictures traced the changes in developing embryos. The volume shook in her hands. She went back to the dorm to tell the others.

At first, Jennifer fell back on her old-style phrasing: she stopped talking of quickie divorces and explored Reunion with Ben and Father's Rights. Jennifer paced and talked a mile a minute about options. About babies and being married. Think divorce, Rachel would say to her from time to time, but Jennifer dithered and whined as though it were she who suffered under a new burden, and not Rachel at all. Rachel longed for Jake's vision, his analytic abilities, but this pregnancy would be just one more point in the failure column to report to him. Dear Jake, I've got this baby in me (no, don't cheer, there's this peculiar ambiguity as to ownership). Is that enough information, Jake? Please advise.

She tore open his letters, hoping for solutions, and instead she found him focused on his own concerns, his voice completely distant from her world. Did he never make decisions anymore, only turn arguments round and round without stop? "Dearest Rachel," he wrote. "I've been thinking about moving. And I've also been thinking about not moving," he wrote. "In favor of moving: The light's lousy in the cottage. Against moving: I'll miss the boat ride. I like the trip out across the water, away from Toronto each evening. I'd much rather feel the rise and fall of the boards beneath my feet than climb up dark stairs in an apartment building at the end of each day.

"We've looked at a few apartments. More to fill up time on a Saturday afternoon than for any other reason. I'm always struck by the odors: cooking grease, male cats, mildew, Lysol, and in one place, cinnamon buns. Always someone else's stamp. I don't feel these places could be mine; that I could breathe deeply in any of them. My cottage smells of summer, of sand and water—comfortable scents." She was gone from his letters now. He had absolutely no idea who or what she was anymore.

Rachel called a gynecologist in New London, the same one Jennifer had gone to for birth control pills. The receptionist told Rachel where to take her urine specimen and when to call for results. Later in the day, when the confirmation finally came over the telephone line (Positive. Positive? Positive.), the receptionist was apologetic. Doctor had no appointments open for two weeks. She wasn't having any problems, was she? No, Rachel said. I'll call back tomorrow.

"Call Ben," Jennifer commanded. "Nothing can be done till you tell him."

He'll laugh, Rachel thought. Hang on, he'll say, and I'll just put Alex on. "Give me the name of your friend who had the abortion," she said.

"You have to call him, Rachel."

"Only to ask for a divorce."

"But if he hears there's a baby, he'll want to get together."

"Jennifer, I don't care what he wants. He's had his chance. He's taken morality and beaten all the life out of it. I don't owe him." Jennifer shook her head in obvious disapproval of her friend's position. "If you don't give me the name of your friend who had the abortion, I'm taking the next train to New York, and I'm going into the first abortionist's office I can find."

Jennifer took her to meet Lucy Barnes from her sociology class.

Lucy Barnes was a veteran of a San Juan abortion. "You miss three days of classes, with much apologies to the professors for stomach flu, and other than that, nobody notices you're gone." Lucy dragged so hard on her mentholated cigarette between sentences, it made a sipping sound. "The girls here are mostly virgins and too stupid to figure it out."

"No side effects?" Rachel asked her.

"Well you bleed of course, you know that," Rachel hadn't known that. "It's like a heavy period. After a week it stops. And they tell you not to have sex for three weeks."

"I could live with that," Rachel said.

Lucy's dark hair was pulled back with a ribbon, showing off her high cheekbones. She was slender, with small, firm breasts, unpregnant breasts, Rachel observed.

"Is it very painful?"

"It's not painless, but it's not bad. He gives you a local, which helps. It's like cramps. Scraping. Bad cramps, I guess, but it doesn't last long. I kept saying to myself, When this is over, I'll be free. It got me through. You just have to remember it doesn't last long." Lucy tapped her cigarette pack against the edge of her desk, popped out another cigarette and lit it against the one that she had smoked down nearly to the filter. She offered the pack to her guests and they both lit up. Lucy exhaled with force, and all three of them watched the smoke rise rapidly then suddenly begin to drift sideways. "But you have to go to this one place. You have to go to the Morgan Clinic and you have to ask for Dr. Ortega. He's American-trained. Very clean, very middle class. He's the only one down there who examines you before he starts. So at least he's sure you're pregnant. You're not just run through his routine so he can make money off you. If it's his day off, go back to the hotel and wait. Go to the beach. Don't go with anybody else." Rachel nodded.

"I should write his name down," Rachel said, and pantomimed scribbling. Lucy pulled a pen and paper from her desk drawer. "I know people who have gone to other places and they're dirty or they don't use the Novocain or whatever it is Ortega gives you. I had a friend from back home who bled for two weeks and had to go to the hospital." Rachel saw the hands of Guernica, oversized, overreaching, and suddenly covered with blood. "Go to Ortega, or forget it." Rachel's hands shook when she wrote down the clinic's street address. Her hands had been shaking almost continuously since she had read the book on pregnancy. Another normal symptom?

When they left, Lucy hugged Rachel. "Let me know how you do," Lucy said. She took thirty-five dollars from a small metal strongbox on her closet door. "This is all I have. I've still got two hundred dollars to pay back on my own Puerto Rican sojourn." Rachel resisted her gift. "Take it," Lucy said. "You're just a pregnant lady if you can't raise the cash." Rachel kissed her and pocketed the money. "Take taxis," Lucy said as they left.

Her friends wrote checks in small amounts, each of them writing several over a number of days. Some they wrote out to cash, some to each other. To avoid suspicion, Jennifer said. Keep the records clean and untraceable.

It was a lot of money, for there was the plane fare, the hotel room, as well as the doctor's fee. There was the train down to the city, too. Meals. I'll scrimp on meals, Rachel said. I'll buy a loaf of bread and some cheese in the market and eat that. Only if you feel perfectly fine, Jennifer said. And not the night you have the abortion. That night you have dinner in the hotel. Room service if you need to.

I'll pay it all back, I swear, Rachel said. For a moment she had thought about dying. Some tiny part of herself seemed to break loose, somewhere high in her chest, and then float off. Hush, she said to her own thoughts.

Jennifer gathered the newest checks and the crisp bills they had been collecting from their trips to the bank and the college cashier. She recorded some numbers on paper, then ripped the paper up. Have you ripped up his address? Jennifer asked, and Rachel said yes, though she hadn't, for she didn't trust her memory under pressure. She had written it small on an index card otherwise covered with Art 315 notes. No one would notice it there. We should destroy any potentially incriminating evidence, one of her friends said. Rachel asked for the money, but Jennifer was reluctant to hand it over. Shouldn't we spread it amongst us till you go? she asked. That way no one will become suspicious. Who will go through my things? Rachel asked. I'll keep it from now on. No need for you to get any more involved than is necessary in this intrigue. We don't mind, these friends told her, each of them, but Rachel insisted. She slipped the money into an envelope, then into the bottom drawer in Jennifer's bureau where she kept her clothes. "It's your safety we're worried about, you know," Jennifer said as she watched Rachel hide the money. "We're not the ones who'll go to jail."

"Would I?" Rachel asked her, her hands still on the drawer. "I'm twenty-one," Rachel said. "Have I lost all my chances already?"

"No, of course not, Rachel." Jennifer put her arm around her friend's shoulder. "I'm sorry I frightened you. We're all caught in the drama of this. We're scared for you, and we've imagined more than there really is. No one arrests people for having money."

"For having abortions?" Rachel felt fear throbbing belligerently at the back of her skull.

"No," Jennifer said. "No." But what did they know? What did she know about any of it?

Jennifer offered to go with her. No, Rachel said. That's only more money. Jennifer issued final warnings: No incisions. Promise, Rachel, because that's too dangerous. No general anesthesia. Only Ortega. Rachel promised. It would be better when she was beyond them, she thought, and on her own. Past their fears which magnified her own.

They had convinced her to take a suitcase. It's more respectable looking than a pack, they said. "I'm getting an abortion. Abortions are illegal in the United States. I'm running away on other people's money. I'm not respectable," she said, as she pushed down on the lid of the valise to close it.

"There's just no need to call attention to it, that's all I meant," Jennifer said.

She hated suitcases. They were heavy and awkward. You had to lift them above your head onto the rack and check them on the plane. She preferred her pack, stuffed like a pillow, next to her on the seat.

On the plane she sat next to a gray-haired woman in a tweed suit who was on her way to Miami to visit her sister. Rachel said she was going to San Juan for quiet relaxation. I intend to feel no pain, Rachel had imagined herself saying to the woman. I've had something weighing heavy on me lately, and I thought San Juan would be a good place to get rid of it once and for all. It didn't seem funny, though, when she tried to say any of it. It seemed too accurate and true. And too bloody around the edges. I'm visiting my cousin who lives in San Juan, she said to her, instead. Whereabouts? the woman asked politely, for she had friends in San Juan, and had visited them on previous occasions, but Rachel said she didn't really know, they were meeting her at the airport. The woman told her of a restaurant that was a lovely quiet hideaway that tourists didn't generally know about, though she thought Rachel's cousins might. Maybe not, Rachel said, they haven't lived there that long. He teaches at the University, Rachel said. The woman told her the name of the restaurant and Rachel took out the Art 315 index card and wrote it in a blank space. Thanks, she said. I'm afraid I've got all this studying, she said, holding up the book on her lap. You go right ahead, the woman said, you mustn't fall behind in your schoolwork.

Rachel said no, thank you, to the offers of food and drink from the stewardess and chirruped goodbye to the woman when they touched down in Florida. She spoke the necessary words to taxi drivers and hotel clerks. But other than that, she spoke to no one else till she reached the clinic.

CHAPTER FIFTEEN

ORTEGA'S CLINIC did not look like an abortion mill, or not like the image of an abortion mill that Rachel had constructed for herself. Knives and coat hangers had dangled in front of her eyes all through the night, but they lifted suddenly skyward on invisible stage wires when the taxi brought her to a building where a young man was sweeping the white steps clean of small debris under a clear blue tropical sky. Where she had imagined a fifth-floor walk-up and dark, bare rooms, she found a shining first floor office with a positive surfeit of nurses. And it was obvious that more than abortions went on behind the examination room doors. The waiting room sheltered men with hacking coughs, pregnant women, and children bright-eyed with fever. She signed her name, Rachel Goodman—it was almost the same as a false name, so little did it seem part of her—at the end of a long list of patients. It was barely past eight-thirty in the morning. She waited then, with the other patients, counting their numbers, estimating exam times, knowing she had hours to wait. The others seemed more prepared. They had food, drink, toys for the children, baskets of knitting to satisfy their hands. She had brought one book with her, but it grew damp in her hand, the shiny paper cover sticking to her palm after a while. She slipped it under her chair once, then picked it up, afraid she would forget it when she was called into the office. Nurses crisscrossed the clinic space, occasionally escorting patients away down a long white corridor.

She watched children toss restlessly from their mothers' laps to the floor, watched the little ones approach one another, then back away without speaking a word. Two woman conversed in a corner—a mother and daughter, Rachel surmised, but except for them, there was no conversation, only an occasional Spanish phrase exploding into the otherwise quiet air. Most of it sounded harsh and admonitory to Rachel; all of it was seasoned with anxiety.

Rachel had a small purse with her. Without the backpack, it had become a necessity. She opened it frequently to see if the envelope of money was still there. Sometimes she looked into the envelope as well, to see the individual green bills which lay inside. Rachel turned pages in her volume of Italian Renaissance drama, but the words jumped around the page, as though she wore someone else's prescription lenses. Meaning refused to be captured under her yellow highlighter. After a while she stood, then walked around the room. Several children rose up and followed her. She led her parade for a time, then sat back down. The group that had followed her sat at her feet and stared up at her. One very small child leaned her face into the leather of Rachel's boot. The mothers seemed not to notice. When Rachel's name was finally called, she had a sense, though it was fleeting, to be sure, that the worst was already over.

Dr. Ortega met with her in his office before the physical exam. He wore a white coat, open, with a knitted sport shirt beneath. He seemed little older than herself. He was attractive and smiling; nearly flirtatious, had this been another setting. On the subject of pregnancy he was surprisingly direct: "You want to terminate, I assume." She nodded in silent response. He took a brief history. They discussed his fee (she was relieved to find that Lucy had given her the correct figure), her recov-

184 ...... *Painting on Glass*

ery, important symptoms she must watch for in the next few days, and the procedure itself. She had difficulty listening. How many times had he done this before? she wanted to ask him. He was too young. He made a joke about college love-ins. She didn't laugh. She wanted to explain how they had manipulated her, that Alex wasn't her fault. "I'm married," she said. He smiled at her.

"All the ladies who come here are married," he said.

When she stood up to be taken to the examining room, she felt dizzy, and the room shook and tottered around her. Just relax, he said to her, there's nothing to fear. He put his hand on her shoulder as they walked down the hall.

She waited for him, naked under a white sheet. It was a clean sheet, though one that had picked up dark stains of humankind here and there through repeated use. She thought about how Americans had converted sheets into gowns, put little ties across the top edge, cut careful slits for the arms. Here, there seemed less attempt at masquerade. A sheet sufficed, so use it.

But the room was cool. Too cool for a naked person under a thin layer of muslin. The large muscles in her arms and legs shook, whether from fear or cold, she couldn't tell. And she wasn't sure what she ought to be doing. The nurse had handed her the sheet and given instructions in Spanish. Perhaps she ought not to have removed her shirt at all. Perhaps not climbed on the table as she had. (Done what then? Stood next to the table with the sheet hanging from her teeth?) She waited. So there would be more hours passed in here, cold, her back beginning to ache against the hard table. Beneath her was another sheet, wrinkled from her squirming to find a comforta- ble position. She had to climb down and straighten it out, then lie back down again. There were U-shaped metal things stick- ing up at the end of the table, and though she had never been to a gynecologist's office, she knew from Jennifer's stories that these were stirrups, and that her feet must eventually slip into them. She wondered if that's what took so long. Was the doctor waiting till she inserted her feet before he returned? She put her feet in, felt the cold, and still he did not appear. She took her feet out and squirmed all the more.

Here was yet another place her mother had never been, never would be. Not Puerto Rico, not an abortionist's office, not even, perhaps a gynecologist's office, although Rachel couldn't be sure of that one. That her mother had never mentioned such a visit only indicated she hadn't mentioned it. Her mother would never have bought a mattress secondhand (Rachel, think of the bugs!), walked out on her husband (men have special needs, Rachel, and you were always so difficult to get along with, remember?), or fooled around with his friend, but then her mother would never have married Ben. Would never, therefore, have had any of these other situations to face.

There was a knock, to which she could muster no language for response, the door opened and Dr. Ortega entered the room. He began, as he had promised, with detailed explanations. "You'll feel me touch you now," he said. Then, "This will feel cold. Try to relax."

The instruments were cold. The stirrups were cold. And weren't there laws saying a nurse had to be in the room during gynecological examinations? She nearly laughed out loud. Yes, she thought, but in the case of illegal procedures, the court is willing to waive the requirement. He asked her for more information. The date of her last period, which she didn't remember exactly. How many weeks pregnant the doctor at home had said she was.

"I didn't see another doctor," she said.

He took her hand and placed it low on her abdomen. "Can you feel this," he asked? "This is your uterus. Quite large, quite firm," he said. Yes, she could feel it. He poked some more, this time omitting the descriptive explanations. When he told her to sit up, she almost said no. She knew that small amount of discomfort had not been an abortion. Had been nothing. Why was he having her sit up? She was still a pregnant lady.

"You're too far gone," he said to her. "Twelve weeks is the boundary marker. After that, we can't do anything for you. You're well past that. The wall of the uterus is softened by now, and with a D and C, it could easily be perforated. For this," he said, pointing at her abdomen, "you need a hospital and induced labor. We don't do that." *We* suddenly. Obviously, this place was too clean, too like home. She'd find someone else. Somewhere else. "There's nothing we can do for you," he said.

"Exactly how many weeks is it?" she said.

"We can't give you an absolute date. Not with your irregular cycles. Fourteen weeks. Sixteen, perhaps. Perhaps not that long." He left the room.

Rachel lay back down on the examining table, staring for a long time at the medications and instruments lining the shelves. Not Alex, then? Why had she thought such distinctions were significant? It was either Ben's sperm, or if not his sperm, his idea.

There was a knock at the door—a nurse, again, speaking Spanish, pointing to the examining table, then back out toward the waiting room, asking, Rachel assumed, if she couldn't have the examination room for the next patient. Rachel went behind the white curtain which hung diagonally across one corner of the room. She felt again where the physician's hand had earlier drawn hers, and it was still there, that round lump, rising, without her knowledge, within her.

When she emerged into the hall, she met Dr. Ortega once more. He led her back into his office. "Everything appears very normal in this pregnancy," he said. "If you choose to terminate it, though, every day, really every hour, counts." He talked about risks in late terminations, drew a curved graph on a piece of paper which he said showed elapsed time and something else, but it looked mostly like a projection of herself, billowing out; her uterus, rising higher and higher. He described saline injections and Caesareans. There was something about live births. No, he had no names of doctors, she should just go to the hospital and go through their procedure for approval for late terminations. "To what doctor?" she asked him (she needed a person, a name, a human being, a photograph, please Dr. Ortega) and then he spoke in Spanish, and though he quickly translated for her, she knew her last chance had crept out the open window of his office along with his attention span. "Just go to the hospital," he said to her. "Explain your position."

"Just," she responded. He was so young. He was probably not a real doctor, anyway. She didn't say that to him, yet he bristled as though he had heard it, pulled his shoulders back and said, "I am sorry." Still, he did charge her for the office visit. Passed her a bill right across the desk. An older doctor would have had the sense to have a secretary or nurse handle such things. She counted out dollar bills onto his desk.

She walked back to the hotel to save money.

What was she saving for? So she could go to a hospital tomorrow? Don't let anyone else do it. She was a foreigner. Alone. Who here cared whether she died under a knife or turned into a vegetable from incorrect anesthesia? Who would ask, on her behalf, that no medical students or interns be allowed to handle her case? Who would be notified of her demise? Who would do the notifying? She needed one person to turn around in her chair to and say, after the doctor had described his procedure, does this seem reasonable and sound, should I go ahead with it? Somebody to help her back into a taxi when it was over. Somebody who spoke decent English.

She had dinner in the hotel. Expensive, and she ate little of it.

Somebody to answer the question: What now?

She drank wine, though it made her head spin as wine never had. Jake, she said, come get me and save me.

Later she said to him, facing into her mirror upstairs in her room, Jake, damn it, I'm all alone.

She filled the bathtub high with hot water and climbed in, but she saw it right away, a uterus poking up beyond the familiar flat contour of her body, pushing from back behind her bellybutton. She slapped at the surface of the water and cried.

She slept badly. She dreamed about her mother. Her mother said she could have her old room back, and when she went upstairs, the old wallpaper, the yellow floral wallpaper from when she was a child was back up. And there was a crib in the room. And the old shelves with the stuffed animals were back up. And she saw there was no bed. No bed for her. Just the crib. And Jake's room was gone. That part of the house had been lopped off. Disappeared.

In the morning, she tried to get his number from information, but the operator couldn't get it for her. Try again later, she advised. Foreign information is difficult. When she tried again a few minutes later she got an operator who spoke English so poorly, Rachel couldn't make any headway.

If only she'd come to us first, she heard her mother say. We'd have told her it wouldn't work. In the night (dream? obsession? true lucid thoughts?) she had crawled through mazes, bumping walls, going backward, till she got beyond the accumulated wrong turns; way back past where her mother might have taken her, back to an error her mother couldn't know and wouldn't admit: She hadn't gone with Jake. She had let him leave and in doing so, had been the true deserter. He had no luxury of deciding to leave or stay. She had let him go to shadows and darkness and then left him there.

In the elevator going down, the elevator operator winked at her, then serenaded her in Spanish. She wept for herself, alone, without rescuer to snatch her from the brink, to bring her back alive and healed; Pauline saved from her perils.

She wept for having let him go, poor Jake, no rescuers, either, no way to climb back home.

Forgive me, Jake, she mumbled as she exited the elevator. The elevator operator bowed deeply. The lobby vibrated with laughter and the colors of resort wear fashions.

If she could have done it any way she liked—if times had been different, if mistakes hadn't been made—she would have followed his route, exactly. She would have taken out those early letters (all of them left behind in New London) and figured out where he'd been those first days of his journey. Which towns he'd driven through, which restaurants he had eaten in. And then she'd have rented a car and started off on his route, up the east coast of the United States, then into Canada, across open country. Jake's route. She would walk into diners where he had been, open a door he had opened a year earlier, and order from a menu he, too, had read over. She would touch something he had touched.

But that was fantasy. That was with time and funds unlimited. She opened the envelope of money again. Strictly speaking, she ought not to be using their money; her friends' money, this way. But she was using less of it than if she had had the abortion. She'd stayed only two nights, not three in the San Juan hotel. And she had to take a plane back to New York in any case. Round trip to Toronto was not going to add that much more to the cost. She'd stay only two days. And she'd call them from Toronto so they wouldn't worry when she was a day late getting back. She'd say everything was fine. I'll tell you the details when I get there.

Look, she would say to them, when I couldn't get an abortion, I needed somebody. And there was a chance that in Canada, with someone with me who knew the place, the hospitals and all that, that I could go through with it. I thought you would understand. I'm going to pay you back, just the same. You can't argue with medical diagnosis, she'd say. It seemed so simple at first, that I would just go see Ortega. Then boom, everything fell apart when Ortega threw me out. They wouldn't like it ("What if one of us needs the money next week?" they'd be bound to say), but it would be over by then. They might fuss and fume, but she'd have been to Jake and back again. She'd get them their money (a loan from Jake, maybe?) and they'd understand. No one else would need it. Use birth control, she'd say to them. Just don't decide, a la Ben Goodman, that birth control is unnatural. It's all cause and effect. Birth control prevents pregnancy. Use it.

No, she wouldn't lecture them. She passed her Miami–New York ticket and cash across the counter to the agent. A Miami–Toronto ticket was handed back in return.

She hadn't counted on the severity of the weather. She knew she didn't have perfect clothes for Canada, but if you're thinking Puerto Rico when you do your packing, you don't tend to think wool coats. Through the windows of the terminal she could see very little, except for the snow, that is. It was not actually snowing, though you had to be told that. It was only blowing. A ground blizzard, the pilot had called it. No cause for alarm.

She had figured she'd tell Jake to bring a jacket to the airport for her—his, Elizabeth's, or even some old extra sweater. The trouble was, she hadn't been able reach him from the airport, a situation which she ought to have foreseen. She chastised herself for not thinking any of it through. What had she done? She'd taken somebody else's money for one thing, and run. He could be anywhere. Anywhere. Gone to Sweden to join the anti-war community there. If she were lucky, he was just at work and would eventually open his front door and dive for the ringing phone (she kept it ringing almost constantly). Why she had imagined he might be home during the day, she didn't know. She'd assumed he worked evenings, late into the night, even, and painted during the daytime. Perhaps because she knew he couldn't paint at night. He was a janitor, and anyone who'd gone to grammar school could tell you janitors worked daytimes, same as school hours, poised in readiness for the inevitable blown lightbulbs or spilled paint. Did the teachers and kids call him Jake? Did the teachers say, "Go look for Jake, Vinny and tell him Lauren has gotten sick to her stomach all over her desk." Did the children avoid him, or worse, were they frightened of him, thinking him mad because of his long hair? Or did they love him, draw pictures with inscriptions To my friend Jake. And did he take home their faces for later, and turn them into cherubs hidden in the underbrush of his paintings?

She had grown used to imagining him feet up, reading in a small room. Sketching, sometimes. Doing rounds once an hour. Not a janitor at all, in her musing, but a watchman.

So she waited in the airport, drinking tea, then gathering her things, going to a phone to try again, and going back for yet another cup of tea. At three o'clock she got teary (school ought to have been dismissed by then, she had concluded) and began to stamp her feet when she heard the rings go unanswered yet again. She moved into the restaurant bar and ordered a glass of white wine and a tuna sandwich. She was very tired.

They don't dismiss him along with the children, you know, she told herself. She laughed then, to think of him bringing up the rear, behind a line of orderly children, then remembered he had been a teacher only a year earlier; head of the line. She saw him sweeping and mopping, turning chairs over onto desks. When he was finally finished, wasn't he likely to stop somewhere and pick up a quart of milk, a six-pack of beer, or something for dinner? This calling and calling could go on forever.

She would go into Toronto and telephone him from there.

She went by taxi to a library. What did she know about Toronto? Why not a library (she asked the cabbie to take her to the most central one)—it was bound to be warm and equipped with a telephone. She was pleased with herself for having thought of it. Once there, she would try to find a number for Elizabeth (what chance of that? she asked herself). He had mentioned her last name, and she could practically see it written out in his broad dark hand. Just nearly halfway down the page, slightly left. An Irish name. And not an O' name. A name of three syllables, and full of vowels. Red hair and Irish, he had said. Elizabeth of no surname. She would know it though, she was certain, if she saw it. She found the telephone directory and nearly wept to see its size (but she had all day and all night, didn't she) and began to go through it, page by page, pausing at every name with an initial E, stopping at the rare occurrence of an Elizabeth, scanning for Irish beside it. Whenever a possible combination occurred, she dialed it. Elizabeth, please, she said. Wrong number. Till Halloran. Elizabeth C. Yes, That was it, she was quite positive. Her hand shook as she dialed that one, only to hear a recording about non-working numbers. She dialed it again. Same recording, this time sounding (silly you, Rachel) a bit peeved at being called up again. She continued through the H's then for a moment, still looking for Irish names, then flopped the pages shut. Elizabeth C. Halloran she said to herself. No point in going on. That was she. Both gone. Presumed dead.

She was too impatient with being in these places; waiting. She couldn't sit still. She would head to the island and wait there for him. Somebody, a neighbor, would take her in, surely.

She made her way toward the lake by ducking into stores and alleyways—anything to cut the wind. She huddled unto herself and alternated her free hand in the pocket of her jacket, pulling the neck of her sweater higher for protection, though each time it slipped relentlessly back down. The suitcase seemed determined to screw her up, catching oddly in the wind, banging into her legs and pushing her off balance. She was crying, though not from hormones, not from self-pity—that all seemed too luxurious under the conditions—now it was a direct effect of the wind and snow striking at her eyes. How was she to survive the ferry ride? It's short, she kept reminding herself. Like Lucy said, you just tell yourself, when this is over, it'll all be fine.

She went into every phone booth she saw for one more try, and for a few moments of warmth. There was almost no light in the sky. She imagined herself on his doorstep, as if she could possibly find it in darkness, frozen and unable to move by morning: What insanity, she said to herself, to think of going out there in the dark. What the hell was she trying to prove? Why had she come to Canada at all?

She put the suitcase down at the curb and stood and watched the cars rush by. She hailed a passing cab, and started laughing when he actually stopped. Her defeat was feeling ever so slightly like victory. She felt the welcome heat of the blower in her face as she lowered her suitcase to the floor. "I give up," she said to the driver. "Take me to a Sheraton or a Hilton so I can get warm."

"Rush hour," he said to her, pointing a thumb toward the endless lines of cars he now tried to merge back into.

"I'm so cold," she said to him, rubbing her hands together, trying to get the pain to go away.

"Where're you from, dressed like it's springtime? Florida?"

"Connecticut."

"Ah. You ought to know better. Americans are a stubborn lot, I've found. Like with that war of yours. Stubborn as hell to be in such a bad war. And you stay in it out of sheer stubbornness."

"It's not my war," Rachel corrected him. "I'm not in favor of it."

"Good, good," he said. "That restores my faith." The meter ticked off red light time. "You'll be comfy at the Sheraton. Magic fingers in the bed, you know. Color TV." Could she use their money for magic fingers and color television? With what explanations? Well, Jake wasn't there, so I had to go to a hotel. You didn't call first? I did try.

"Is there a Y?" she asked the driver.

He laughed. "Bit of the other end of the scale," he said, "no bellhops, no working elevators."

"More affordable, though," she said, aware of the incongruity of arriving at the Y in a taxicab. The important thing was that she get to lie down somewhere. To lie in the dark for half an hour and get herself back to feeling whole. She had never, never been this tired.

"Sure?" he asked her solicitously.

"Yes."

"Some turning around to do, then," he said.

When she entered the building, the smell of chlorine swirled round her like damp dream memory, alluding to old, but familiar places and times. Getting back to basics was how she thought of it. There was a room at a very good price. The woman called it a cubicle, and Rachel pictured a closet-sized enclosure with a ceiling fan. A door that closed onto quiet darkness. She picked up a pool schedule before she headed upstairs. "Who says you have to go to San Juan for a resort vacation?" she said to the attendant at the desk. The woman nodded. She expected the elevator to be broken as the cab driver had said it would be, but it wasn't. It was slow and it was bumpy, but it carried her to the fourth floor well enough. There was a telephone in the hallway on the fourth floor—she wouldn't even have to go back down to make her calls.

A cubicle, it turned out, was a space between partitions within a very large room. Each cubicle had a bed and an open metal box next to it. It all looked something like a hospital room, only larger. Sheets, towels, and blankets were piled at the end of the unmade beds. Blue striped ticking mattresses. A woman was asleep in one of the beds already. On a few others, women lay stretched out, one reading, the others only staring. One clutched her striped pillow to her chest. None of them acknowledged her presence as she passed. It was just as well. She wished there were more privacy, but she was so exhausted, she really only cared about getting her body down on that mattress. She had tried not to stare into the others' spaces, so her glances had been quick, but it did seem to her that most of the other occupants were much older than she. One woman played a radio, though not too loudly. In one cubicle, several woman sat on one bed talking; playing cards, maybe, she couldn't quite see. Rachel found cubicle seven and put her suitcase on the floor next to the bed. She shook out the two sheets (neither was a fitted sheet, of course) and started to spread one of them over the mattress. "I'm Anna," a voice behind her said, and Rachel jumped at the sudden words.

"I'm sorry." Rachel held the sheet against her chest and tried to smile. "I didn't see you there." The woman was very thin, her fine, straight hair blonde but dark-rooted. She wore heavy black eyeliner on her lower lids as well as her upper, as though her eyes had been circled as part of some selection process. She wore no other makeup. Rachel couldn't guess her age; less than forty, more than her own age.

"I'm in charge," she told Rachel. Rachel smiled again—or still—she felt trapped in that space, that stance; she wasn't sure what this Anna meant. Was she a staff member, or self-appointed ruler? And what was she in charge of?

"It's not funny," Anna said.

"I didn't say it was," Rachel responded. She needed to rest, not deal with territorial silliness. If she were polite enough, acted serious as hell, perhaps old Anna would take off.

"You're in bed twelve, down by me," Anna commanded. "Where I can watch you."

"Seven," Rachel said, though it wasn't really audible. She fumbled in her pocket for the paper the woman downstairs had handed her. "Seven," she said, and held out the paper with its inked-in number.

"Twelve," Anna repeated. "Fold up the sheets real neat like, pick up your suitcase and move there." Then Anna held out a knife. Long, shiny. She held it casually, as though it were an incidental accoutrement, not actually threatening Rachel with it, not clutching it hard-fisted and extended toward any of Rachel's vital organs, veins or arteries, just holding it up where Rachel could see it. She could see this: it was a kitchen knife. A real kitchen knife for slicing turkey and steak. It wouldn't fold up and go out of sight. Where did Anna keep it? Obviously not in a pocket.

Rachel folded sheets, Anna watched. Rachel tossed the options about for a few seconds. Surely she would rather take her chances on freezing to death than on getting knifed. (I avoided an abortion with statistical risks in my favor for sleeping next to a crazy with a kitchen knife?) She picked up her suitcase and went to bed twelve. Anna stood at the opening to twelve and watched again. Rachel shook out the new sheets. Two other women looked in over Anna's shoulders. When the bed was made, Rachel sat down on it. "Unpack," Anna said. Rachel opened the suitcase and took some things out: a pair of slacks, a striped blouse, a nightgown, comb and brush and put them in the wire basket. Anna walked over to examine the rest of the contents of the suitcase. The small purse lay concealed inside the jacket Rachel had folded across the end of the metal bedstead. Rachel tried to keep her eyes away from it, but couldn't—without the money and without Jake, she'd be entirely stranded. Anna turned over one of the books in the suitcase. "College girl?" she asked. Rachel nodded. Anna laughed and left the cubicle, the cohorts who had gathered with her now following behind. Rachel waited a few minutes, then quickly repacked, though she didn't snap the suitcase closed, knowing Anna would hear the noise. Then holding the suitcase beneath her jacket, she walked rapidly from the room.

When she reached the staircase she ran. She heard Anna shout from above, "Hey," and heard her start down the steps. Rachel kept going, running, nearly tripping part way down the third floor staircase and she heard Anna shout "Asshole, hey you, asshole!" What an echo! Rachel thought and then she rounded the second floor landing, sliding past two men with gym bags, and though she couldn't hear any thunderous hooves following behind, she didn't slow down, for they might be descending by elevator. She didn't stop at the desk to get her money back—the woman had informed her of the No Refund Policy when she had paid. Was that because she knew about Anna? And she kept going, on out the door, till she found a phone booth (Anna wouldn't follow her out into the cold, would she?) and she cried till she had no breath left; this time from wrenching, bottomless self-pity. Rachel imagined the words she ought to have spoken (shouted) to that jerk at the desk: What kind of a place is this that knives are allowed? That such emotional extortion goes on? Words she would never say because she would never go back. She unfolded the jacket (she hadn't had time to put it on, hadn't, for the first time all day, noticed the cold) and found the purse. The envelope was growing ever more slender, but it was still there.

When she got her breath back, she would walk down towards the dock; towards the ferry, and take it, damn it. What else was left as choice? First, though, she'd dialed his number once more. Each time she heard the unanswered rings, they seemed more startling. Sharper. They hurt her all over. She tried Elizabeth's number again, and hung up before the recording had a chance to play through completely. What would she do once she was on the island? She called information and asked if there were a new number for Elizabeth. Sorry, the operator said, no other listing. Can I help you with anything else? Rachel started to cry all over again. Come and get me, she wanted to say to the operator. Give me a coat to wear. Tell me where he is. "I wish you could," Rachel said, "I've been trying to reach Jacob Marsh on Ward's Island all day. Would you check the number for me?"

"One moment, please." Was there a chance she had misremembered? Burn all the records, Rachel, his mother had said. Why had she followed such demented advice? It had seemed so right back then. Like draft cards going up in flames. Like spite against the government for having forced his exile. Now it seemed Jake had gone up in smoke and the federal government was still remarkably healthy. The operator read back the same number Rachel had been trying all day. Memory had served her. "I'll try it for you," the operator sang out. The phone rang as before. She imagined his cottage shaking from the noise. Shattering and falling into pieces in the snow. "Are you sure it's Ward's Island?" the operator asked? "I have a new listing for a Jacob Marsh on Bloor."

"Try it," Rachel told her. There were two rings, and his voice. His voice so clear, so real, so unexpected, she couldn't speak. "Hello," he said into the phone. "Hello."

"It's Rachel," she said in a just audible gasp.

"My God, Rachel," he said. "You're our first call on our new telephone. How are you?"

"I'm here."

"Is this your party?" the operator interrupted.

"Yes," Rachel said, and then, "Thank you."

"You're where, Rachel?"

"Toronto."

"Oh God, Rachel, Toronto? Where?"

"In a phone booth. Here, Jake."

"Do you mean it?"

"Oh Jake," she said, "come and get me."

"Tell me where you are," he said, and Rachel let the phone hang swinging through the booth, left her suitcase, jacket, and purse on the floor of the phone booth while she ran back into the snow to the street corner to find out where she was.

CHAPTER SIXTEEN

SHE SAW HIM drive past once, go round the corner and come back, saw there were no spaces where he could possibly park and that she damn well better get out of the telephone booth and flag him down but then she saw him do a U-turn, almost kill himself and about six others, so she grabbed for her suitcase, but it was stuck under the damn seat. You're a real jerk, she started shouting at herself while she was pulling and tugging at the bag and it wasn't budging an inch, and she saw he'd stopped the car across the street, right in the traffic lane, and was running toward her. And then there was this moment when he reached the booth that came right out of old time comedies, though she didn't laugh—she was a lot closer to smashing glass with her bare hands than she was to laughing—when they both tried to get the glass open, pushing and pulling against each other, and she saw he was laughing at first, then both of them were crying and finally they figured out to push in on the center and she was out.

She was shaking and her teeth were chattering and he said she should get in the car and get warm, but all she wanted to do was hold him there, kiss him, make sure he was real.

He kissed her face and he took off her hat and kissed her hair. "Same hair," he said, "nothing different," and he slid his fingers into the curls. She tried to tell him it was longer, but she couldn't talk. He was saying her name—and she his, though no one could have known it for the crying, and then he told her she had to put on his coat and he lifted her arms down gently and he slipped his coat off, though by then she'd gotten her arms around his neck again and wasn't about to let go, so he had to put the coat around her shoulders. When he made her put her arms into the sleeves, she put her hand on his chest and said, "You'll freeze." She was hiccupping while she spoke, the way a child does who's cried herself out, and he said, "You're the one needs warming right now. Let me get you home." So she let him.

He brought her, weeping and shivering and wearing his oversized jacket, and just generally a horrible wreck, in to meet his friend. And there was Elizabeth, all vibrant red hair, opening the door to them. She understood, now, why he had chosen her: such color was an aberration Jake, as artist, would have found irresistible. Rachel reached her hand out to touch Elizabeth's, and as they embraced, she saw how white her complexion was, and knew that this was the delicacy Jake had seen and written about to her. "Here she is," Jake said, though Rachel couldn't tell which of them was being introduced to the other.

"Beautiful hair," Rachel said, catching some of Elizabeth's in her hand as she spoke. Jake had his arm around her, and she turned and leaned her weight into him, touching now, the familiar wiry beard, stroking the scratchy fisherman knit sweater, all of it so very good to feel again, and he leaned his head back as though he were watching her (just the way he always had) and stroked the hair away from her eyes ("I'm not a dog," she used to say to him), smiling, shaking his head. "I don't believe it," he said, holding her tight against him. It was a good old Jake embrace. No one else hugged as though it were a major commitment of energy and emotion.

And meanwhile Elizabeth had gathered clothes for warming Rachel. She waved an oversized sweatshirt and thick white socks over Jake's shoulder at Rachel in a funny way that made her laugh, but she wasn't letting go of him just yet. Jake still had her encircled in his arms and was rocking back and forth, serenading her with that rumbling noise he made out of contentment. "I do love you," she said, and he kissed the top of her head, then rested his cheek in her curls.

Elizabeth said, "Enough is enough, Jake, let the poor girl sit down and get warm."

"I'm warming her," he protested, but they hobbled together, arm over arm, to the chair, anyway. One chair in the whole place, Rachel now saw, and had to laugh. No other furniture except three snacking tables set up around the room, to mask, she supposed, the emptiness of the place. Jake sat at her feet (no other choices but the floor, here) and Elizabeth said she'd heat up some soup for Rachel, but Jake said, "No, she wants coffee with five sugars, don't you?" and Rachel said, yes, that was really what she did want, and she put her hand on Jake's head, caressing curls, still not believing. How had they let it be so long?

"Five?" Elizabeth questioned her.

"He taught me that," she said, tilting her head toward him to incriminate her friend. "Because I hated the taste of coffee but liked the idea of ordering it in restaurants."

"And now you like it?" Elizabeth asked.

"With five sugars, I love it."

"Five sugars it is, then," Elizabeth said and headed for the kitchen.

She'd almost stopped crying, though when Elizabeth left the room, she started again because she thought how what she really wanted was to be here on a visit, to just love him and Elizabeth, and go for walks and to a museum, and out for dinner together, and instead she'd come dragging an awful agenda behind her, like a sack of dirty clothes, so oversized and lumpy, she had trouble getting the unruly thing through the doorway.

"And toast with butter," he said to her, pantomiming slathering huge amounts of butter over a tiny piece of bread, and she nodded, but when he began to get up (and leave her alone) she put a little downward pressure on his shoulder and he didn't resist. He started to explain about their move to Toronto, how they'd only just started living full time in the apartment three days ago when the bed arrived. Then that booming voice of his, singing, "If we knew you were coming . . ." finding just the right funny song for punch line, the way he always used to do, and they were laughing together, singing the words about baking cakes, and she said in her best fake southern accent, "Don't you all mind about that, I have always vastly preferred the taste of toast to cake." He sang "Toast for two, and toast for three," to the tune of "Tea for Two," and she thought, watching him soft shoe his way to the kitchen, now that I'm here, even with the bad news, it'll be all right.

Though she tried not to listen, the distance between her chair and the kitchen sink was just not that great, their whispers, not that soft. She heard Jake tell Elizabeth he was sorry. "The lack of warning," was one of the phrases she heard. Well yes, Rachel thought, there had been no warning. She had apologies to make. She would explain how she had tried (and tried and tried) to call. Elizabeth's overheard response to Jake was forgiving. "It's not a problem," she said. Rachel considered putting her fingers in her ears, or singing aloud to herself. But the whispering grew more wispy, lost in the space between Elizabeth and Jake, she supposed, muffled by embrace and kiss, more than likely. Good, she thought. I don't want their secrets, as well as my own, just now. And she would apologize for this untoward and dramatic arrival.

They paraded back into the room, Elizabeth with the coffee, walking slowly, watching the level of hot liquid rising and dropping along the edge, Jake with thick sliced toast with butter covering every bit of the surface (just as she liked it).

Jake stretched out on his side on the floor, his head propped up on his hand. Now? Was this her moment for confession? No, later, when she had him alone. Elizabeth would have to be told, of course, but for starters, she'd like to make her revelations to Jake only. She sipped at her hot, sweet drink.

"Lots of nice big windows in this place," Rachel commented after glancing round, finally. "I bet you get light through most of the day."

"Lots of good light," he said. "And the white walls help. I wish you could have seen it before—the walls were all different nauseating shades of blue. We painted everything before we moved in. We had to, we'd never have been able to survive otherwise. We took it because of the studio. And the ceilings. They're higher than you usually see, which I liked." He turned on his back and shaped the room out with his hand as he spoke.

"The studio was a mess," Elizabeth said. "The worst room in the apartment. It'd been used as some kind of junk room with rags and papers all over, and one of the walls was bulging and a child had done squiggly crayon drawings all over the walls."

"I practically had to rebuild an entire wall back there. But it was worth it, it's a fabulous room."

"Let me see it, then."

"Do you feel all right?"

"Fine, absolutely." She put the coffee down on the table and Jake stood and led the way.

It was a wonderful room, that studio, boasting enormous oak double-hung windows stretching nearly from floor to ceiling on one wall. Their brass locks had been polished to shining. Between the four windows on the south side, she saw his penciled sketches: a figure, turning, it seemed, from one panel to the next. "A triptych?" she asked.

"Of Elizabeth," he said, nodding.

"And a fresco," Elizabeth announced and Rachel turned and saw her arm extended to another window she'd not yet seen. "Oh Jake," Rachel, whispered, "it's quite a triumph."

"I love it," Elizabeth said. It wasn't a real window she stood next to, but a painted replica of those on the long wall. The brass lock of this pseudowindow gleamed, somehow, just as brightly as the real stuff of the other wall and the glass appeared to catch light on its smooth surface. "How'd you make it look so much like glass?" Rachel asked him.

He shrugged. "Luck," he said. "I had an idea about using gray to do it and it worked." There was no view through the other windows in the dark, but through this window, there was daylight. Two vibrantly colored birds hovered in flight above a meadow, and two cows, charmingly wobbly, grazed in the grassy area. The meadow sloped down to a becalmed body of water. "Your lake?" Rachel asked him.

"He's brought Lake Ontario all the way out to the Annex," Elizabeth said. He explained to her then, with the animation she loved when he talked art, how when the reconstruction work was finished on the wall he'd added a thin, finer layer of plaster across the center portion of the wall. Elizabeth had kept it wet by spraying it with water from an old Windex bottle. "You have to work really quickly and maintain a very thin layer of color," he said. "That's why the cows are so pathetic looking. You can't go back over anything on plaster. There's no repainting or rethinking." He angled a light in toward the wall, and the colors glistened with gem-like brilliance. "It's like no other medium." She heard the awe with which he viewed his own creation.

"The bedroom's small, and there's no shower," Elizabeth said, "but Jake loved the light in here so much, we decided it didn't matter. Wait till you see it in daytime."

"I think this room was originally designed as a studio," Jake said. "There were obvious, logical places to put up racks for canvas," he said, pointing to where he'd done exactly that.

"The landlord doesn't know about the fresco," Elizabeth explained to Rachel.

Jake had seated himself on the floor in front of his painting and the women took places on either side of him.

"I told him I was painting the flat. That's all I've done."

"It makes me nervous that you didn't tell him exactly how you've painted it, though." Elizabeth put a hand on his shoulder.

"He's enhanced the value of the place. The owner should be very glad to have an original Marsh."

"Of course it's unsigned," Jake said.

"Sign it, then," Rachel insisted.

"Too late," he said. "The plaster's dry."

"Use a pen, then. A pencil."

Elizabeth reached over to the work table for a drawing pencil and handed it to him. His hand moved quickly along the inner edge of the trompe l'oeil windowsill, forming the letters of his name. He sat back to examine his addition to the painting. "The pencil makes it look like a cob web, especially in the corner there." The women agreed.

"The final perfect touch of realism. Lovely," Rachel said, and Elizabeth echoed the sentiment.

When they'd gone back to the living room, she saw from the way they glanced at each other, then at her, the way they shifted with restlessness, rearranging themselves first next to each other, then apart, that they were growing weary with the waiting she was asking them to do. With dancing round the obvious. That this was not the usual friendly visit was clear. They wanted to know. They were waiting for explanations. Reasons for and duration of stay. "You've got one hell of a cold city here," she said, and Elizabeth was off and running on a "you-think-this-is-bad" saga of winters past. In the pause that followed those stories, Jake took Rachel's cup and went back to the kitchen to refill it. Rachel began to tell Elizabeth about the crazy person at the Y, about how incredibly terrified she was, stretching it, elaborating (not that it wasn't horrible), but sending words out fast and hard, blocking Elizabeth's advance, just a little longer. Tomorrow. When she was rested.

Jake returned to the living room and handed the replenished cup to Rachel. In the silence while she drank, she saw him move closer to Elizabeth and grab for the conversational initiative: "How long were you planning to stay?" The suddenness of it startled her. These were words about boundaries. He wanted circles drawn round her and tickets handed out for Limited Engagement Only.

"Just two days, maybe three." She paused, listening for the sound of her answer. Her words had a casualness she wished were real. "And I should call my roommates so they don't worry." She had made a dreadful, selfish miscalculation. If they could, they'd send her to a motel, close their door, and get back to their lives. They didn't need tales of marital woe, an unwanted pregnancy, and related hysteria. Had they heard the absence of Ben in her statements? She would add his name, patch the breech for the time.

But Jake was quick, shrewdly on the defensive: "And Ben?" he asked.

She passed a hand across her eyes, then lowered it again. Time in. Anyone not on base is it. "I'm sorry, Jake," she said.

"You're split then?"

She nodded. "Split," she repeated. "Kapowee. Over."

"I thought that might be why you were here. Why the change of address. I'm sorry," he said.

"And pregnant."

"Oh no," he said, and she heard how his words sounded like a weary, rasping moan.

She lifted the cup and saucer from her lap and lowered it to the floor. "I'm a real mess, Jake," she said. She saw Elizabeth, eyes closed, slowly shaking her head. "Can I get an abortion here?" Rachel asked, and she heard herself giggle with dreadful inappropriateness.

Elizabeth let out a little melancholy laugh. "You're not going to have the baby, then?"

Rachel shook her head. "I don't know what to do. Everything's so magnificently screwed up in my life. I wanted an abortion. It was completely settled. Then I went to Puerto Rico and the doctor I went to said I was too pregnant for the simple procedures and I had to go into a hospital and file papers and face official committees or something like that and I don't know—I got scared. So I came here. If I'd had someone to go to the hospital with me, I'd have been all right," she explained. "I just couldn't face dying by myself."

"Dying?" Jake said, taken aback.

"I was scared, Jake. The possibility felt so real, I could feel it breathing on me. I couldn't go through it alone."

No one spoke. Then Elizabeth lifted her hand, as if to beg a turn, and said, "Sometimes a baby can help pull a marriage together."

"No," Rachel said and shook her head vehemently. "I don't want to be pulled back into this marriage. In this case it would be pulled under. Ben's crazy."

"Mental hospital stuff or something more benign?" Jake asked.

"Maybe not certifiable, but I think he's getting close. Or trying to get close, I'm not sure which. He has no core, Jake, no central portion that's always there, always identifiable as him. Only his unpredictability is predictable."

"Is he violent?"

"Not physically. But he was sometimes mean as hell, Jake. He told his friend to seduce me. I don't know, is that violent, or just indecent? He wasn't there, himself, of course, so I guess he doesn't feel responsible. And he wanted to bring his girl-friend home to meet me, the bastard."

"Jesus, Rachel, this sounds unreal." Jake walked across the room and picked up his cigarettes from the table. "So you mean you slept with this other guy," he said from his new position way over by the windows.

"Ben was never there, Jake. I never knew who he was going to be when he walked through the door. He left me on my own." She watched him take a cigarette from the pack, tap it hard against the windowsill, then bring it to his lips. "Yes," she said. "I slept with him."

"Forgive me, but all of this seems sudden and not entirely explained, somehow, Rachel. You're rushing. You need to go over all the options."

"What other options? I can't go back to Ben. He wouldn't want anything to do with a baby, and he'll claim it isn't his, anyway, though it is. What else is there? Go home to mother?"

"Stay in Toronto, maybe? Keep the baby."

"I don't want a baby, Jake," she wailed at him. "I don't want his baby. I feel I've been invaded by Ben. I don't want him controlling me this way. I have to have an abortion. It seems sudden to you because you just heard about it. But I've been over it all, Jake. I promise you I'm not doing it without plenty of thought. I thought too long. That's why I couldn't get this settled in San Juan."

Why was her timing always so lousy? Why was she always, always, in the wrong place at the wrong time? She'd chosen a moment when he had no need for her. No use for her. She was poor little sister arrived home in dire straits, yet again. And, as always, in the morally inferior position. Compared to Elizabeth, who was she? She should just leave them to one another and go off somewhere and have the baby, like Elizabeth said. The choices were narrowing down with fearsome speed. "Listen," she said. "I'll go back tomorrow. I'll get a little sleep and take off. And there's nothing to pack, even," she said laughing at how funny it seemed, how far she'd come, how long she'd waited, and how wrong it had all been in her imagination. She'd seen it in such neat and tidy terms. Get to Jake. He'll fix it. Hah! No neat and tidy here, was there? She wished they'd never seen her like this. Wished she were gone already and the crying (damn, she'd been so sure she was past that) began just as fiercely again, and then Jake was kneeling beside her chair, lifting her face toward him and he said, "We'll help you." Then he was shushing her, and she put her arms around him and Elizabeth was there, next to her, too, and she said of course they would help her. Of course they would, she said.

Elizabeth said she'd heard of a kind of mythological figure called The Angel who was supposed to reside in one of the northern suburbs. "A semi-retired doctor who's known to specialize in 'appendicitis,' " she said. So while Elizabeth went to the kitchen to call friends who might know somebody who might know something, Rachel found a way to begin to laugh about herself again. "I guess you'd call it a traditional wedding," she said to her friend, "you know—marry in haste, repent in leisure. I was the all-time prize-winning nitwit, Jake. If you'd been around you'd probably have seen his craziness. You're good at knowing what people are really like. Maybe I'd never have married him if you hadn't left."

"I could have put on my black and white striped shirt and played referee, you mean?" He pretended to bring a whistle to his mouth and formed the referee's hand signals for out of bounds. She laughed at his performance.

"I wish you'd been there, Jake," she said and pulled gently at the curls along his neck.

"And you wouldn't have listened to me any more than you ever did. You've always been on your own about relationships."

"Maybe," she said. "I couldn't have done any worse, though."

He put his hands behind him and leaned back so he could see her. "Are you legally separated now?"

"Do you mean, did I see a lawyer? Is that how you make a separation legal?" He nodded. "No, then it's not legal. I guess I have to find out what I'm supposed to do. I have to find out about divorces when I get back. You know, living with Ben was like having an adversary from a cartoon. I never knew what clever new thing he'd be surprising me with next. Do you think Road Runner Syndrome is grounds for divorce?" she asked as she laughed at her own joke; laughing too long, too hard, till she couldn't stop and tears rolled down her cheeks. "Do you hate me for screwing up like this, Jake?"

"Of course not."

"I did so want you still to like me."

"Of course I still like you," he said and raised her hand to his lips. "Old habits die hard."

She brought his hand to her own lips.

Elizabeth came back into the room, her address book hanging from one hand. "No luck yet. Darcy's at a conference and won't be back till Wednesday. Ellie said the only guy she knows is in London."

"Ontario?" Jake asked.

"England, I'm afraid."

"Cynthia might know something." Elizabeth looked at her watch. "Is it getting too late to call?"

"No," he said. "You can call her." When Elizabeth disappeared again into the kitchen, he turned back to Rachel. "Are you sure about going the illegal route?" he asked her.

"You of all people should understand, Jake. The laws are ridiculous. They don't allow for choice. All I want to do is live my life the way I want to. To make choices."

"I understand that, Rachel, but there are risks, physical risks. You just don't know what you're getting when you bargain for an illegal medical procedure."

"I'm aware of the risks. You and I can evaluate them together." Then, bending low, bringing her face to his, she whispered, "I want to be free of him. I want to go back and start over. Jacob, help me with this. I'm afraid to be alone." She touched his cheek with one hand. "Help me?" she pleaded. He lifted her hand away from his face and she thought she was going to start crying all over again, but he kissed her mouth before she had such a chance.

CHAPTER SEVENTEEN

*C*YNTHIA didn't know anything about The Angel, but she gave Elizabeth her friend Eva's address. Eva put them on to Linda, and Linda said she'd get back to them after she called somebody else. It was one A.M. before the telephone chain wound its way back to them and they got the name of the doctor and the town he practiced in. "We all need to get to sleep," Jake advised, once the cheering was over.

"I'll get a sleeping bag for Rachel," Elizabeth suggested.

"We should let her have the bed, really," Jake interposed.

"Yes, take the bed," Elizabeth said, brushing her hand rapidly from side to side as though erasing her previous suggestion from an invisible blackboard. "You'd be more comfortable that way and we're used to the sleeping bags. We haven't had a chance to get addicted to the bed yet." Elizabeth's face flushed as she spoke, presumably, Rachel thought, from embarrassment over appearing less self-sacrificing in her hospitality than Jake.

"I can't take your brand new bed," Rachel said with firmness. "It'd be a terrible waste of space, anyway, to have one person in a big bed like that. It's meant for two; for you two." Elizabeth busied herself then with straightening some magazines that lay upon the table. Was it the revelation through this talk of beds of the sexual nature of Elizabeth and Jake's relationship, then, that had caused the blush?

Jake touched Rachel's shoulder. "You've had a lousy couple

of days, Rachel. Take the comfort tonight."

"No," she said, covering his hand with hers. "I won't take your bed. But if you've got two sleeping bags, I can put one on top of the other and make it softer."

"We've got two," Elizabeth told her.

"I've been using just a sleeping bag on a bare floor lately, so two quilted bags over carpet will seem like luxury."

Together, the three of them laid out her odd bed, Jake fetching an extra blanket, Elizabeth a few towels. There were hugs all round, and Elizabeth and Jake headed off for their bedroom. It was an effort then, to find the nightgown in the suitcase, to open the suitcase, for that matter, and to concentrate on what she sought, but she did find it, and with towel, hairbrush, and toothbrush in hand, directed herself to stand, just one more time, and to go into the small bathroom at the other end of the kitchen.

It was an oddity, that little bathroom with its wooden floor, tub on legs, and an oval mirror hung from cord of gold twist but with its reflecting surface turned to the wall. That there was a mirror at all, she knew was a concession to Elizabeth. "I took down the mirror," he'd written, so long ago now. "I thought the glass might show I'd faded, so I'd rather not look." Rachel turned it around so she could see her face. It was an archaic glass, rescued, undoubtedly from the back room of an antiques shop. The wooden frame, once gilded, was now graying and cracked along most of its surface. The silvering was scratched away in several places and so thin in others, she seemed almost to disappear. It made her face seem puffy, her eyes distant. She touched a hand to her check to feel the curve of it. Is it me, still? she asked the image. How much can I change and still call myself Rachel? She turned the mirror back, saw that the cord showed no wear, wondered, after months or years, when constant turning had worn it thin, when the mirror slipped to the floor and shattered, whether it would be replaced. Whether a new one would hang with permanence, facing outward, daring Jacob to look. She washed her face and brushed her hair without benefit of reflection. How on earth was she going to sleep? The fatigue was so intense, she'd never drop off. Her legs and groin ached the way they had the time they'd tried to climbed Mount Washington. Her head hurt with a dull, sad pain that seemed to be an independent creature taking up residence in her skull, uninvited, just as the seeds of another creature had taken over in another region of herself. She wondered if she could scout up some brandy from a kitchen cabinet, but as she turned the knob to leave the bathroom, she reconsidered and decided to slip as quickly as possible into her sleeping nest, close her eyes, and not open them again, whether sleep came to her or not.

In the dim light of the candle Elizabeth had left burning next to the sleeping bags, Rachel saw Jake, seated on the floor, a bed pillow on his lap. "For you," he said, holding it out to her when she'd reached him.

"It's yours, isn't it?" she asked, not yet taking the offering from his hands. When he nodded she said, no, she'd be fine, look how cushiony the bags were if you slipped down below the opening. She patted the quilting to show him, then lifted the top edge and slid down into the red and green plaid.

"I can share with Elizabeth," he said, laying the pillow next to her head.

She put her hand on it to push it aside, but that odd mixture of softness and resilience that only a brand new pillow has, melted her resolve. "Thank you," she whispered, and drew the pillow under her head.

In the candlelight, his curls seemed white, not blond at all. She laughed aloud, and pulled a strand of her own hair out to the side for him to view. "Am I gone all white in this light, too?" she asked him, and he nodded.

"I'm glad you're here," he said and took her hand in his.

"I am, too."

"I sent the new address to you, but just a few days ago. You'd have been in transit by then, I guess. I was still going out to the other place every couple of days to get my letters, so it didn't occur to me you needed to know. I'm sorry about that— if you'd had the address, you would've been saved about six hours of torture."

"Jake, I'm all right now."

"We only disconnected Elizabeth's phone today. Mine is supposed to shut down tomorrow. It was very bad timing."

"It doesn't matter." She covered his hand with her other one. "Really. It doesn't matter since I did find you."

"Yes. Sleep well," he said.

One of the candles, a mere stub to begin with, had burned down. The other now allowed just enough light so she could see him move across the room, open the bedroom door, and disappear. The bedroom was already dark. She heard him fool with the knob, perhaps even a lock, heard the bed frame slide along the bare floor in response to his weight and then silence. She blew out the remaining candle and listened again. A few whispers, a few more squeaks of the bed, but it was too hard, too very hard to concentrate, and she slept.

When she woke, it was light, and she saw him standing, barefoot, in tee shirt and jeans, his back to her, in the kitchen. He was standing watch over his brewing coffee. She saw how he ran his open hand back through his hair to "comb" it, as he always had, and she waited, still in her sleeping bag, while he waited, for the smell of coffee to begin to fill the room. He took three mugs from a cabinet, then came out into the living room. "You're awake, then?" he asked in a quiet voice. She nodded. "Your hair is lighter than I remembered, even in daylight," he said.

"Yours, too," she said. "Memory doesn't suffice, does it?" He shook his head and smiled.

"Maybe I'll get the portrait going again," he said, "now that I've seen you. Maybe I've just had the coloring off."

"The wedding portrait, you mean?"

"Oh shit," he said with a laugh. "No need for wedding portraits, is there? I haven't even packed up the sketches yet. I guess I won't bother now."

"No, don't bother," she said, reaching her hand out to him. He held her hand between his own. "It's so good to be here, finally. To see you." she said.

"Did you sleep?"

"Enough. I'll sleep better when this is all over. Is Elizabeth still asleep?"

He nodded. "I'm always up earlier than she is. I usually put up coffee and then she gets up. She needs the definite promise of food and drink to lure her out of oblivion. Do you want to try to sleep more? Should I go away?"

"No. Absolutely not." She pulled herself up to sitting and leaned back against the armchair.

"Coffee, then?"

"Yes."

While he poured, she emerged from her cocoon, pulled the surplus blanket around herself, and followed him to the kitchen. He set their cups on the table. "And toast?" he asked.

"I should have brought you Thomas', shouldn't I?"

"I get this fresh bread in town, now," he said, as he sliced into it. "I almost don't miss the other stuff anymore."

"Next time, English muffins, I promise."

"We get good marmalade here," he said, pushing a crockery pot across the table to her. "British style." She scooped an ample serving onto her plate while he adjusted the toaster gauge. "Light and soft, right?" She nodded.

"You seem exactly the same to me," she said. "It's a little like passing back through time. It's hard for me to believe anything at all has happened since I last saw you."

"I believe it," he said.

"Your beard's all different," she said, her fingers touching the bottom edge of it. "Isn't it strange that it would be so different, this time."

"It's a thoroughly uncultivated beard."

"You're so negative, Jake. It's just unrestrained, that's all." She combed her fingers through it gently. The toast popped and they each took a slice.

"I think of myself as different," he said as he distributed orange rind across his toast. "Being here, having to be here, changes things: when I think about my past, it seems physically unreachable. I think in third person sometimes, like, 'He went to Yale.' 'He taught school.'" She laughed and touched her lips to his cheek, just above his beard.

"Don't you think some of that is just being older and having other times, other things you've passed through? Having a past?"

"Maybe. But it feels just the opposite; as though I have no history, and it scares the hell out of me. It's as though I'm thinking about someone I knew and not myself at all. Seeing you is good, though, Rachel. It's like confirming that I really had a past. That I had such a friend as you."

"Have such a friend," she insisted between bites of toast. "I'll start crying again if you speak in past tense that way." She put her hand on his shoulder and studied his eyes. She saw blue that was the same color as her own eyes. "Please say we still have one another," she begged.

"We still have one another," he said, but she heard, in the

way he looked toward the doorway, the other words that he would surely begin to say to her. Words about growing up and growing older. Lofty phrases about how some people's lives, though seemingly similar, could never be made to mesh. Most of all, words about Elizabeth.

And then they both heard Elizabeth moving about in the bedroom, opening drawers. She passed through the kitchen, greeted them both warmly, and moved on to the bathroom. Jake filled the third cup and brought it to the table.

We're actors in an Italian farce, Rachel thought to herself, rushing madly, not from one side of the stage to the other, but back and forth across the Canadian highways. Gathering magic potions procured from pharmacists, fooling the other characters with quick changes of identity: husband and wife at one moment, brother and sister at the next, and old friends again when alone, expeditiously switching back and forth without the aid of disguise or costume. How she wanted to laugh at it all, to take the tension that lay just below the flesh of her face, and turn it into laughter or tears. But there wasn't time.

Rachel slept next to him in the front seat of the car in the interval between the second pharmacy and the third doctor. They had travelled two hours northwest of Toronto only to find the doctor, the so-called Angel, was ill himself, in-hospital recuperating from emergency surgery. A very elderly doctor who was filling in for him examined Rachel, wrote a prescription, and advised her to consult another doctor back in Toronto. "He's familiar with this kind of case."

"What the hell does that mean?" Rachel demanded of Jake when they had returned to the car. "Does he or doesn't he do abortions?"

"We'll see, Rachel," was all he answered. She must be calmer, she knew, so he would be calm as well. So he would not give up on her. The doctor's prescription turned out to be for iron-enriched vitamins. "To be taken once a day for the duration of the pregnancy."

"These will help make the pregnancy healthier, right?" she asked the pharmacist.

"Make you healthier. So the baby won't drain all your nutrients away." She told him to forget the order. She didn't have the money just then, she said, and she'd be back to pick it up in a few days. They rushed from there back to Toronto where the next doctor suggested they "help nature along" and wrote out a prescription to be taken at intervals of four hours along with castor oil and hot baths. Rachel was furious. "This has about as much likelihood of working as any other old wives' tale does. I might as well stand on my head and drink water from the wrong side of a glass." Jake got back on the phone, calling now, all the American exiles he knew, getting another name and scheduling another office visit. This doctor explained the law, the narrowly defined circumstances under which abortion was legal in Canada. It was "approaching too late," he told her.

"Just approaching?" she questioned him. "Shouldn't I be doing something now, today, then?" He gave her another prescription and told her to come back in four days. "I want an abortion," Rachel said to this doctor, "not medication. Won't four days be too late?"

"Let's not rush," he said

"I want to rush," Rachel told him.

The doctor responded curtly: "Then I'm not the man for you."

As soon as they were back at the apartment, Rachel dumped some of the pills from each bottle onto the kitchen table. They didn't appear to be the same medication. Their shape, color, and even the directions as to how and when to take them differed. She'd take both kinds, she told Jake. "It'll be twice as strong and twice as likely to work."

"Or twice as likely to blow you up," he said. "Who knows what that'll do to you?"

"What choices are there, now?" she asked him. They were both exhausted. All the doctors had said the pregnancy was proceeding normally. "Like we're supposed to be pleased with that analysis. All this running and waiting in offices, and still pregnant," she said. "Nothing's happening," she screamed. She crawled, fully clothed this time, back into her sleeping bag. He got back on the phone.

"I give up," Elizabeth said.

"Because you're Catholic," Rachel accused. She heard Jake slam the phone back down. She was coming loose at the center, ready to send pieces of herself flying out like missiles with hurting powers.

"Rachel, you've got to calm down," he admonished her. He had his arm around Elizabeth.

"I'm sorry," she said. "I know I'm behaving badly." If the two of them were to take hold of her, pin her hands down at the sides, pull her back to some center, perhaps she'd be whole again. She slid her head down below the opening of the bag.

"Little Rake," he whispered to her. He was kneeling beside her. He lifted the quilting from her face. "I'll take care of you," he said. "I'll get you out of this, somehow." But that only made her cry.

Elizabeth was gone from the room. "Tell Elizabeth I'm sorry," she said.

Elizabeth came up with one more lead. There was a doctor in Buffalo some people went to. One of those city doctors with an enormous, drop-in, half-the-city-clientele. But for the right fee, he did wonders, she'd been told.

"I can't go across the border," Jake said. "Do you feel well enough to drive yourself?"

"I'll take her," Elizabeth offered.

"If we're just in a car, crossing at Niagara Falls, no one will stop you, Jake, will they?" Rachel questioned him.

"They might."

"With all those tourists, how would they have the time and energy to check? We'll pretend we're newlyweds, carry a suitcase, kissy-face a bit." She pursed up her lips and made noisy kisses into the air.

"Where's the marriage certificate?"

"They don't ask for that kind of stuff, Jake. We say we left it home. In New York, we'll say. I haven't the faintest idea where my marriage certificate is. Please, Jake, I can't go alone."

"They ask for birth certificates or some other proof of citizenship when you cross the border. I'm on their special list. I'm a fugitive."

"He can't go, Rachel," Elizabeth broke in. "He could be arrested. I'll take you, if you like." She saw Elizabeth stand between them, cutting them neatly apart as though she had shears designed expressly for that purpose.

"I have no choice, then, but to go with Elizabeth?"

"No."

And then she grabbed for Elizabeth's hand, kissed it, and tried to tell her she hadn't meant to put it that way, hadn't meant to be unkind. Elizabeth said not to worry. It would all be over tomorrow.

She tried to nap. She tried to give them space. "You two, go out someplace, I'll be fine," she said. She meant to laugh, but it came out a wrenching, twisted sob. Elizabeth made her a dinner she couldn't eat. She took the long, scalding baths the second doctor had directed. Jake fiddled with the radio dial.

Rachel hung over the toilet, gagging, hoping they'd left the kitchen for the living room or bedroom, so they wouldn't hear.

"Rachel," he said to her while she paced beside the kitchen table and he and Elizabeth tried to eat dinner. "Are you still sure about this?"

"Yes," she whispered. It was time for another pill. She poured water into a tall green metal drinking container. She forced herself to drink all of it. One of the doctors had said to keep her fluid intake high. The metallic taste lingered on her tongue.

"All you've eaten today are those pills," he reminded her.

"It's all I can eat," she said.

After the next bath, she got dizzy.

"Don't make them so hot," he pleaded with her.

"I can't do this anymore," she said. "I feel so horrible. No more medications. Now I've got diarrhea from them. And I was retching the whole time I was in that last bath, Jake. I think this whole prescription business is just supposed to give you something else to think about so you won't think about abortions and so it'll be too late to do anything, eventually."

"I think it might be better if you stopped the pills," he said.

"Maybe," she said. Everything was whirling: her stomach, her brain, all going round and round like a high-speed tape with no stop button to press.

"Please, Rach." He stood behind her, both hands on her shoulders. The spinning sensation was slowing. She leaned back against him. "Please," he whispered and she agreed. She went and sat in the chair by the window and she did calm down for a while, and even slept a little, sitting up, but when she woke up, it was time again for the pills from the bottle with the blue label, so she went to the kitchen to get them, and Jake was there, but the pills weren't. "I thought you said you were stopping," he reminded her.

"I know I did, but I have to keep taking them. It's possible they'll help, and if it's possible, I have to keep going. Please," she begged when he didn't respond, "tell me where you put them." After a moment, he opened a cabinet over the refrigerator.

"You're sure?" he asked her before he handed them over.

"I'm sure," she said, and she filled the green metallic vessel yet again.

Still later, she lay on top of the sleeping bags in the dark, too jumpy, now, to crawl inside. Her fearful thoughts produced offspring more monstrous than themselves in the black night. The doctor in Buffalo now appeared before her in a bloodied butcher's apron, cleaver in hand. "This isn't the Garden of Eden," he said to her when, in her twisted, imagined dialogue she asked him whether he would use any anesthetic. She got up off the floor and turned on a light. And then another. She would sit up through what was left of the night, she told herself, though, at the moment, she was unable to stop pacing long enough to sit. If there were to be no anesthetic, then being exhausted wouldn't be so terrible, would it? It wouldn't make her any less likely to die, she didn't think. She heard the bedroom door open and turned to see Jake in red pajama bottoms.

"I saw the lights pop on," he told her.

"I'm too keyed up to sleep."

"Should I sit with you for a while?"

"Thank you." They sat together atop the sleeping bags, backs against the chair. "If I knew this would really be over tomorrow," she said, "that this doctor in Buffalo would do something, I'd be OK. But it seems like I might be shuffling back and forth like this for days or weeks and still end up pregnant. I'm at the point where I don't care if this Buffalo place is dark and dirty, I just want action. Closure."

"You're not afraid anymore, then?"

"No," she said, choosing the word out of the air, someone else's word, no doubt, for the fear was thick and sticky in her mouth like suet. She gagged on it and gasped for air. He had his arms around her then and she tried not to cry too loudly, not to wake Elizabeth. "Have the baby," he said quietly. He was stroking her hair.

"No, Jake. There's no way to do that."

"We'd work out a way. I can't send you off like this to a hack. Take another turn, Rachel." He pretended to read from a card in his hand: " 'Have a baby, stay in Toronto.' " After a moment, he added, "We could be a family."

She shook her head, and touched his face. "Thank you," she whispered. "As ever, you are my too gallant savior."

"And?"

"And, no. And try to be quieter," she whispered. "Poor Elizabeth will misunderstand your chivalrous gesture."

"Marry me, Rachel," he whispered and ran a hand into her curls.

She touched his cheek. "Oh Jake, it wouldn't work. Not with other people's babies and other people's lovers."

"When there's no perfect answer, no easy choice, it's a question of choosing best options, you know that. Think about it." He kissed her and she wanted to hold him there, to pretend that it was true, that they could make it all right if she would say yes. That they could just fling open the bedroom door and explain, in perfect ease, to Elizabeth, that there'd been a change of plans. She kissed him once more.

He rubbed her back and massaged her shoulders so she would relax. He made her lie down so he could put the blanket over her. She dozed and saw her parents and his parents pass by, solemn, clothed in black. She saw their faces, lined up in a row like gargoyles over a doorway, their faces gray, pitted stone, their eyes wide, their mouths open in bewilderment. She passed through a high stone archway and saw she was alone. When she looked back, Elizabeth and Jake were receding on the back of a train, flying away out of sight. She woke herself with her own garbled shout of denial. She saw that he lay sleeping, stretched out beside her.

"Jake?" she whispered, and he opened his eyes.

"Are you OK?" he asked her.

"I'm fine," she said. "Jake, it won't work."

"Why not?"

"All this medication I've taken has probably done damage to the baby. It's too late for other choices."

"We'll talk to somebody, a doctor. We'll see."

"They'll tell us it's OK, Jake, because of the law. Nobody legitimate in the medical profession can afford to deliberately encourage ending a pregnancy, you know that. They won't even use words like abortion or termination."

"Somebody'll give us medical information. Statistics, chances."

"Options."

"Yes."

"If you take medication to terminate a pregnancy, it has to do damage." Now she was crying all over again and the sobs kept rolling against her ribs, one after another, defying her need to say one last thing. But she did say it: "That medication was intended to destroy." And he did hear it, she was sure of it. He held her close, and in time, she slept again.

CHAPTER EIGHTEEN

SHE WOKE with pain. She reached out for him (she had seen him there earlier, next to her on the floor, she was certain of it), but he wasn't there. Of course: gone back to his bedroom. He couldn't sleep on the floor all night, could he? The wrenching sensation stopped, and she fell asleep once more.

Next time the pains woke her, they were quite different: pitch-dark and intense as though they meant to pull all her insides out with them.

Holding her breath did nothing to abate the torment; rocking gave her no ease. She crawled deeper into the sleeping bag till her head was fully inside, closed her eyes, and managed to drift into sleep once more before a new spasm jerked her awake. She crawled further down, curling herself tightly around her center of agony. What a fool I am, she told herself: No more pills. No more.

It was hot inside her cocoon; stifling. Maybe she would die, or at least pass into a state of unconsciousness from lack of oxygen. Perhaps that would free her from the misery.

With the next pain, she felt a rush of wetness between her legs, and reached down to touch herself. She crawled her way out of the sleeping bag clutching at fabric and carpet as if she were pulling herself up the face of a steep mountain and thrust head and hand outside into the air of the room. Even without light she could see the dark color of her hand and could feel the next wave of blood as it flowed out of her. Her arms and legs were shaking. Stop, she commanded her body, but it paid her no heed. She was like a captive of a large, hungry animal: she would be shaken and shaken till she capitulated. Am I dying? she wondered. Her jaw trembled so badly, it set her teeth to beating out a persistent rhythmic clatter. What would Elizabeth think now? As if it hadn't been bad enough that she'd come crying and moaning into their lives with too much business of her own, but now was bleeding all over the sleeping bags and carpet. She couldn't wake her on top of all those other wrongs, but then the pain started again, black and endless, and she called his name, though she hadn't meant to, and he came out of the bedroom, Elizabeth right behind, pulling a robe around herself. Jake called the hospital—she heard him say his wife was pregnant and bleeding—and they said she must come in immediately. Elizabeth said she should wear Jake's robe and put his jacket on over that and sit on a towel in the car, because it would be easiest and fastest, but Rachel said she couldn't go like that in just a robe and a jacket, but then she got another contraction and Jake got on one side of her and Elizabeth on the other and they propelled her out the door and carried her to the car. Elizabeth tried to help her arrange the towels under her in the back seat, but Rachel said, "It's all right, Elizabeth, I've stopped bleeding now, anyway, it's all right, it's all right," protesting like a madman, she knew, but it was awful to have people see you when you're falling apart. Then Jake got in the front and Elizabeth stood by the car waving as they drove away, and she waved back, and the towel was already soaked before they'd gotten halfway down the street. She told him she was sorry she was ruining his car. And his robe and his jacket. And he said none of it mattered, everything was going to be fine. But when they got stuck at a light, he pounded his fist into the steering wheel and shouted, "Change, goddamn it, change already," so she had to say to him, "I'm OK, Jake. There's not even that much blood now."

In the emergency room, they gave her a shot for the pain, and it was better after that. She wanted to ask them: Did the pills do it? But she was afraid; she didn't know the rules here. They might take out notepads and pens and call in the police if they knew about the pills. "Did you do anything to bring this on?" they asked her, and she said no, and she cried, though she thought it was from relief, more like laughter accompanied by ornamental tears.

She loved the nurses. And the doctor. There was an aura around them; a shininess that emanated from their smiles. Whenever she looked up at them, they smiled back at her. They told her it would be all right. Everything would be all right. They called it a spontaneous miscarriage. The nurse she liked the best was the one who told her she could have more babies. "This happens to lots of women, and they go on to have perfectly normal babies," she said. The nurse squeezed her hand. There was something about the way they cleaned her up, bloody mess that she was, so gently, so carefully, with their damp cloths, that made her feel as if she were a new, helpless infant, and content to be just that. When they had lifted her onto a bed with fresh sheets, the nurse who had taken her hand in the worst of it brought Jake back into the room.

He stood by the window as though distracted or maybe even wary of her. That frightened her, so she held her hand out to him, and motioned for him to come sit on the edge of the bed. She'd expected to see him laughing and cheering, perhaps even waving a banner ("We won"), but his expression was disturbingly empty. He sat next to her and pushed the hair back from her forehead. To her relief, he laughed when the curls came tumbling right back down. "I need a trim," she said.

He leant close and whispered his words, though the nurses

had departed, and the small recovery room was empty but for them: "It's all over. You're not pregnant anymore. Life is simple again."

"And I don't have to go die in Buffalo." She whispered, for she, too, was accustomed to conducting a life of secrets. She reached up to touch his face.

"I know."

"You're not angry with me, are you?" she asked.

"No, why do you ask that?"

"You seemed so sober when you walked in here."

"It was sobering, Rachel: a hospital, blood, you in pain."

"It's over now."

"I'm beginning to feel that, but I had to see you first to take that in. Now the tension's starting to go. The anger, too. A person can get pretty angry at the way the world is run; at the pettiness of the law and all that."

"And sad, too," she said. "When I was on the operating table, I didn't want to be losing the baby. The nurses and the doctor didn't want me to be. We all wanted it to be right. To have it be a real baby. There was a terrible sense of disappointment in the room. I didn't want them to know I'd ever wanted to end the pregnancy." He was nodding as she spoke. "Did I do the wrong thing, Jake?"

"No, no." He stroked her hand. "Chances are you didn't do anything. The doctor said the pills were probably a low hormonal dose, or even a placebo, and wouldn't have brought this on."

"You told him about the pills?"

"Only in a vague sort of way. I said it was an unplanned pregnancy and that a doctor had given you something for it. He seemed to know exactly what I was talking about, though as you said, he didn't name it. But he was quite firm about saying it would have happened anyway. He called it a blighted embryo. All that mad running around we did wasn't necessary, apparently."

"All that gagging and retching was just diversion for a winter afternoon?"

"I guess so. For what it's worth, the doctor said you could try to start another pregnancy in a few months." Jake paused. "Actually he said we could try again. It made me think of The Parents."

"Listen, when the nurse said to me, 'you and your husband can still have plenty of healthy babies,' there was a funny, upside-down moment when I thought of telling you, not Ben. I'm sure it was the drug they gave me—we should find out what it was because it gave me the sweetest high."

He brought her hand to his mouth and kissed it. She'd seen how the nurses wrapped the real babies in receiving blankets. How big the eyes looked peeking out from tiny faces. She wanted to hold one of them. Hand it to Jake.

"Didn't we almost get married last night?" she asked him.

He laughed. "I think so," he said and smiled. "We were rather filled with despair and dementia, I'm afraid. I forgot, for the moment, the little legal detail that you're already married."

"It didn't seem important at the moment."

"Anyway, things have been dramatically simplified since then."

"And the moment is past. Elizabeth will be pleased to have you back."

"Yes. And to have you well and unpregnant," he said. "Did the doctor tell you that you have to stay here for the morning?" She said he had. "Then he says you're to go home to bed and take it easy for a few days."

"I need a shower. And food. I'm starving, Jake. I haven't eaten in twenty-four hours."

"The shower'll have to wait, I'm sure, but I'll go get sandwiches and I'll pick up some clothes from the apartment."

"Don't be gone long," she said.

"I know," he said, rising to stand at the side of the bed, "you're starving."

"Yes." And she didn't want to be there alone with baby voices, so soft, yet fierce, all up and down the corridor.

"Try to sleep while I'm gone. I'll call Elizabeth to tell her you're all right. I have to call in sick again at work, too."

"You'll get fired."

"I'll try not to. I'll sound very, very sick," he said, affecting the voice and stagger of the mortally wounded.

She reached for his hand as he began to walk away. "Jake," she said. "Miscarrying, at least, is legal. I've done something right, finally, haven't I?"

"You've done fine," he said. "Legal and right are not synonyms, you know." Then he touched a finger to her lips as if to hush her.

Later, as promised, he brought her clean clothes, sandwiches, a message of good cheer from Elizabeth, and a colorful shopping bag from the hospital gift shop. "Remember the Fireman's Carnival?" he asked with an enormous grin.

"Of course."

"Remember how I never won any stuffed animals for you?"

"Because you wouldn't play the games, Jacob. You wouldn't even try to knock the bowling pins off the shelves or get the rings around the candles."

"Right. You remember."

"I most certainly do, you stubborn thing. And?" She gestured for him to continue talking.

"Well I decided to make up those past sins to you," he announced and upended the bag over her lap, letting fall a stuffed mouse, rabbit, puppy, and two bears with knitted sweaters and ski caps.

"Oh, Jacob, you are a love." She hugged one of the bears to her chest and then kissed its nose. "Better late than never, as always." And though she tried to get it out of her head that stuffed animals were really for babies, she couldn't help thinking, seeing the bear in the pink sweater and the bear in the blue sweater, about people bringing these bears into the rooms down the hall to celebrate pink births and blue births. And that just lead her to wonder whether the doctor might have known whether her baby was a boy or girl and she asked Jake if he knew, and then she was crying, and the poor bear (that at least made her laugh) got squashed between them when Jake tried to hug her.

He said he would take the animals back to the shop if they upset her, but she protested, no, the sadness came in waves, just like the pain had before. "I'm all right again," she insisted. "Besides," she continued, "I've waited a long time for you to bring me these prizes, so I'm not letting go without a fight." The memory of the carnival made her laugh; blew the despondence into particles fine and light as talc. "You wouldn't play because you said the games were fixed and impossible to win."

"They were."

"Then why'd I always see other girls walking around with the animals?" she teased him.

"Ha!" he said with exaggerated vehemence. "They were shills. They worked for the carnival. They were there to make you think it could be done."

"I don't believe you," she said and remembered those were the exact words she'd said to him years ago (though then she'd ended by sticking her tongue out at him). "So find somebody else to baby-sit you," had been his wicked retort before he'd disappeared and left her to find her own way home. She'd told on him. The Parents had listened, nodded, then gone on with the task at hand. There had been no higher source of wisdom or governing body of justice to fall back on in those days. None now, either, sad to say, in their wider, real world, when the subject matter was the two of them. "Hey, Jake," she said, "I believe you."

"How about if you believe me and I believe you, from now on?"

"A deal," she said, and they had the bears shake hands on it.

Going out to the island was a sudden, last minute idea. He opened the door to the car to let her in and he said he was glad the wind had died down, and then commented that the still days, like this one, were the ones he liked best going out on the ferry, the kinds of days he was likely to miss most.

"Would you take me out there?" she asked when he'd slid in on his side of the car.

"Now, you mean? You're supposed to be resting in bed."

"Can't I rest there? There's a bed or couch there, isn't there?"

"Both; bed and couch, but there's the crossing, too. You'd have only an uncomfortable low ledge to sit on the whole way out. There aren't any real benches on the launch."

"But it's just a few minutes, isn't it? The weather's turned mild, it'll be an easy trip."

He put the key in the ignition, but only held it there, not turning to start. "And then you'd have to walk to the cottage . . ."

"I'll go slowly. I'll take it at a crawl. And I'll rest as long as you like, once we're there." She put a hand on his shoulder. "Please, Jake. I want to go out there and see where you were all the time I was back in New London, only conjuring you up out of memory."

"You're not too tired?" He looked directly at her and she saw he was ready to assent, saw, too, that he wanted her to go there with him.

"I slept while you were gone, and I rested flat out the rest of the time. I'm fine."

"You're sure?"

"Cross my heart and hope to die," she said, marking out an invisible X across the left side of her chest. He started the car.

I know this place, she said to herself as they entered the cottage. "This is the playhouse, Jake. This is where we used to hang out, only it's grown-up size." She took off the jacket she'd borrowed from him and tossed it to the couch. "It's so familiar."

"It's not really like the playhouse," he protested. "That was a tiny little place, with the roof practically touching our heads once we were grown. It was one room."

"Oh, come on, you know it's a carbon copy made big." She took in a deep breath. "It even smells like it, the way the smell of lake and sand have settled into the boards. Most people hate that musty smell, but I love it." She leaned her head back to look at the ceiling. "The roof's built in the same way with the beams visible and kind of makeshift. And it has the same small windows that don't give any air. The same spiders, I'll bet. I should have known you'd get a place like this. I should have figured it out when you wrote that it was on an island." She walked through the living area, touching the windowsills and door frames. "I know it's much bigger, and it's got a kitchen which we never had, but it's the same. It's funny to see all the furniture here, though; it seems incongruous. It should have a blanket and the little table you made and that's all." Enough walking around he said, reaching for her hand. He insisted she lie down on the couch and went to the bedroom to get a blanket for her.

"There's no woods here the way there was at home," she

shouted after him. "I thought from your paintings there were huge trees here. I'm too literal, I guess."

He smiled and tossed the blanket to her. "Artistic license. Autobiographical borrowings. A little of here, a little of there."

"You've got yourself a much larger body of water here than back home. I do think Lake Ontario outclasses our pond."

"More houses here, too. More people in summer."

"Still, it's a good hideaway, isn't it?"

"It got to be a bit too much of a hideaway after a while." He sat down in the armchair.

"For Elizabeth, you mean?"

"Well, for the two of us. You cut yourself off from the world when you live here. That's why we moved into town."

She put her hand up to the glass of the window behind the couch. "There's a shadowy light here that makes the place look almost surreal. It's beautiful, though."

"I'd emphasize shadow, not light, in that description," he said and laughed. "On a day like the one you arrived, when the wind is so high off the lake, it's real drafty in here. Papers'll blow right off the table. These places weren't meant for year-round living."

She sat up to catch the view out the window. "It'd be better, of course, if you could see the lake like you could from the playhouse. But still, it beats the hell out of city streets."

"You really think it's like the playhouse?"

"Definitely the same architect," she said and laughed.

He brewed tea for them and they drank it together and didn't speak. They listened to the sound of the water on the shore. "Now I'm tired," she said to him. "Now that I'm finally lying down, I don't think I want to get up again."

"I shouldn't have let you talk me into coming out here." He put his teacup down beside hers on the table. "I'm a bad guardian to give in so easily to your whims."

"And yours," she pointed out.

"It is nice here, isn't it?"

"Very. My dream of cozy." She pulled the blanket closer round her.

"I guess I could try carrying you to the boat." They both laughed. "We'll take one of the last boats so you have maximum time to rest."

"Maybe I should just stay here tonight, Jake. Elizabeth might be glad to have her privacy back."

He slapped at his jeans pocket, found his pack of cigarettes and took it out. "I don't want to leave you here alone."

"I'm not an invalid. I'm just tired. I'll call if I need you."

"I've had the phone disconnected."

"Oh, and so you have. How easily we forget. But I'll be all right, anyway, Jake. And I'll be more comfortable here because there's a bed for me." He offered her a cigarette, but she shook her head.

"Don't you think you'd be more comfortable if you were with other people?" He moved to the couch and sat in the space she'd left when she drew her knees up. He lit the cigarette and pulled the saucer that served as ashtray closer.

"I'd be more comfortable in a bed than a sleeping bag. But you're welcome to stay and be other people for me, if you like."

"I don't think I can," he said as he stretched his arm along the couch back. "With the phone out, there wouldn't be any way to tell Elizabeth. Why don't you come back there. Elizabeth and I can take care of you. We can do a little old-fashioned hovering."

"Elizabeth doesn't need me there, Jake. I'm just making her nervous."

"She likes you."

Rachel shook her head. "She's lovely and polite, Jake, and

she's dying to do what you want and expect her to do, but she's worried I've come to spirit you away. I know it. Besides, I acted so out of control the whole time I was with her, I'm embarrassed."

"Those were extenuating circumstances, she knows that. And you're fine now."

"But I don't want her put out and having to do for me. I want to make up a little for crashing and breaking into her otherwise settled life. And if I'm alone, I can stretch out and sleep late, and I can cry, if I need, without worrying that good guests don't act unhappy."

"All alone?"

She nodded. "Yes."

"I suppose it'll be all right," he said shaking off the long ash that had formed on his cigarette, and she failed to suppress a giggle of pleasure at winning the special hideaway for her very own. "Thank you," she said.

"What about meals?"

"I told you, I'm not an invalid. I can either come out to Toronto for dinner, or if you want to get me some groceries, just a few basics, I'll make some simple meals. Mostly I'll just lie around and read. Think. Mourn the baby when I need to." She held the edge of the blanket to her cheek and was quiet for a moment. When he left, there'd be no more voices in the rooms. "Is there a radio?"

"In the bedroom."

"I'll be fine, then."

"It's true that it might be easier on Elizabeth," he said quietly, almost as though he were talking to himself. "I won't be able to be out here with you during the day. I have to go back to work tomorrow or some other exile will have my job by noon."

"I don't expect you to be here."

"I'll come out after work and bring some food."

"Is there anything left here, now, that I could call dinner?"

"I'll see. We didn't move any kitchen things yet." He crushed the cigarette out in the saucer, then checked his watch.

"Would you rather get back now?" she asked.

"Today's Elizabeth's late class day. She gets back after eight."

"I'll let you serve me, then."

He made a salad of what he called found food: artichoke hearts, baby shrimp and canned new potatoes. There were melba toast crackers and beer to go with it. He gave her a complete inventory of the rest of the food supplies. She would be able to have toast and marmalade for her breakfast, canned ravioli for lunch. He would be back by supper time the next day, he said, with a supply of more appealing food.

Once he was gone, she fell asleep briefly on the couch, then woke, anxious to walk again through the cottage. She felt no fatigue anymore, just the silvery clean edge of exhilaration. Everything is as I would have imagined it, she thought, with his crossword puzzle book on the floor by the couch and his art books tumbled together on a bottom bookshelf. There were a few small paintings: the island dock, the cottage deep in shadow, and the empty beach. Canvases leaned against the wall, sketches hung with pushpins in kitchen, bathroom, and living room. There was his dark blue comforter on the bed. His choices of spicy condiments on the shelves, and jars of sweet relish and ginger preserves next to the marmalade in the refrigerator. The box of pastels, used and broken, which she had given him for his last in-States birthday lay half scattered, half in the box on the table by the bed where she was to sleep.

At the apartment, there had been a painting of Elizabeth: a white face caught in motion, a fiery flash of hair; all of it lit from behind with burning white light. Here, at the cottage, there were no paintings of Elizabeth, though one small water-color of Rachel hung in the corridor between kitchen and living space. The painting made her look like a nineteenth-century noblewoman; elegant, distant and, she thought, much too pale. She found the photographs of the two of them, Rake and Jake, mounted in primary colors. Rachel was intrigued by how similar their expressions appeared, how alike their poses for the camera.

In the stack of canvases, she found the one that was to have been her wedding gift. It had more abstract elements—at least in this stage of noncompletion—than any of the others she'd seen in either the apartment or cottage. In the center, there was blur of movement, a suggestion of two figures dancing in a circle, hands lifted together. The partially painted background had large blocks of red and blue that spread all the way to the edges of the canvas, pushing outward against its confines. Despite the broad, less detailed work of the painting, he'd still given her that ambiguous pouting smile that he always did. It was very much like her. He'd made her hair a flash of yellow, but so warm, she wished, as she touched her hand to her hair, that it were truly the color she bore in life. There was a wash of gesso over Ben's face. He'd tried it once, or perhaps twice, or more, and decided to begin again. She realized now that the sketches that hung through the cottage were the studies for this work; all details that were or weren't on this canvas: hands, hair, faces, even what she believed was an early incarnation of two figures seated together, hands clasped, on a bench. Ben's face (she assumed it was Ben, the woman, herself) was turned slightly to the side, in order to avoid the facial detail of which Jake would have no knowledge.

She returned again to the pile of canvases. All the others were empty. The colors of the one he had begun had a vibrance she'd never seen in his work before. She would try to get him to take what he was doing there with the volatile, moving planes of color and go on with it in something else. She turned the painting to face outward, then sat on the couch to examine it some more. Despite Ben's presence, or near presence, in the painting, she still found it a remarkable piece. Perhaps there was a way to complete it, a way to focus on the strangeness of the dance they had performed together.

It was a wonder to her that she felt so comfortable in the cottage, with sketches of her husband all around, but they were Jake's visions of him, not the real Ben. They were imagined and idealized. The coloring, the beard, the slender build matched Ben's but could also have been the general features of many, able to be claimed anytime. Jake himself could be described in the same terms.

No, this place was comfortable because Jake had shaped it from all that was familiar to her. It was formed of his breath, his thoughts, and the impress of his body on every piece of furniture. She walked through the house, touching the sticks, strings, and mud of his nest. She could stay here forever now that things were settled and she was Rachel again. Just Rachel. Rachel Rothstein. She could stay in this place that took its meaning from his life in it.

Time—the times, the turbulence that had twisted the path of his life—had taken them and put them on separate planes. She occupied his space, but only after he had abandoned it. Had she come here (oh but for a lousy couple of bucks) that night she'd run to the bus station, would they move in a common orbit now?

She hoped Elizabeth had never lived out at the cottage. She didn't want her to know these details of him so well or to know this place as her refuge. He'd said they'd felt isolated out here. They? He had to have meant: Elizabeth hadn't liked it out here. Jake had chosen this place because it was home. She was certain of it. And she was certain that he had felt her presence in this place. They had, after all, grown up together in it.

By the time she crawled into bed, she was exhausted again, the energy of moments earlier now transformed into nervous irritability. She lay awake in the dark, trying to identify the unfamiliar noises in and around the cottage. It was a lonely place, suddenly, this summer bungalow in the middle of winter.

She thought to take comfort in remembering the doctor and nurses of the early morning hours, but when the figures she dreamed up moved toward her, they wore the shapes of nightmare figures from a Fuseli painting.

She made a place for Jake in the bed, creating him out of air, so that she might lean into his body during the night and feel the length of him alongside herself. In the darkness she listened again and heard the gentle repetitions of water against shore, and caught the sound of his breathing, slow and even, as it is in sleep, beside her.

CHAPTER NINETEEN

*B*Y THE NEXT DAY, Rachel felt good enough to bundle herself into Jake's sweater and jacket and to walk the short distance to the lake. The water had carried the usual odd assortment of tree limbs up onto the shore. She gathered these, wondering if any of them had started from American soil, and formed them into a make-shift seat at the water's edge. Like a raft, she thought, waiting in dry dock for the journey to begin. She knew, from years of practice in childhood, that if she stared long enough at the water, she'd begin to feel as though she were floating along the rolling surface of the lake. Everything was easier when her mind drifted with the gentle rise and fall of the water. Even thinking about seeing Ben once she was back in the States seemed not so impossible as it once had.

Who would Ben be then? Such tricks with costumes and mirrors he was able to play. How unfortunate that when their paths had first crossed, he was playing draft evader. By now, he might have enlisted in the Marines. She wondered: Was he so clever that he'd known her weakness, right from the beginning, and then played on it, as on a musical instrument? Had he known that any reference to her distant friend, even if clichéd and superficial, had the power to draw her attention? No matter that the actual resemblance between Jake and Ben was as worldly as the headbands they wore and as easily cast off. And what did that make her? The naive mark, watching the show, believing it all, clapping like a crazy, begging for more. Have you ever thought about being an actor, Benjamin? she would remember to ask him.

Late in the afternoon, Jake came out, as promised, to the island. She laughed to see the supplies he'd brought: a few oranges and bananas, a quart of milk, a loaf of bread, and a dozen eggs. Would it be French toast, then, or pancakes for this winter dinner? "How are you feeling?" he asked as he placed the groceries in the refrigerator.

"Much better," she said. "I feel recovered. I took a long nap."

"Good," he said. "I thought if you weren't too tired, you could come back to the apartment for dinner." She was disappointed. She'd imagined them preparing a meal together, taking onions, garlic, spices, and meat, or as a default those eggs, fruits, and bread, and changing it together, turning it with cutting, stirring, and heating into smells and tastes they could relish together.

"Elizabeth isn't a complainer, but I think she's feeling left out," he said. He folded the brown bag and stuck it in the small broom closet by the stove.

Rachel told him it would be fine, of course it wasn't really fair to Elizabeth, the other way, was it, both of them out here all evening. No, he said and he went into the bedroom. Why did he walk away from her with just that one word? She followed him, stood in the doorway to the bedroom. "Are you angry with me?"

He turned to face her again. "No."

"Then why'd you walk away?"

"I didn't walk away. I wanted my tobacco. I don't do dope anymore, you know. It's too chancy here. With a drug conviction, I'd lose immigrant status. So now I smoke odd-flavored tobaccos and get hostile when I can't find them, sorry. I looked all over the apartment and it's not there. I thought maybe it was still here. With two houses, now, it gets confusing."

She felt the color rise in her cheeks. "It was selfish of me to stay out here," she said quickly. "I thought it would be better for Elizabeth, but you're right, it must look to her as though we were deliberately cutting her off."

"Yes," he said. He shut one bureau drawer and reached down to the next one. "I mean, no you're not selfish, you chose to stay out here for perfectly good reasons, but if you're feeling up to it, I thought we could all have dinner together, that's all. No heavy meaning, you know, Rachel." He found the tobacco in the nightstand. "Ah," he said holding it up for her to see before he folded the pouch in half to fit into his back jeans pocket. "It'll just be easier, I think," he concluded.

Marry me, he'd said: But in crisis, Rachel, remember. Neither of them would be so foolish as to think such thoughts in daylight.

On the way to the ferry dock he showed her how simple the route was. "Straight down this street, right turn, straight on toward the lights of the dock. Reverse that coming back out. There won't be very many other cottage lights on, so you'll find it easily, I think." She understood that she'd be coming back on the boat by herself.

"You can borrow the electric lantern to light your way," he told her when they were on the boat. "Will you mind going back by yourself?"

"No. It'll be easier for everybody," she said.

"Elizabeth put up a pot of chili," he informed her, and she could tell from his accompanying sigh that there were to be no other new restrictions. Dinner together. Boat ride alone. Yes, it was fair. And better.

What she had wanted was time alone. Time to begin to piece it together, to say, Why do I always come back to you? She wanted to know if he knew the answer.

But now she felt again, what she always felt with Jake, the sense that she should be on her way. That she should be making it on her own. Grow up, Rachel. She leaned against the railing of the boat, bracing for the crash of the launch against the wharf. It would be better if you left, he would say, though perhaps not till tomorrow or even the next day. It would be just as well, once she was physically up to it. Schoolwork and all. It would be less confusing. They rocked forward with the impact, then back. She thought to ask him, And if I grow up, won't you cast me out all the sooner? but chose, instead, to walk in silence along the ramp to shore.

We'll write, though, won't we, she thought to herself as he pulled slightly ahead of her. It was a cold evening and they moved quickly up out of the terminal, running to warm themselves with the heat of their own muscles. We'll write that we miss one another, and we'll leave each other, so we can miss one another. She'd always worked on this principle: if she left, he couldn't get tired of her.

These had been her plans: to sit next to him in the dark (the playhouse hadn't been electrified). To be like they were. To figure it out.

Elizabeth: you worry in vain. We haven't the means for seduction. We'll write letters again. He'll say he misses me. You won't mind that, will you Elizabeth? She had stopped to catch her breath. Ahead, in the light of a street lamp, she saw Jake, bent low against the wind, waiting.

Rachel sliced bread while Elizabeth grated cheese. "Tell me," Elizabeth said, "has Jake always been capable of eating three dinners?"

"Definitely," Rachel answered. "If he eats at six o'clock, he's in the kitchen at nine, and on the phone to the pizza place by eleven."

"Then it isn't just the Canadian air?" Elizabeth wanted to know.

"No. It's class-A gluttony."

"I hear you, you two," Jake said, emerging from the living room. He reached for his jacket where it lay across the chair and tossed it over his shoulder. "If you're going to malign me like that, I might as well leave. I don't like to be called a glutton."

"Would gourmand be better?" Rachel asked, tugging gently on the woodsman's shirt as he tried to walk away.

"Only slightly," he said, turning back to her. "I'm not sure I like my women reducing me to such simplistic terms." Though she knew he was only continuing in the game of their joking banter, his words, *my women*, sent of wave of warmth through her.

"I'm sorry I teased you," she said and touched his face with her fingertips. His hand moved lightly through her hair. It was their apology, each to the other, she knew, for drawing apart. The harshness between them softened, and their hands met and held, for just a moment.

"If you still feel like leaving, you could go get us some beer," Elizabeth suggested.

"You'll miss me when I'm gone," he said, and the women laughed again as he went out the door.

"He's a good friend," Rachel said.

"And he says the same about you. He really adores you, Rachel." She saw in the blinking of Elizabeth's eyes; in the way her hand brushed repeatedly at a stain on the counter, that there were questions; fears.

"I don't want you to worry about us, Elizabeth. We're friends. We were never lovers." Rachel felt the silence then between them, a silence she hadn't anticipated. She'd thought Elizabeth would say, Oh yes, I know, or, I'm so relieved to hear you say that. Rachel held her breath, waiting. She watched the cheese in Elizabeth's hand grow smaller and smaller against the grater. When there was nothing left to grate, Elizabeth reached for a mottled blue bowl that sat up on one of the shelves, then transferred the cheese from the wax paper into it. "The cheese looks nice in there," Rachel said, feeling the leaden stupidity of her words, when talk of other things hung over them so heavily. Rachel wanted to leave the room. The only hope left for her now was that Elizabeth had suddenly gone inexplicably deaf and hadn't heard anything she'd said. Or that Rachel hadn't said anything. She'd only thought about it. How had she managed, so quickly, to make a bad situation infinitely worse?

"He said you once were." Elizabeth's voice was soft, the syntax twisted enough, so that Rachel needed a moment to pick up the thread of meaning. "Were lovers," Elizabeth added, with obvious difficulty. She glanced at Rachel, then away.

"One time," Rachel said. "When we were very young. Much too young."

Elizabeth nodded solemnly and took three plates down from the shelf. "That's what he said, too."

Rachel wanted Elizabeth to say it was all right. "We chose to be friends, not lovers." More nodding. "The old mystical journey just wasn't so mystical for us, I guess," she said, not at all sure she should be making jokes, but wanting laughter badly. Elizabeth smiled.

"It's none of my business, really," Elizabeth protested.

"Sure it is."

"It feels like it is," Elizabeth said, and they laughed in relief that they had finished with the subject. Jake came through the door and wanted to know what was so funny, but they wouldn't let on, keeping the laughter going by saying "just mystical talk, nothing you'd be interested in." Elizabeth cast a conspiratorial smile Rachel's way and they laughed together.

During dinner Jake read them parts of a letter from his mother. She'd written that she wanted him to get a Canadian gardening manual and check the date for the last possible frost in Toronto and then write and let her know what it was so that she and his father could come visit after that date. They'd all laughed over it and Jake explained to Elizabeth about how Grace turned reclusive around Thanksgiving and rarely went out alone in the car till April first because of her fear of snow. "It's very funny," Elizabeth said, "but I do hope she realizes she'll never see her son again unless she gets herself up here. It's time for her to accept that he's become a Canadian." Rachel was startled by the statement. Did she hear an eagerness in Elizabeth's voice? It sounded to her as though Elizabeth relished the idea of keeping Jake in exile.

Rachel mentioned it when Elizabeth had gone into the bathroom. "She seems determined that you're here for life. What's this Canadian business? I know it's a cliché, but time moves on, wars end, and all that. The raven that says Nevermore was only a figment in a poet's imagination, Jake, wasn't it? Why is she so determined to make you Canadian? What if you go back? She's not going with you?"

He pushed his chair back so that it balanced on two legs. "I'm Canadian now. I have to be," he said.

"I'm not talking about immigrant status and legal definitions, Jake. You can't erase everything you were. Not spiritually, anyway." She leaned toward him across the table.

"I think I'll be here for the rest of my life."

"Come on, Jake. Administrations change. The world comes full circle and all that."

"I have to tell myself it's forever. I have to believe it's forever, otherwise I only wait. Waiting isn't living."

"What about hoping, Jake?"

"There are other clichés, too: Time heals all wounds. You know that cliché, Rach."

"But that's what it is, Jake, a worn out cliché."

He let his chair down hard and sudden. "Clichés usually spring from old, too familiar truths."

"They're not truths."

"What's not true?" Elizabeth's voice startled Rachel. She had returned to the table.

"Clichés," Rachel told her, and she felt her pulse race.

"Just some bullshit," Jake said. He leaned his chair back again and put his hand on Elizabeth's back.

"What?" Elizabeth persisted.

"We were just trading clichés. You know, where there's smoke there's fire. Where there's dinner there's dessert. We were wondering whether that was true."

"It's true," Elizabeth said, but Rachel saw how she kept looking first at her, then at Jake, and back again, trying to snatch from the space between them the real words that had been there moments before. Jake's hand stroked Elizabeth's back as she stood next to him and Rachel saw her body ease under his hand. Rachel was an interloper, sure enough. She tried to smile, to will her lips to such action, but one side of her mouth resisted more, making her smile decidedly uneven. But it was a smile, nonetheless, and under the circumstances, a hell of a lot better than tears. She rose and cleared the table for dessert.

Elizabeth said, "You two sit down and talk while I do the dishes." Rachel wanted to say, "No, I can do dishes, too, watch Jake, you'll see," but she stopped herself. Some terribly small, infantile part of her had escaped into the open for a moment, but then crawled back into her psyche, bent with shame.

Rachel pushed her chair back from the table. "You could

show me what you've been working on," she suggested to Jake.

"With the moving," he said once they were in the studio, "I've done very little. Just the fresco and the sketches for the wall pieces. There's not much to show that you haven't seen."

"There's the painting of Elizabeth," she said, pointing to where it hung.

"That's from the cottage, actually. I put it up there, thinking I'd finish it, but even though the light's good here, it's an entirely different light. Too different. I don't think I'll be able to finish it."

"Go out there on weekends and work on it," Rachel suggested.

"No," he said, sitting down on the floor in front of the portrait. He opened the bottle of beer he'd carried with him from the table and poured it into two glasses. "We're giving that place up at the end of the month. And anyway, Elizabeth gets weary of posing. It's not really fair to make her do it, especially on weekends."

"I'm sorry you're giving up on it. I like it. You've got about twenty different shades of red working together in there. Colors that aren't really in Elizabeth's hair, but the painting makes you believe they must be."

"Yes," he said. He stood up and adjusted the light over the painting. "Do you get any sense of the hair having buoyancy?" He moved his hands in easy circles. "Like it's floating, maybe?"

"And of the figure turning with it."

"Yes," he said, nodding.

"The white makes that happen. The white and the red fight, I think."

"I wanted that." He stood to one side to examine his work.

"And you did it in the wedding picture."

"Oh yes," he said with a laugh. "You've seen that, then? My great abortive attempt."

252 ...... *Painting on Glass*

"And mine."

"I thought that was going to be good, but what the hell, you can't have everything."

"You should finish it."

He laughed. "The meaning's gone. There's no energy behind the image anymore for me."

"Couldn't it be a portrait of someone else? A portrait of a marriage, a relationship, I don't know. I like what you were doing with it. I like the way the people move through that color. Can't you just make it two anonymous people? Or you and Elizabeth, maybe."

"Maybe." He sat back down next to her.

Elizabeth came in with another bottle of beer, another glass. She stopped next to the fresco. "Here's my favorite," she said.

"That was a real trip, painting that," Jake said.

"You should have seen him do it, Rachel. He did it so fast. It was like the pictures were in his hands." She held her own hands before her, as if they, too, possessed a magic. "It was like the images flowed out onto the walls."

Jake laughed. "Talk about me more, you two," Jake said. "I love being a latter-day Michelangelo."

Rachel was startled, then, to see Elizabeth put her hands to the fresco. First she traced the shape of the birds, then seemed to pet the cows. As Rachel watched, Elizabeth moved her hands from one object to another in the painting. The second time Elizabeth reached out to stroke a cow, Rachel looked toward Jake with raised eyebrows. He smiled and shrugged. She understood: he didn't want to be the one to have to come down hard on Elizabeth's naivete. "You know the oils in your hands can muck up the paint," Rachel said and Elizabeth drew her hand back as though the bushes she'd caressed had pricked with real thorns.

"I'm sorry," she said first to Rachel, and then to Jake. Rachel saw the surprise in her face as she shrank back from the painting.

"It doesn't really matter," Jake said. "It's just a wall decoration, not a painting."

"You never said it was bad for the paint." Why not? Rachel wondered. He'd certainly explained it all to her enough times. "Does it wreck up the paints?" Elizabeth asked him. She moved a blank canvas out of the way so she, too, could sit on the floor.

"It can, theoretically, because there's so much oil in your hands, but it doesn't matter."

"But why didn't you ever say so? I feel like such a jerk."

"Because I liked it when you touched it. It was cute."

"I don't want to be cute, Jake."

"I don't mean cute, Elizabeth, I've used the wrong word."

"What's the right word?"

"I don't know. Endearing."

"Not much better, is it?" she said to Rachel. "I'm endearing, now."

"I meant the gesture was endearing," Jake said.

"Is that better, then?"

"Hey, guys," Rachel said. "I'm sorry. I spoke out of turn. Like Jake said, it's just a wall decoration."

"Right," he was quick to add. He reached for Elizabeth, though from where he was, he was able only to grasp at her foot, which she pulled back. "Come here," he said, but she shook her head, then reconsidered and slid over closer to him. He put his arm around her and offered her a sip of his own beer. He kissed her cheek while she drank. Rachel drank from her glass, her eyes closed. Did she know him anymore? Why was he so disengaged from his art? Why did he accept so easily giving it up? Was it because of Elizabeth that yet more plans had evaporated? Was it all just so much cuteness, now? There was a silence in the room broken by their uncomfortable shifting about. She had not meant to make things so awkward. She would talk then, filling the air with words, even if the patterns they built up were mere patchwork inanities.

"You know someday this fresco will get painted over," Rachel said. "A family will move in here who will think the colors are too bright. They'll get white paint and cover it over."

"And then their children will take nice bright crayons and color over that." Elizabeth said.

"I did it as a joke, so I've no right to complain. Just to be able to see cows out on the streets of Toronto is enough reward for me for my efforts."

"You should get a commission in a public building," Rachel said. "Someplace where you won't get painted over."

"Maybe I can interest the Ontario Gallery of Art in my work. I'll be the Orozco of Canada."

"Maybe you could be," Rachel interposed. Elizabeth laughed lightly and Jake pretended to choke on his beer.

"All right, not the art gallery, first off, but you can start somewhere. Advertise. Go for the rich people. Private homes. You know how to put up the plaster, and everything. You'd be considered a real find, Jake."

"You mean I'm a regular interior decorator."

"Your first clients might think of you that way, but as your name gets known, you'll get more autonomy."

"As in 'Sorry, I don't do artichokes on kitchen walls?' " Jake interrupted.

"Yes. And as in, 'This is my art, take it or leave it.' And then the library comes begging you, 'Please, Mr. Marsh, couldn't you just manage a small area of the entryway,' and then the airport wants you to do its waiting room, and you're too busy to take the art gallery, after all." She pretended to brush paint in broad strokes across the wall. "It takes time, of course.

Eventually somebody else does the replastering, you know. You just show up with the paints at the last minute.

"It's a dead art, Rachel."

"Isn't it what you always wanted to do, though?"

"Long ago," he said.

"Not so long ago," she insisted.

"Definitely before the war."

"I'm beginning to think there isn't anything left in you that predates the war."

"There isn't," he said with a harsh-edged laugh.

Elizabeth looked at her watch, "Jake," she said and pointed to her timepiece.

"Right," Jake said. "Last boat time," and the three of them rose from the floor. Time to take little sister home, Rachel said to herself.

There was plenty of time to catch the boat. She could have asked him some of the questions she had. They could have talked of themselves; could have selected from a complete array of conversational topics: their past, their future, in comic or serious mode, alike. Yet they sat together on a bench and barely spoke. They didn't touch. She knew if she were to begin, she would say only this: "Can you come across with me?"

She pulled off her glove and reached a hand—a real hand, flesh and blood—for his. He wore no gloves, preferring to thrust his hands deep into his pockets as he walked. He slipped his fingers between hers, and their palms met and held tight.

The boat had docked. "Tomorrow," he said, as he slid his hand away, "you should make a plane reservation." She nodded. "I guess I have to do it," he added suddenly. "I'm the one with the phone."

She stood on the Toronto side of the boat as it moved out across the harbor. He disappeared almost immediately back through the gates toward the street. He hadn't waited to watch the boat pull away. It was too cold for that sort of thing.

On shore she held the lantern by its wire handle and swung it forward and back from the end of her hand, first lighting her way, then casting what lay ahead into darkness. Each time her way blackened, she felt a touch of panic, but she welcomed the focus; it left no room for other thoughts.

She kept the music loud and the lights high. She found his wine (behind the books, exactly where he'd always kept it) and poured herself a glass. His wine. His house. His books. She ran her hands over the spines. He was not an organizer; not taken to alphabetizing or categorizing, yet she'd seen him pull a book he wanted from his shelves without a moment's hesitation. He'd developed his intellectual radar by sitting and looking at his shelves; clearly, they were his favorite still life. Perhaps it was the artist's eye for color that was at the heart of his grouping, but if it were, she failed to see it; colors and sizes mixed together, but for the oversized art books that were relegated to the large bottom shelf. She had to search the shelves for the volumes she wanted. It took time, but she found each of them: the T.S. Eliot with hers and Jake's earnest marginalia to "Prufrock" and "Four Quartets," *Secret Agent,* the Conrad novel they'd taken turns reading aloud in the playhouse, and the oriental poetry collection she'd given him. She found, too, though she hadn't been looking for it, the collection of D.H. Lawrence stories he'd mentioned in the letter that had the sketches. She opened the pages carefully, and found, every thirty pages or so, a drawing. His drawings of her. These were more hurried than the ones he'd sent her. Not so concerned, as he had self-criticized, with getting every line just so. These were the hand of someone working quickly, of grabbing at an image or idea before it disappeared. Before it woke. But they were the sketches of a lover, surely; sketches in which the pencil had lingered over lips till they were too full, over a curve,

till it begged a hand to test its shape. And there were two
pictures of her with eyes open. One, still lying down, but
seeming to come awake, another of her sitting, her legs drawn
up and encircled by her arms. She had no memory of posing
for him. These were fantasy eyes he'd drawn; eyes that invited
and assented to an off-stage lover. Was it true? Had she wanted
him then? Has this gone on so long, Jacob Marsh? Her fingers
followed the lines that came from his hand and that were her.
She put the sketches carefully back into the book, approximat-
ing the places from which she'd removed them.

She poured herself another glass of wine, sat down on the
couch and pulled her legs up under her. She stripped off layers
of memory as if they were items of clothing, till she saw him:
A browned summertime body. She remembered how the dark
blonde hair fanned out in a diamond shape around his navel.
She could see him rub his hand across his chest and abdomen,
feeling the shape of his own musculature, as he walked from
the pond.

And now? Did he still nourish fantasies complementary to
hers? Had he seen her standing naked, as she had seen him,
in the bedroom of the cottage?

In the morning, then, he would call the airline. By evening,
she might be home. She laughed, trying to place herself.
Where was her home, now? She'd find a corner in Jennifer's
room again, or perhaps Christine's this time. It hardly mattered where.

He'd appear in the doorway, a ticket in hand. Hurry, he'd
say, and she'd grab her things, and the dialogue wouldn't quite
mesh with what she'd had in mind, but the scene would have
its own momentum by then. Just as at the hospital the nurses
effortlessly spoke their lines to her though she wasn't the char-
acter they supposed. And the baby? Just a wisp of a story line,
an aberrant line of dialogue. My baby. Your baby. His baby.

Whisked off and out of the scene, never having existed at all. The plane leaves in an hour, he'd say. Why were their cues always slightly off, the pages of the script so hopelessly out of order?

CHAPTER TWENTY

*H*E HAD AN IDEA, he said when he arrived, of how he wanted to sketch her. She saw he had no ticket in his hand; no envelope sticking out of his back pocket.

What if she stayed one more day, he proposed. She laughed and put her arms around him. He would come out very early in the morning, if that was all right with her, so he could see her when the light was most vivid in the cottage. If she could stay through the weekend, he would do a series of studies because he'd had some ideas that had to do with the playhouse image and the old blanket that she'd jogged his memory about. The stuff she'd said about the cottage had brought together a lot of images. "It started to come to me when I was on the boat. I get my best ideas, then," he said. She saw herself shaking a blanket and spreading it out across the floor. She could feel the rough wool, see the familiar blue and white stripes down near each end. And she saw the blanket, caught on a breeze as she shook it out, then laid it on the sand.

"What about your classes?" he asked her. "I don't want you screwing up your whole academic life just because I've got an idea about a sketch."

"I just have my senior seminars now," she told him, "and they meet only once a week. I've made excuses for one round. If I need to, I could call the art department and explain I've been detained or stranded or kidnapped, or something that sounds pressing and non-negotiable for the second round. They'll let it go," she assured him.

"We're only talking about a day or two," he said.

"Right," she said. Whole days, though, days when he would come out with the first morning boat.

"I might move the big chair over to the window." He studied the room for a moment, then did just that and motioned for her to sit in it. "We'll see how the light is tomorrow," he said, "but I think it'll do wonderful things to your hair."

"That's good," she said, "because I definitely need to do something about my hair, it's a horrible mess." She combed her fingers through the tight curls and giggled.

He sat down on the arm of the chair. "Tie it back," he said, reaching behind her to catch it in his hands.

"No," she said, "I'll cut it off I think."

"Don't cut it," he said, his hand tracing patterns as gentle as whispers of suggestion along her neck. She leaned forward and kissed his mouth. She almost said, "Don't worry, I won't leave," for the words seemed right in that instant, but whispered, instead, "I won't cut it."

"Elizabeth's gone out to get Indian food for us," he said.

"Yes," she said, "we should get going."

She woke early, but only barely early enough to shower and dress before he arrived. She had gone into one of his drawers to borrow a shirt, or perhaps only to touch his things. She looked through them all, lifting them, sliding her hands between, and holding them in a pile against her chest as she decided among them. She settled on a blue and red plaid flannel that he had worn in New Haven and that was nearly threadbare at the cuffs. She was buttoning it up when he came through the door. "How do I look?" she asked him, turning around, modeling his shirt for him.

"Like the old days," he said, and she knew he was remembering how she used to raid his bureau of shirts, and perhaps, even, of how they'd fought, long ago, how he'd twisted her arm, hard, behind her back because she once took a shirt without permission. Now he ran his hand along the fabric between her elbow and wrist. He seemed to study the flannel, tracing the intersections of plaid, waiting to say something more.

"What?" she asked him, her own hand closing round his arm.

"Is there coffee left?" he asked and when she said there was, he went to the kitchen to prepare it.

He didn't talk while he worked. Sometimes she'd ask him a question, and he wouldn't hear. If she persisted, of course, he'd eventually respond. But his intensity pleased her. She waited. They could always talk later.

At midmorning they walked out to the beach. "We should go back to Toronto for dinner, I suppose," he said, tossing pebbles across the surface of the lake. "We could go to Chinatown."

"Maybe I won't come tonight," she said. She walked along the edge, kicking sand up with her toe. "Elizabeth's so uncomfortable with me there, Jake. She barely ate anything last night. When you went out to buy wine she told me her friend Catherine was wondering why I'd had to come all the way to Toronto when there must be underground networks for abortions in the States, good as there are here."

"Screw Catherine."

"I don't care about Catherine, Jake, but the point is Elizabeth does. Or she cares about me being here."

"What'd you say to her?"

"I told her I'd only come because I was crazy. Because I was alone. I said it was a mistake."

"No it wasn't. It was absolutely fortuitous. Something told you to wait as long as you did. To go this roundabout route so the pregnancy ended on its own, naturally."

"Do you really believe that?"

"Yes."

"I came here, you know, because I knew you'd take me in no matter what my story; because I knew you'd be there in precisely the way I needed you."

He put his arm across her shoulder and they stood at the edge of the water. "Did you say that to Elizabeth?"

"No."

"I think that's just as well. When I got back last night she was sitting in the kitchen. She wanted clarification. Definition. I keep telling her we're not lovers, but I have to tell her over and over. I don't think she believes it, though she says she does." He took her hand. "I considered coming out here this morning and telling you to forget it, but I wanted to do the sketches too much. I want to have them. So I asked Elizabeth to come out here with me, but she said she couldn't; she needed to study."

"I really need to get out of your life, don't I?"

His hand tightened on her shoulder. "Look, it's not your fault." She laughed and shook her head. "Or not entirely," he said with a smile. "I'll finish the sketches. Then you'll go, and we'll be OK."

"Sure?" she asked him.

"I'm sure." They walked back to the house with their arms around each other.

During the afternoon she read, sometimes lying down on a blanket on the floor, sometimes in the chair. She was no longer posing, only there for his occasional reference. One time he laughed and she looked up asking, what's the joke? And he passed her what he'd been working on: a drawing like the photograph that was on display in both their parents' homes. Jake and Rake, sitting in the big brass bed, side by side. "Isn't that what it looked like?" he wanted to know, as he stood behind her, looking over her shoulder as she examined it. "Yes," she said, "you've caught that spacey, noncomprehending, why-are-you-adults-all-laughing-at-us look? on both their faces."

"Our faces," he reminded her.

She laughed. "It's hard to connect with them, though, isn't it?"

"Yes," he said as he tacked the drawing to the wall. "I always wanted that photograph. This'll have to do instead."

In the course of the day he'd finished more than a dozen sketches and begun twice as many more. He'd left them here and there, all through the room. "Any major successes in that lot?" she asked him.

He gathered the drawings together, then shuffled through them. "Lots of good material to take off from. I want to do a series of small paintings from these. And I got much more done than I thought I would. One day's posing is going to be enough."

"I don't mind it," she said. "You can do another day if you like."

"Look at all this," he said and passed the sketches to her. No, she'd say, and convince him there really weren't enough: What? None of me standing? she'd ask. None of me talking, doing things, but just sitting, over and over, lying down, what can you do with such a limited range? She might say, don't you want me at the table, or maybe hanging out wash, or rowing a boat, something more? Only just a little bit longer, she'd say. But it would be hard going: the look of satisfaction he wore told her he was entirely pleased with his efforts.

"I can make a plane reservation, then," she said. He nodded, though she wasn't sure he'd heard her, for he was back at one of the sketches, redoing the lines around her mouth. She lay back down on the blanket. Why not stay? she asked herself. Chances were (though she hadn't mentioned this to him) all her professors wouldn't be equally understanding. Some or all were likely to make it difficult for her to finish the work on schedule. She might not graduate. So then why go back? Why not stay here for a while longer—where else was there for her? She wouldn't stay forever, maybe a few weeks. She'd watch spring come in, then take off, once she'd figured out where to go next.

When the light began to fade, he called it quits. "Want some wine?" she asked him. "The former tenant seems to have left a bottle tucked away here," she said as she pulled the books off the shelf.

"You've been exploring, I see."

"It was an easy kind of detective work. That's where your wine always is. Always was. Behind the books."

He smiled. "I'll have some," he said. "And I'll see if I can find any crackers and cheese."

"There's no cheese. I ate it."

He brought a box of crackers and two squat juice glasses from the kitchen and came and sat with her on the blanket.

"A good day," he said. They clinked glasses. "To high productivity and artistic output. I only wish I could get paid for this," he said. "What bliss it would be to love one's job."

"It's only that you're not paid *yet*. That's down the road." She raised her glass again.

"The woman has faith in me. Thank you," he said and brought his glass to hers again. "When will I get paid?" he asked her.

"In time. I don't know. When you have ten paintings to

bring round that'll make the gallery owners have apoplexy in their mad passion to get an exclusive on you."

"Time is never, then."

"Sure it is."

"Bullshit," he said and she pretended to mock offense at his language. "Time's a lousy cheat. We plan and we never get there, do we. I mean what have we achieved, you and I, that we once had our sights on? I want more simplicity. I want promises that I'll make it."

"I promise."

He laughed. "Would that you could," he said and reached a hand to stroke her hair. "Thanks, though," he added.

"That's OK. I figured it was time for me to start offering profound advice and all that. You've always gotten to play the teacher. I just wanted my turn."

"What profound things have I taught you, little Rake?"

She considered for a moment. "How to smoke."

He guffawed. "High-level stuff."

"Do you remember when you taught me to smoke those noxious unfiltered Camels?" He laughed and nodded. "Remember the time you got that fabulous hash and we fell asleep in the playhouse and The Parents came out looking for us?"

He shook his head as he smiled at the memory. "The poor things never suspected. Not even a word about the sweet smelling tobacco."

"They were too relieved to find us fully clothed, to think of other causes."

"They wouldn't have cared at that moment, I don't think, if we'd shot up with heroin."

"Oh heroin they'd have minded. They knew about the evils of heroin."

"Wish I had some of that hash now, believe me," he said. He lay on his side, propped on one elbow.

"Wish I had more time like this with you." She reached for the cracker box and shook out a half dozen onto the blanket. "Jacob," she began, then hesitated before her announcement. "I've been thinking about staying." She felt the words flutter in the air like colored doves released from a magician's hat. He ran his tongue over his lips but said nothing. "I feel so comfortable here. Because of the water, maybe." She heard the doves flap their wings, heating the air with their unison attempt to gain altitude. He turned over onto his back and rested the glass on his chest. "What do you think about me staying?"

"I think the timing's terrible," he said. She bit into a cracker; found it soggy. "You've got your last semester to finish. Don't screw yourself up again."

"I don't see it as screwing myself up. I see this as a quiet place where I can pull myself together. What if I get back to Connecticut College and they say, sorry, too late, you're not going to graduate."

"You said you could work it out."

"I said I thought I could."

"Well you can't work it out if you don't try, Rachel." He reached for a cracker.

"They're stale," she said, but he ate it without complaint. "Is it Elizabeth you're worried about?"

"That's a part of it, of course. I obviously can't ignore her in this."

"I swear to you, Jake, you'd be free to have your own life. All I want to do is pick up the lease on this place. I want to be alone, not tagging along with you two." He shook his head. "Maybe I could talk to Elizabeth, explain that it would be a kind of retreat for me; a healing place. We wouldn't even have to see each other." This last statement was so wickedly untrue, she colored to hear herself speak it. "Or we could get together once in a while. Chinatown, a concert, that sort of thing," she amended her stance.

He turned his eyes upward and laughed. "That doesn't make any sense, Rachel. She'll pack up and go."

"Would you want me to stay?"

He sat up and reached for the wine. "Your plan, if you'll forgive me, Rach, is ridiculous. Like I said, it doesn't make sense."

"I'm not talking sense, or straight and narrow correct choices, I'm talking about want, Jacob. Would you want me to stay?"

She brought her palm to his chest and moved it slowly across the surface of his shirt.

"Rachel," he whispered and she heard something in the way he breathed and the way her name became a question, that Yes, he wanted her to stay, and he was touching her hair, saying her name again. She tried to remember what it was she would say to Elizabeth, the rules and boundaries by which she'd just promised to abide, but his hands still held her, and he spoke her name again. For herself, she found only vague whispers of rambling, incomplete sentences.

Her fingers moved over his lips, his moustache, and his beard. He kissed her, then drew back, but she wanted more, his whole mouth first, then his top lip, his lower lip, then she had to see if his tongue was waiting. Her clothes felt so hot and thick, and she said "Make love to me."

"You've just had a miscarriage, Rach."

"Then almost make love to me, Jake." She leaned back, drawing him down to lie with her.

"Elizabeth," he explained, and Rachel decided they'd wait after all, just kiss once more, maybe twice more, but she couldn't tell where the kisses began and ended, so had trouble counting. His hand slipped between the buttons of her shirt and his fingertips reached for the curve of her breast.

"Rachel," he said in a whisper that was hot and sweet against her lips. Her name, now, not Elizabeth's. Her fingers were at the buttons of his shirt, her lips on his neck. He touched her face, kissed her mouth, and ran his hand over her hips, and she was aware of the hardness of her bones, the softness of her flesh under his touch. She moved under him, calling to him with kisses and the touch of her hand, whispering his name. She said, It's all right, isn't it? and he answered, Yes, yes, but she saw them then, in that other time, one other time when she'd asked him to love her, and she said, I mean because of Elizabeth, though it wasn't because of that, she said that only because she hoped it was. He looked toward the door when she spoke Elizabeth's name—not that she would have been there. He said never mind, and hushed all the other things she had to say, as well as the fear, with kisses on her mouth and her neck, and then he looked up again (Don't remember!) and she wanted to grab hold of him, tighter, tighter than before. Then he stopped, like an animal who's caught an unexplained scent on the breeze; wary, frozen. She watched him, waiting now. His fingers played over the soft flannel of her shirt as though he'd lost track of what to do next, of where to go from there.

He brought the buttons and buttonholes of her shirt together. It was a tedious job for him; his fingers worked slowly. Neither of them spoke. Her eyes stung with tears when he ran a hand across her chest in a gesture that was much too much like a waving of goodbye.

"Do you love her?" she asked. Not: Do you love me—a harder question, and one against whose answer there might be need to cover her ears.

He touched her hair one more time; two fingertips to one wayward curl. "I don't know. My whole life is constructed around her now."

She saw the space between them, but didn't move closer, only willed their bodies to touch again, the space between them to vanish, the ache within her to leave. "Constructed how?" she asked him. "Do you mean like a set of building blocks? Is Elizabeth a fortress of some sort?"

"Maybe." He sat up and found his glass of wine. "I'm an exile, Rachel. I'm here. I'm Canadian. I can't go home. Not with you. Not with anyone. I need a fortress, maybe. Shit," he said. "It's so screwed up." He put his glass down on the table and lowered his head to his hands. She raised herself to sitting, moving closer, for she wanted to touch him, to console him, but what she feared was this: that he would feel her hand upon him, and brush it away. Or worse: that his eyes would stop meeting hers. "Look," he said finally, "you and I have been through a lot together. Lots of troubles. Usually yours, of course. But I can't always drop everything the way I used to when we were kids. If I drop Elizabeth now, I'll be alone, and I don't want to be." He pushed his tumbler back and forth along the table. "If you stay, you know we'll be lovers." She nodded, just once, and didn't look at him. "And then like the last time, we won't be lovers." Yes, the cold, somber memory of themselves as failures. She started to protest, to tell him past was past, you can't talk about things that happened a hundred and fifty years ago, but he hushed her. "Elizabeth will be long gone by then. That's too hard an exile for me. As long as you're here, I'm hanging on to Elizabeth by a thread. And you're going to leave, Rachel, because you have your own things to get on with." He brought the glass to his lips and waited for her response.

"I'm not talking about leaving. I'm talking about staying. I need to be with you, Jake."

He took in a slow, deep breath. "Things haven't changed, Rachel. There's always that sense of urgency with you. Then it fades. It always does. It's an old, worn-out role, this problem solving that I do for you. It has no more usefulness than The Parents' fantasy about us."

"The Parents' fantasy is a fantasy. But there's real stuff

between us." She gestured with vehemence, her hand moving to his chest, then hers and back again. "Didn't you ever think, even for a moment, that we would get together?"

"A thousand times."

"And?"

"And we didn't. So it's fantasy, too, isn't it?"

"Why didn't we ever get together?" she asked him.

He laughed "You always had someone else. You married some other guy, Rachel."

"I'm getting a divorce."

"That's beside the point. I wanted you here, and you married some other guy."

"I wanted you, Jacob."

His laugh was harsh. "Then why'd you marry him?"

"Because you were gone—forever, it looked like. Because he seemed a little like you. Because I was an ass, Jake. I wanted him to be you. I wanted you."

She turned her nearly empty tumbler on its side and spun it on the table. Droplets of red liquid flew from its center. "Look," she said after a few moments had passed and he still hadn't responded, "this is turning into a real disaster. Maybe you should go and I should forget the Chinese food. I'll see you tomorrow. I'm sorry. I didn't plan it like this, believe me. I didn't mean to ask you to make love to me, Jake. I didn't mean to screw things up with you and Elizabeth." He nodded, but didn't meet her eyes. "We're a sorry pair, you and I, because I do love you, you know, Jacob, in a mad way. But you're right, we must like parting and writing 'regards' and 'best wishes' better than anything else. Missing connections every time: Whoops, sorry, can't make it, I've just gotten married." She laughed, but heard in his strained breathing that she was making him angry with her banter. "I am sorry to have made a mess of things."

"Rachel, the time for us to be together was when I first came to Canada. That's when I needed you in my life. I needed you badly then. Your letters," he said, "made me think you'd come. But I gave up. I made the break. Since then," he gestured broadly, "things have happened." He stood up and she saw how tightly his hands gripped the back of the chair. She thought to stroke down the tendons that rose so fiercely under his skin, yet didn't. "Why didn't you come with me, then?"

"You never asked me."

"The hell I didn't," he said, his hand now a fist on the chair back.

She sat up straight and hurled her words at him: "You didn't ask me, Jacob Marsh."

"What the hell did I come to New London to see you for, then?"

"To say goodbye. To tell me about how it was killing you that your girlfriend in Boston wouldn't go with you." She stood up, the better to aim her accusations at her target. "The one with the Irish touring cap. What was her name?"

"Theresa."

"Yes, Theresa." She leaned toward him, and she heard his breath, short and firm, before she continued. "You asked Theresa to go with you, remember? I wasn't the one invited."

"I did ask you, damn it. I guess you just didn't have any desperate needs and problems just then, did you?"

"What can I say to you?" She grabbed at the blanket, letting the crackers scatter along the rug, folding it as she spoke. "You're always right and I'm always wrong. You have the superior intelligence, judgment, the whole works. I'm sorry I didn't understand you really meant me to come to Canada even though you said it was somebody else you wanted here. And I'm sorry I came to you for help with the pregnancy—like the doctor said, I would have lost the baby just fine and dandy all on my own without your help." She tossed the unevenly folded blanket over the chair. "You're right. I need to grow up. I need to get out of the wrong place at the wrong time. But listen to me, Jake, I'm not going to play the bad guy anymore. I'm not giving you anything else to charge to me as guilt." She strode to the door and gripped the knob. "Go take Elizabeth to dinner. Get it all patched up already. Tell her you've got it all straight with me. Tell her there was never anything between us except for some teasing and fantasy and colossal amounts of misunderstanding. Time for movin' on, Jacob." The door stood open.

"Don't be an ass, Rachel."

"Time to stop telling me how to behave, remember?" She flung her free hand high above her head. "Time to be on my own. Go back already, will you?"

He tossed his jacket over his shoulder and turned to speak to her. "Just go," she said, and shooed him, with her hands, as though he were a disobedient dog, out the door.

CHAPTER TWENTY ONE

*F*OR A MINUTE in the airport, she thought she saw
him. She started to laugh and almost shouted his
name, but then she saw how the woodsman's jacket
had fooled her, that the man wasn't nearly as blond
as Jake and that he was considerably older.

This is the way you wanted to do it, she said to herself, so
this is what you get. No leave taking. And certainly no fanfares.

She hadn't left immediately after their shouting and tossing
up of hands. No, she'd waited the time she knew it would take
him to walk to the dock, think it over and come back. Then
she had waited longer even than that, till he would have had
time enough to get to Toronto, board the next boat back and
ring her doorbell. But he hadn't done that. Then she had
checked the ferry schedule he had on the refrigerator door
and for good measure, she had waited for one more boat.
It was then that she had packed her suitcase and written
the note.

She had hesitated about leaving so brief a message, but what
need was there for her to summarize the heat of their encoun-
ter, and what else was left to be said? "You were right," would
be enough. He was right. If he wanted to be left alone, she was
only making an ass of herself hanging around. She was always
thinking, this year will be different. This year I'll catch up,
somehow. As her mother had explained to her when she was
five or six, Jake will always be the older one, Rake, you'll never

be as old as he is. But she was always running to catch up to his bigger stuff. He painted and she studied art history. He burned his draft card and she stuffed envelopes. If he'd been a doctor, she'd have been the nurse, tagging along behind, imitating, but not quite coming up to the mark. She was always playing the fool, the comic relief.

She did have to get on with her own life, he with his. He'd been right. Wasn't that what she'd written in the note?

She stopped and put down her bag in the middle of the terminal. She tried to remember the exact words she'd said, the last words, for last words at partings could be so important, but they eluded her. Would he remember them? All she could recall was the sound of the door as he had shut it—not loud, really, not a slamming, but the dull sound of a swollen door stuffed back into its frame. A slow leaving, not taken on the run. If she'd called him back? If she hadn't left? Oh hell, she said aloud, and shook a fist into the warm air of the terminal.

She couldn't sit still on the plane, going over it still another time. What had he said in New London? "Come with me?" Were those his words? No. He hadn't. They'd joked, yes, said The Parents could round up the caterer, formal attire, band, and guests in a little under two hours if they gave them the chance. Laughter. He gave her hair ribbons. And he told her what his father had said when he'd gone home to say goodbye: "Will you ask her to marry you?" More laughter.

"What'd you tell him?"

"I just said I couldn't ask you yet. The timing's not right, I said." Belly laughs so bad they had to hold each other up. "We can't spoil the charade now, can we?" Hysterical laughter to the point of tears.

Was it possible he'd asked her?

No! He made the whole damn thing up. Made up those words in his exile, and wove them into a fantasy to fill the Canadian winter air. How else could he play out the miserable, all-suffering, deserted expatriate?

Had he said it? Had he laughed when he said it so it seemed a joke? She remembered the hair ribbons, the way she'd stood next to the car and tied them through her hair. She remembered that they'd kissed.

Damn you, Jake, I'd have come. I swear it.

And now? What exactly had she brought on herself? Run off (yes, just as he said, predictable, predictable) and he'd go out to the cottage in the morning, expecting her to be there. It wouldn't occur to him, would it, that she'd deserted. Go have dinner, she'd said. And what had he said? Come with me? No. Who could ever remember any of it? she thought in despair. Have dinner. See you in the morning. And she'd run off.

Though she had the window seat, there was nothing to see in the darkness, till finally, there were the lights of the airport, pulling her in along their gaily colored chains. At customs, she looked for him again (fantasy of fantasy), as though he could have gotten there ahead of her, and would be standing just past the gate, waving.

Other people were met and embraced. They came through the gates, one arm stretched out, the other holding a shopping bag filled with gifts or the new baby the relatives hadn't yet seen. What did she have to bring back, and to whom? At least I'm not pregnant anymore, she thought. Here I am, the modern woman arrived home with a clean swept womb. She remembered then the sound of the doctor's instrument; the sound of a straw in an empty glass. And she thought of a toddler, hands held high, saying, "All gone."

It was good to be back. Or perhaps it was just good to lie down after not sleeping all night. All the girls on the corridor came to her in the morning, cutting their classes to get her story. She drew it out in a shamelessly long-winded tale, giving details and dramatic enactments of scenes in doctors' offices and in the hospital. They held her hands and told her it was a fairy tale ending, with no abortion after all, no dying, only legal emergency room procedures costing a fraction of a Puerto Rican abortion. "A veritable happily ever after," Jennifer proclaimed it.

"And I'm barely bleeding anymore," Rachel told them brightly. And she would pay them back soon, she promised. They said they knew that. The important thing was, she was safe. Jake was the big brother of the story. The savior. How they all wished for someone like that, they each said. A man who's a friend without all that other crap. And she told them how the good thing about friends was that they had no secrets. We always know what the other one's thinking, long before it gets said. Yes, Jennifer said, but secrets are what make for excitement. They're the heart of romance, she insisted. So you choose, Rachel said. Friendship or romance. Her words sounded leaden and unbearably stupid to her. But they nodded. Yes, they said. Everyone knows, you choose. She lied to them: she knew nothing about him, nothing about what he thought. Had she known he wanted her to come? If he'd asked, would she have?

Rachel's narration did not include the final scene in the cottage. In response to their queries, she did say that Elizabeth was very nice. Very good for her old friend. And there were two other small lies: she said she had wanted to get back as soon as possible (because of classes, a fact that was understood without her having to mention it) and that Jake had driven her to the airport.

When she thought of him after that, she thought of him with Elizabeth. Though there was this about how she saw them: they didn't touch very often. When she'd actually been with them in Toronto, it had been so, too. And she'd rarely seen them kiss. Funny, because Jake was something of a toucher, reaching out all the time, underlining his offers of support with a pat on the back, an arm around the shoulder, a hand to her cheek. When she thought of Jake and Elizabeth now, they were in restaurants. Chinatown, of course, for that was the unfinished chapter. She took them through the meal in her mind, ordering for them, tasting dumplings in hot sauce along with them. The next time she'd watch them pause over steaming samosas in an Indian restaurant, then order stuffed cabbages at the Hungarian place they might have gone to had she stayed.

And she saw the cottage, empty. There, she saw him alone, coming through the door, finding her gone. Going through the cottage, not believing it at first, thinking she was at the beach, then believing. Then nodding. Oh yes. Of course. He would see she had put the wine away, the crackers—those that hadn't been ground into the rug—would be back in the box, and the glasses would be washed, though not returned to the cabinet. He would see that she had not stayed for dinner. The shirt, the flannel shirt that she had appropriated from his drawer that day, he would see lying across his bed. Most times, he would put his hand on it.

Sometimes when she imagined it, there was the note, just as she'd left it, taped to the inside of the front door: "You were right. Sorry. Thanks. Tell Elizabeth thanks. R." Sometimes there were other notes there, the ones she tried to write then ripped up, and the pieces of which she'd put into her suitcase. Sometimes there were new notes. "I love you," one said. When there was a note, he always found it as he was leaving. His hand always lingered on it, and he always read it through several times. He always took it down before he left, folded it and put it into his pocket. Sometimes Elizabeth found it later in the day. Once, there was no note when she retold the story to herself. In that version, he realized the whole thing was a dream he'd spun out of snow-filled air.

After a few days back at school she began to see him moving out of the cottage; boxing up books and wine and kitchen things. Lifting the comforter from the bed, packing the canvases in brown paper. Once she let Elizabeth come along for that, but Elizabeth was too cheery, too pleased with the task. The next time, it was just Jake again, and he paused over things, held onto them and remembered old connections. In the end, though, it all went in the wooden wagon he kept under the house, got pulled to the ferry and carted up the stairs to the apartment. All that was left was that smell; the musty, summer place aura. After that, she saw the door of the cottage was barred, the windows boarded up.

These were daytime thoughts. By night she rarely dreamed of him, and was glad of it, glad there were no twisted images haunting her in the dark. She didn't sleep remarkably well in those first weeks after Toronto, but woke whenever there was a voice in the corridor, the sound of a motorcycle outside. She learned to distinguish one dog's bark from another on the nights when she couldn't sleep at all. And she did have one dream. She knocked on his door and said, "Here I am, back again." He opened the door, and she could see over his shoulder that it was really his room back home. He spoke in the singsong taunt of childhood: "You forgot to say, 'May I.' " She couldn't remember for a minute whether you were supposed to say Mother, may I, or Father, may I (it was a boy asking, after all), but he laughed and said "naaah-naaaah-na-naaaah-na," and closed the door before she was able to say anything. Then she grabbed onto the knob and tried to open the door, but it was locked. When she woke, she couldn't catch her breath for the longest time.

CHAPTER TWENTY-TWO

*I*T WASN'T EASY finding Ben. Alex said it was a long, long story, so why didn't she come to New Haven, and he would take her out to dinner and tell her all about it? She hung up on him.

The next time she called, Alex was very charming, but also, quite obviously high. He said Ben had gone to California. Northern California, he said. He'd dropped out of Yale, but he was in some kind of special novitiate program. "You mean he's studying for the priesthood?" she asked in amazement.

"Not *the* priesthood," Alex said. "Not Catholic stuff. Eastern stuff. Centering. You know, getting in touch with the inner child crap. Taoism, Baoism, one of those."

"Where is it?"

"Where's what?"

"This priest place."

"California."

"California's a big state," she reminded him.

"I told you. The North."

"Does it have a name?"

"I told you that, too, Rachel, love. The Novitiate. Sounds official, doesn't it?"

"Yes."

"I might go out there, too."

"You should," she urged him.

The Novitiate had a phone, but the woman who answered

("Bless you, how may I help you?") said novices could not take
calls. Rachel took the address and wrote, maintaining what she
thought was a pleasant and not too formal tone. She asked Ben
to agree to a divorce. He wrote back immediately. "I don't
want you to be unhappy or constrained," he wrote. "What is
this life if we are bound against our will? I embrace any decision
you make regarding our union." He told her he was studying
the art of healing. The Novitiate, he said, was a wonderful
place where spirituality and therapeutic techniques were beau-
tifully married. She might be interested in knowing, he said,
that he was studying self-healing, and he was becoming a much
better person. Because of the religious nature of his studies he
expected to avoid the draft, though the Novitiate was still so
new, nobody knew yet if it would qualify for divinity school
status. He had no intention of making it easy for the draft
board to find him—he'd left no forwarding address, nor had he
told his parents where he was. He hoped she wouldn't turn
Judas to his Jesus, he added. And he was in love with a woman
named Sunrise. "She took that name for her novice-tag," he
explained. "You're a good person, Rachel," his letter continued. "Let me know when the divorce is definite. Blessings,"
he wrote, and below that, "Quester," which she assumed to be
his novice-tag.

To Jake, she wrote long letters that went unanswered. Still,
she kept on, writing small details of her life, sometimes nearly
transcribing classroom discussions when she had nothing else
to report.

After the third unanswered letter, she went home for a visit.
She went into his parents' house, stopping in the doorway of
his old room, resting her ear against the frame, listening as one
listens for the sound of the sea in a conch, for his voice.

Grace was anxious for news of her son and kept Rachel with

her for hours in the kitchen, pouring her more tea, feeding her more of her special five-layer chocolate cake that had been Rachel's favorite as a child, till, even to Grace's mind, there was absolutely nothing more to tell.

Rachel walked down to the beach and stood as close to the water's edge as possible without getting her black leather boots wet. She watched the water touch the shore and then recede. Advance. Retreat. Approach. Avoidance. These were rhythms she understood. Rhythms that, Jake, too, knew intimately.

She stayed till it was dark and cold, till the pond was no longer visible. Till she could imagine the pond was Lake Ontario; the house behind her, a Wards Island house. And she remembered how he had told her, when they had stood on the shore of his lake, that he often thought of escape by water: nighttime, an open boat.

He told her how Dan Stevenson, a fellow exile, had been arrested at his father's funeral. The feds had been waiting for him. They had a special unit, Dan said, that read the obituary pages of all the major newspapers in the country just waiting for such chances of nabbing you. "I have seen California, once more," Dan had written to Jake from jail. Dan hadn't said whether he thought it worth the sacrifice. Neither had Jake.

Jake often dreamt of running across an open field, he said. It would be light—full sun or flood lights—then suddenly dark; darkness palpable as water against his skin was how he put it. He'd blink hard, repeatedly, to clear his sight and still he couldn't see anything, but only feel the pounding of his blood and the aching in his chest as he gasped for air. The flight was never terminated by either capture or escape; only by his waking.

It was like running in circles, he said to her, thinking of going back. He might as well shout out over the lake for the ones on the other side to come and get him. They couldn't hear at that distance. They couldn't see. So they weren't coming. He was a set piece in the game. She was the one moveable piece. And she had gone flying off into space. She shouted his name in the dark, as loudly as she could, out across the lake.

She wrote, "Forgive me," on a piece of paper and sent it to him. It was her first mention, oblique or otherwise, of their standoff. Clearly, she couldn't storm the game board that way, but if she were to move with caution, perhaps she could proceed in little bits and pieces, one square at a time, across her side of the board, till she had edged up as close as possible to his side. So her voice could be heard across the distance.

His letter arrived so soon, she thought perhaps the two had crossed in the mail: "Forgive me," were his only words.

"Am I still allowed to say I miss you?" she queried.

"Of course you can say you miss me. I miss you," he replied.

"Tell Elizabeth," she wrote, "how much I appreciated her help. I would like to tell her that she saw me at my worst, in one of my frenzies, as you might put it, Jake, but it was still me, no matter how I try to portion it off. I mean it though, when I say I'm sorry I behaved so badly." She wrote that Ben had agreed to a divorce. That she had spoken to a lawyer who had "started the ending rolling."

He wrote that he was spending more time at the cottage again. "Elizabeth is trying to finish her master's thesis and doesn't need me around. I moved some more things out to the apartment, but there's just so much you can take when you're limited to the capacity of a little red wagon." She began to send her letters to the Wards Island address.

She sent him a check to cover the emergency room expenses. He wrote back that he'd ripped it up. "Don't worry about it," his note said. "There is no owing, no obligation."

She mailed a letter every day and got one back as often. Each sent answers to the other, then each asked more questions.

She wrote: "Jacob, was there ever a time you loved me?"

"I love you," he wrote back. And: "In the morning, I time my departure to coincide with the arrival of the mailman. I save the letters for the subway, then read them there."

She made appointments for job interviews in Boston. "I don't mind if it's menial and mindless for a while. It's been a long year. I'm hoping for some empty-headed job at one of the galleries. Then when I'm ready to be challenged again, I'll be in the right spot." She got several offers, including the one she was most interested in—a clerical job at Harvard Art Department. She accepted the position.

Rachel went to Boston to look for an apartment. "The pickings are slim, to say the least. Erin Reilly came along with me," she wrote to Jake. "She's used to a bit more luxury than we were shown. She thought we were going to get air-conditioned, carpeted places with swimming pools. We've got a 'maybe' possibility in Cambridge. I'd be able to walk to work, but it's more money than we ought to spend for less space than we'd wanted. We'll have to share a room. The landlord wants a couple ('single girls have wild parties, etc., etc.'), so he's holding out on us for another two weeks."

"I've signed another six-month lease on the cottage," his next letter said. "I'm moving back out there. When I told Elizabeth, she said she was glad it was definite and settled; that for weeks I'd been leaving her without really owning up to it. I hadn't meant to cause her additional pain that way, but apparently I did. So it's definite and settled. She's got a roommate lined up for the apartment."

Their letters now were sometimes only a single sentence or two: questions tossed out across the void. They had shed all the traditional parts of letter writing, casting aside the how are you's, the asking after others, the rhythm, the timing and pauses. To hell with balancing news and response to the last letter. They were down to essentials. They now had conversations, interrupted between each speaker's line of dialogue, while the statements and questions were hurled headlong over the miles, from one to the other. She hated the dreary hours till his next words arrived.

The day the letter arrived from the Cambridge landlord saying she could have the apartment, she found another letter in her post office box, this one from Jake. "I have to go to Canada because of the war," he wrote. "Would you go with me?"

She went directly to the campus store and bought a packet of stationery. She wrote only this: "Jake, I would. R."

That was what it was about, then: simple questions, simple answers.

Four days went by with no letter—he had stopped writing. He'd written nothing since that last question. Then Sunday intervened, bringing no mail, and the waiting was hell. Increasingly, she began to see that she had erred in thinking his question serious. We are such jokers, we two, she thought.

The letter, when it did arrive was too thick, too like a business communication. It would contain lengthy explanations of how he hadn't meant quite what she thought. Her throat grew so tight she could barely swallow, and her face was hot with anticipated shame. She carried the letter back with her to Jennifer's room and held it close against a lamp. If she could see the message through the envelope without having to open and unfold it, the rejection might be easier to take, she thought, muted as it would be by the screen of the envelope. What she saw, though, was not his usual legal sheets, but something red with official looking printing on it. So she opened the envelope. It contained an airline ticket dated June second, the day after her graduation. "Not much time, you scoundrel," she said aloud. "Aren't you a bit presumptuous?" she asked and shook the ticket at an invisible companion. She laughed at the two of them. He'd inserted a piece of paper into the folder with the ticket. It read, "I love you, J."

She did not write back: they were done with letters, now.

It was a morning flight. The first thing she saw as she flew into the city were the islands, spread out like filigree across the dark water. She was almost sure she could tell which house was his from the air.

For a moment she thought she saw him standing on the beach, waving as she flew on overhead, but that was just a passing illusion. He would be at the airport already, would have been there for at least a half hour before arrival time, close by the gate for international arrivals, and he would guide her passage into Canada.